TRANSNATIONAL PEASANTS

TRANSNATIONAL PEASANTS

Migrations, Networks, and Ethnicity in Andean Ecuador

══ David Kyle

THE JOHNS HOPKINS UNIVERSITY PRESS   Baltimore and London

© 2000 The Johns Hopkins University Press
All rights reserved. Published 2000
Printed in the United States of America on acid-free paper
1 2 3 4 5 6 7 8 9

The Johns Hopkins University Press
2715 North Charles Street
Baltimore, Maryland 21218-4353
www.press.jhu.edu

A catalog record for this book is available from the British Library.

Library of Congress Cataloging-in-Publication Data
Kyle, David.
   Transnational peasants : migrations, networks, and ethnicity in
Andean Ecuador / David Kyle.
      p.   cm.
Includes bibliographical references and index.
ISBN 0-8018-6430-5 (hard : ak. paper)
   1. Ecuador—Emigration and immigration.   2. Ecuadorians—Foreign
countries.   3. Emigrant remittances—Ecuador.   4. Ethnicity—Ecuador.
5. Ecuador—Social conditions.   6. Ecuador—Economic conditions—1972–
I. Title.
JV7491.K95 2000
325'.2866—dc21

00-008909

An exclusive new preface to the 2003 edition is available at:
http://www.press.jhu.edu/press/books/titles/s03/s03kytr.htm

CONTENTS

 # MAPS, FIGURES, AND TABLES

The world is changing, and so are the world's migrants. This book examines two types of cross-border migration that are relatively novel: first, long-distance migration facilitated by human smugglers and a range of other "migration merchants," and, second, entrepreneurial transnational migration by relatively common people not employed by transnational corporations or organizations. The Ecuadorian province of Azuay exemplifies the first type; it is the site of a large-scale, clandestine migration flow to New York City. Migration from this region took off so rapidly that in a single generation Ecuadorians went from obscurity to its present status as one of the largest immigrant communities in the New York metropolitan area. Though human smuggling is not a new activity in human history, it has for the most part been confined to helping people cross a single border by overcoming natural barriers and evading enforcement agents. Today, however, we find globally organized networks of migration merchants profiting from the global demand for both legal and illegal migration services; many are engaged in the financing and facilitation of the surreptitious crossing of one or more national borders at great distances, thus allowing even cash-poor rural smallholders the opportunity for a household member to work abroad illicitly. As is the case in Azuayan migration, the business of migration is often a part-time activity of return migrants and nonmigrants who, far from being full-time criminals using the latest technology, help distant relatives, neighbors, and coethnics out of Ecuador at prices below that of professional migration merchants. The export of labor from Azuay, which has some features of indentured labor, is a profitable commodity for migrants and nonmigrants alike.

The second region, Otavalo, which lies several hundred miles to the north of Azuay, is the site of an ethnic economy based on the manufacturing and brokering of its own indigenous and other group's ethnic clothing and handicrafts, which are sold abroad on several continents by their own Quichua-speaking merchants. A more recent cultural commodity offered by this region is the performance of folkloric Andean music in the streets and plazas of several countries. Such cross-cultural brokering is thought to be one of the most common social institutions for trade historically; but it is an activity that largely died out with the rise of industrial military power, which was used to effectively create colonies rather than trading partners, and, somewhat more recently, with the development of highly rationalized global markets dominated by transnational corporations. Why do we need cross-cultural traders when we can either simply take what we want in the name of national interest or buy it in a shopping mall? Though much has been made of the technological revolution as the driving force of "globalization," this is not sufficient to explain current forms of transnational activity engaged in by contemporary brokers from more humble origins; to understand contemporary forms of transnationalism, we do well to examine the underlying sociopolitical forces that created and destroyed past cross-cultural trade networks.

Apart from the relative novelty of these two types of long-distance migrations back and forth from remote, rural locations, what is most surprising is that they both originated as mass migrations in the same country at about the same time. Furthermore, while there are significant differences between migrants and nonmigrants in the four rural sending communities examined in this book, the sociodemographic characteristics of migrants in both regions, such as levels of human capital, are very similar; most migrants are young adult men with modest levels of education, from traditional households, and engaged in a combination of farming, handicraft manufacture, and wage work. Either they or their parents are considered *campesinos* (peasants).

What accounts for this regional variation in transnational economic strategies wherein one group sells its labor and the other its cultural commodities? For one thing, past migrations in the Andes, including those that occurred centuries ago, continue to affect the patterns of current migrations. They do so in at least two ways: by shaping socioeconomic development patterns and by creating ethnic identity, which, once constructed as positive or negative within a local context, is slow to change. While contemporary migration abroad from these regions adds another layer of complexity to each region's ethnogenesis and social stratification, it typically does not represent a fundamental break with the past precisely because most are leaving not to start a new life but to better the one they already have back home. In addition to past migration and ethnic makeup, unique historical local and global connections are potential resources available to a would-be migrant. Other important factors explaining this subnational regional variation are the economic and political decisions of local elites in and out of one's own ethnic group and the timing of their success or failure. Even within the highlands, which is distinctive socially and economically from the coastal and Amazonian regions, different elite families in a linear chain of valleys have pursued a range of economic, social, and political strategies in different historical periods. The various migration experiences of regions, their ethnic makeup, historical connections to outsiders, and their unique economic histories and repertoires have produced the contemporary differentiation of migration patterns by region and community we see today in Ecuador.

Yet, while this comparison of two divergent sending regions in the same country yields insights into the historical and proximate causes and organization of transnational migration from these two regions, it also calls into question general theories of international migration. Because of the relative novelty of these and other emerging types of migration and the dynamic state of the world political economy at the turn of the millennium, I argue that we need more basic research on migration in both sending and receiving regions and less theory building, much of which is built on the empirical foundations of what we know from a handful of cases, especially Mexico. Far from ignoring theories of migration, I reach this conclusion because I have tried to draw on the insights of the primary theoretical approaches to migration in both research design and analysis—and the outcome has been mixed. Because of the obvious novelty of several aspects of these two migration flows from Ecuador, I collected data at several conceptual levels (individual, household, community, and region) using multiple methods in order to engage diverse theories of migration, which differ in the types and scale of the data they privilege. Though theories of the causes of international migration are often viewed as competing, each had something to contribute to our understanding of these two migrations new to the research literature, although no one approach came out unscathed. This is the highest praise that any theory can be given—that it helps us to understand not only the patterns found in an existing body of data from which it was created but also offers valuable guidance into where to look next time. However, the two migrations explored in this book force us to rethink our basic distinctions between legal and illegal, labor and entrepreneurial, economic and political, temporary and permanent migrations. In short, just as migration theorizing is coming of age, the world has changed.

However, change does not necessarily imply linear evolution toward completely novel forms of social activity; it also implies a reemergence of much older forms of cross-cultural brokering in new guises.

===

I owe numerous debts to people who have helped me, knowingly or unknowingly. A grant from the Program for Comparative International Development of the sociology department at the Johns Hopkins University allowed me to make a preliminary trip to Ecuador for several months. Primary funding for a year of field research in 1992 and 1993 was provided by the Social Science Research Council and the American Council of Learned Societies, with assistance by the Mellon and Ford Foundations. In Cuenca, I am deeply indebted to those who assisted me in data collection in numerous ways, especially Libia Cajamarca, Patricio Carpio, Zoila Gomez, Ana Loja, and several students from the Universidad de Cuenca and the Universidad de Azuay. Professor Alejandro Guillén and the staff at the Instituto de Investigaciones Sociales (IDIS) at the Universidad de Cuenca provided critical intellectual and social support during my first stage of research in Azuay. Both the enjoyment and quality of my fieldwork was greatly enriched by my *jorga* in Cuenca, the members of the band Utopía. I especially want to thank band leader and politician extraordinaire Gerardo Machado for his generosity. In Otavalo, I probably would not have been able to conduct research at all without the experienced guidance and social networks of Lynn Meisch. Similarly, Linda D'Amico in Peguche provided some practical suggestions that helped me negotiate local culture. I was ably assisted in conducting survey research in Guanansi and Peguche by the members of the Centro de Desarrollo Comunitario Incapirca in Peguche. My greatest debt of all is to the members of the four communities of this study for their openness and generosity.

I want to thank the following people who read chapters or discussed major areas of the study and gave helpful comments at early stages of the study: Christopher Chase-Dunn, Mary Crabb, Patricia Fernandez-Kelly, Lynn Meisch, Sidney Mintz, Deborah Truhan, and especially Alejandro Portes as my mentor throughout the period of field research and dissertation writing. I am deeply grateful to John Dale, Lyn Lofland, Robert Smith, and David Spener for reading the entire book and offering insightful suggestions, many of which I have gratefully incorporated. This book has been made readable by a wonderful copyeditor, Katherine Kimball, and the guidance of Henry Tom at the Johns Hopkins University Press. Any flaws of the book, however, are all my doing.

Much of this book was written under the roof of my immigrant parents-in-law, Pietro and Luly Siracusa, who provided the perfect environment in which to write (and also to forget about writing). Above all, I'm deeply appreciative of the intellectual and emotional support of my partner, political scientist Christina Siracusa; I dedicate this book to her and to our two children, Alan Pietro and Ana Cristina, who find ways to put manuscript pages to more productive use.

TRANSNATIONAL PEASANTS

CHAPTER ONE

Introduction: Transnational Peasants?

> International migration has never been as pervasive, or as socio-economically and politically significant, as it is today. . . . Never before has [it] seemed so pertinent to national security and so connected to conflict and disorder on a global scale. The hallmark of the age of migration is the global character of international migration: the way it affects more and more countries and regions, and its linkages with complex processes affecting the entire world.
> —Stephen Castles and Mark J. Miller, *Age of Migration*

If anyone embodies the age of migration as described above, it is Jesus. I first met Jesus in Tomebamba, a village sitting atop a temperate plateau in highland Azuay, Ecuador. This is not a community on any tourist map, and even if it were, few would find the dirt road leading to it out of the nearby town. The community is a small museum of rural Andean architecture from premodern to postmodern, ranging from thatched huts to red-tiled cottages to multistory angular houses with large glass windows and imposing concrete fences. The rusting support rods protrude from roofs like invisible flags signaling vertical progress.

Jesus had gone out of his way to get my attention as I walked along one of the short roads, gawking at miniature mansions amid cornfields. Eager to tell an unsuspecting American of his amazing life, he led me to his home and poured a beer. With permission from the French restaurant in Manhattan where he worked most of the year as a cook, Jesus was home for the month of May to see his family and to oversee improvements to their ever expanding two-story house. Like the house he was continually constructing but had rarely lived in, Jesus's life had a permanently unfinished quality; he had no clear exit strategy from the binational life he had built over the course of eleven years of shuttling back and forth between his two countries. After months of dreaming, he was "back home" among the three young children he barely knew, apart from the videotapes his wife had sent him. At the restaurant near Times Square (which I later visited), he was known as a hard worker who showed up on time six days a week. Playing at his feet now were the reasons for his eleven-month sacrifice. For most of us who do not keep households in two countries, Jesus's bittersweet life seems to be a high price to pay for a handful of weeks each year on top of the world. Yet, so many Ecuadorian migrants—mostly from Jesus's province—have been leading similar lives that by 1993 they constituted one of the largest groups of undocumented migrants in New York state—and at the same time have made remittances one of the major sources of hard currency for Ecuador. In 1995, in response to this new reality of migration and the lobbying efforts of migrant leaders in New York City, Ecuador changed its laws to allow dual citizenship with the United States. It is precisely this type of political imprint that lead Stephen Castles and Mark Miller (1998) to declare ours an "age of migration."

The way in which this study evolved ultimately shaped the research design, and it provides an introduction to the goals of the remaining chapters. During a visit in 1990 to Cuenca, Ecuador's third-largest city, in the province of Azuay, I learned that the local topic among professionals and cabdrivers alike was what sounded to my ears like "la YANY." I asked a *taxista* what it meant and was told, "Tu sabes, yo amo Nueva York—Y♥NY." Everyone I met talked about who was in New York or about to go there, what they were doing, and when and if they were coming back. Unaware of mass international migration from Ecuador, which at the time had not been systematically researched, I was intrigued by the mysteries of why and how so many left this region of Ecuador—and came back—and was quickly motivated to plan a study: Why this region of Ecuador? Why New York City (then in a deep recession)? Why not Quito, or even Los Angeles? Why, and how, do so many, especially from rural communities like Tomebamba, shuttle back and forth without settling on one side of the border? Historical waves of immigration coming from rural areas of Europe have left an imagery of peasants forced from their beloved lands. Yet, it was difficult to see how large groups of Ecuadorians were being forced to migrate, since, on the contrary, many were rural landowners risking the countervailing force of the U.S. Border Patrol. Were there, in fact, historical or social forces at play that transcended individual migrant decisions?

Much of the time, social forces operate as invisible structures, which we can only partially discern and which we easily forget about in everyday life. Fortunately for scholars of migration, the social forces leading to mass international movements of people in this century have not been so subtle.* Numerous sociological studies have continually underscored the role of economic, political, and military disruptions (often at the same time) such that a mass exodus was nearly a foregone outcome of actions taken in distant national and foreign (hegemonic) centers. For example, emigrant countries' close contact and conflict with the United States typically begins well before migration to its shores, not after; nearly all Caribbean and Central American emigrations fall into this category (e.g., Cuba, Puerto Rico, Dominican Republic, El Salvador). Explaining international migration from some countries is even easier, in that we deliberately recruited their citizens en masse when U.S. employers needed them (e.g., Mexico, Puerto Rico) or when in all but name they were refugees escaping violence (e.g., Haiti). More subtle is the role of large-scale transnational investment in manufacturing or agricultural regions in producing international labor flows; however, once again, the disruption of the local economy and of local households is usually obvious, for example, in the practice of hiring only young women in "export processing zones," leaving the men to look for work elsewhere. In short, the "core" of advanced countries dictates, if not directly, then indirectly, the neocolonial terms of immigration from its semiperiphery.

Yet, these past patterns of immigration from Latin America, and the sociopolitical theories developed to explain them, only imperfectly fit the Ecuadorian case. Ecuador is one of the few countries in Latin America that the United States has not occupied militarily; and the province of Azuay has been no bastion of U.S. investment. It was not immediately discernible how any core (and New York City is the quintessential core) was forcing this remote province into mass labor migration. I considered alternative theories of migration, especially from economics. Is Jesus an example of a more individualistic immigration reality based on rational calculation, more in step with the age of globalization every contemporary CEO and head of state invokes? Much like the truly global awareness in the last century that all peoples of the world could mate and produce children, perhaps a global awareness of wage

* This chapter is intended as an introduction to the volume rather than a scholarly summary of theories of international migration, which are considered more systematically throughout the book. For a thorough summary of social scientific theories of the causes of international migrations, see Massey et al. 1998.

differentials in labor markets, finally linked by airline routes, produced a type of economic migration open to nearly anyone on the planet who possessed ambition. In talking informally with return migrants in Azuay, immigration often sounded more like a gold rush than a means of survival. Their stories had all the elements of a rite of passage rather than forced labor: the dangerous clandestine journey; the character-building stage of at least two or three years of mind-numbing work away from loved ones; and finally, the triumphant return, much wiser and, especially, richer. Certainly, the wage differential was enormous. With an average monthly income in Ecuador of around $60 a month in the early 1990s, a migrant could reasonably expect to earn at least ten times that amount as an undocumented laborer working in the back of a restaurant or factory.

It was also clear, however, that there was more to migration from Azuay than simply a monolithic wage differential and the advanced technology in travel and communications said to be driving economic globalization. Consider two facts: first, Tomebamba is attempting to catch up with late-nineteenth-century technology: in 1993 (a decade after Jesus first left for the United States), only 2 percent of households had a telephone, electrification had arrived only fifteen years earlier, and indoor plumbing was a novel feature of only the most recent migrant-built houses. Historically, then, did anything connect Azuay to New York City? If there is a single phrase that captures Azuayan life it must be this: "Nothing ever replaced the hats." Since the middle of the nineteenth century, Azuay has been synonymous with Panama hats, finely woven straw hats that get their name from where they first became popular rather than where they are made. The cottage industry, which dominated the city and countryside alike, has hobbled along since the 1950s, when it lost its global market demand. As it turned out, the Panama hat trail led to New York City, the center of hat importation and global brokering. But how did the path taken by hats lead to a mass migration to the same destination? Certainly, with several layers of middlemen between them, peasant-weavers could not have known the New York importers. Where in the long story of globalization do we begin in order to explain Jesus's transnational lifestyle, connecting midtown Manhattan with Tomebamba?

Another intriguing feature of this region became clear: mass migration abroad is an uneven process affecting only some communities in Azuay, and few regions in the rest of Ecuador. Nearby coastal regions of Ecuador, with some of the most squalid conditions in Latin America, were not sending migrants in numbers large enough to transform local society, as was the case in Azuay. Even more intriguing were preliminary reports from some of the most remote communities in Azuay that so many urban laborers and rural small-holders were leaving for New York that by 1990 no men were left, and the communities were turning into "villages of women," while other communities were hardly touched by migration. If migration was caused by the push and pull of a large wage differential spurred on by a regional economic crisis, why was migration abroad so geographically uneven? While the broad causes of emigration from most countries could be traced to a combination of economic exclusion and political repression, the unevenness of international migration patterns had been noted and examined by migration researchers. The sociological literature on immigration since the 1970s prominently features the role of social networks in patterning, expanding, and sustaining migration to such an extent that it becomes self-reproducing, apart from the original conditions that led to it. Often, the first person to migrate from a village became a "pioneer" for the rest of the community, which soon followed. Thus, social capital, built on dense social networks and trust, explains some of the unevenness associated with migration flows from the same country or region.

Without further research, there was no apparent reason to favor one theoretical approach over another, and so I designed this study to consider multiple theories of immigration from the social sciences, which are different, in part, because they focus on different conceptual levels of analysis (microeconomic versus macroeconomic). Thus, the study design investigates sociodemographic characteristics and processes at the individual, household, community, and regional levels.

I could not stop thinking, however, about another part of Ecuador, the region surrounding the small town of Otavalo, in the northern highlands. Migrants from this region were Quichua-speaking handicraft merchants (men and women) and folkloric musicians (men) who traveled abroad and returned after several months of selling their wares and playing music in streets, malls, festivals, and plazas around the world. Otavalans, from several villages dotting a valley of spectacular volcanoes, flaunted their foreign exploits and commercial prowess among the many foreign tourists visiting from cities many of the Otavalans knew intimately. This seemed to be an even better example of transnational migration, but it certainly did not bear much resemblance to the labor migration of Azuay, since the majority of Otavalans were not traveling abroad to work as laborers. Even to the most casual observer, something is going on in Otavalo and nearby villages that is unique within Ecuador and even most of Latin America; here is an indigenous group of native peoples who not only produce cloth and handicrafts in household-based workshops and small factories but, more importantly, also retain control of the marketing and selling of the products on a global scale. One does not need a formal study to see that the story in Otavalo is clearly not the typical one of outside middlemen reaping most of the profits from a cottage industry. In addition, from my preliminary research in Azuay I knew that some of the wives of migrants to "la YANY" were knitting sweaters for Otavalan merchants, who would make the twelve-hour trek to rural Azuay to buy them and would then sell them abroad as their own, perhaps in Amsterdam or Los Angeles.

The case of Otavalan transnational migration raised several intriguing questions related to regional integration under the long process of uneven globalization, but the main question was this: how has ethnicity, specifically ethnic identity, shaped the two divergent patterns of transnational migration in Azuay and Otavalo, developing in both cases into a mass migration of rural inhabitants from the same country and at the same time? Another feature of Otavalan communities evident outside the tourist market in town was the diversity of economic activities found in its numerous communities that were identified as Otavalan. Some were the merchant-migrants traveling abroad. Others were agriculturists attempting to survive from a small plot or communal land and perhaps sending a family member to work in one of the household workshops owned by members of the wealthier, merchant communities. Thus, just as in Azuay, migration from Otavalo appeared to be an uneven activity.

Though the task was daunting, I decided I simply could not understand one region without also examining the other. Apart from the theoretical interest of comparing Otavalan and Azuayan transnational migrants, such a comparison provides a check against overgeneralizing the experiences of a single region. In addition, a comparative study is more likely to avoid the tendency to rely on one-dimensional cultural arguments that draw support from detailed accounts of the traditions and ideology of a single ethnic group.

The emerging focus on ethnicity and preexisting economic activity in each region also led me to choose research sites that differed along these lines within each region. For Otavalo, I chose one agricultural community, Guanansi, which had been part of a local hacienda, and one community at the heart of the merchant-weaver economy, Peguche. Similarly, the complexities of Azuayan social life, in large part built on past waves of immigration and colonization of the region, meant that its rural inhabitants were also far from an undifferentiated mass of peasants.* Some villages were considered ethni-

---

* An important caveat to this book is that it is not about peasants or, more specifically, theorizing and debating whether peasants exist (if ever they have in Latin America) and,

cally homogeneous, while others contained a combination of whites, mestizos, and *indígenas* (indigenous people). Ethnic identities stemming from the colonial period also indicated which set of economic activities were appropriate for group members. Poor rural whites, for example, were more likely to engage in a range of self-employed and skilled activities other than hat weaving or working as day laborers. That is, *caste*, though too strong a label for the Andean region, comes closer than *class* to capturing the salient ethniceconomic social divide in the regions of this study.

Unusual for the province of Azuay, Tomebamba is known as a homogeneous community of indígenas, probably because it is one of the very few left in the province with elderly people who still speak Quichua, the language of the Inca. Since the middle of the nineteenth century, the community of Tomebamba has supported itself by weaving straw hats, an activity that still occupies most of the women's hands and those of their children for much of the day. Considered neither "Indian" enough to be of touristic value nor mestizo enough to gain local respect, Tomebamba suffered the fate of other hatweaving communities even more intensely. Yet, unlike Tomebamba, the less isolated village of Quipal, also in the province of Azuay, has more varied ethnic groups and economic activities. By choosing communities that varied in ethnic makeup in Azuay and in economic activity in Otavalo, I could better

---

especially, how they have changed. I use the term *peasant* as a rough translation of *campesino*, the label given to most of those in my study by urban dwellers (and many of the subjects themselves), reflecting their rural (in Ecuador) residence, agricultural activities, and ethnic identities. I do not wade into the huge literature and debates on peasants, since it would only marginally advance the primary research question at hand. More important, if I were to underscore, even through a deconstruction, the "peasant identity" as such of the subjects of this book, the diversity of their backgrounds, identities, and lived experiences would recede into a new, but still common, socioeconomic category. The oxymoron, *transnational peasants,* is meant to underscore the tension, even ridiculousness, inherent in conceptualizing a household as peasant in one context and transnational in another and is not meant to signal the transnationalization of "the peasantry" as an evolutionary trend in global capitalism (however, see Kearney 1996, for a Herculean effort at "reconceptualizing the peasantry" precisely within the context of transnational migration). Social science, reflecting the societies in which we live, has a well-developed language for classifying people into static categories (and it is easy to add more of them); these are often the categories developed by states. But our typologies fall well short of adequately describing what is at the heart of most dramatic narratives, namely, how people negotiate and overcome their ascriptive statuses and the expectations of others that surround them.

evaluate transnational economic migrations abroad as they are situated in multiple regional, national, and even global social structures and ideologies.

Whatever the initial social forces leading to Jesus's migrating back and forth, any professional observer of immigration to the United States can imagine the rest of the story: his transnational commuting will soon be over when his wife, Ana, and his children join him in Queens. While that may or may not come to pass, it certainly would not happen so cleanly in Tomebamba, owing to the gendered nature of migration in that village. Ana had only rarely left the province of Azuay, where she took care of their three children, wove straw Panama hats for local brokers, and tended to an assortment of plants and animals. She was the sister of Jesus's first wife, who had died several years earlier. Ana knew very little of Jesus's New York world: his certificate of English proficiency from a Queens night school, which hung prominently on the wall, could equally have been, for her, a certificate for having walked on the moon. For the men of Tomebamba, most of whom knew the New York subway system better than the plat of Cuenca, dual-household life led to new forms of control over women—they collectively conspired to keep many of their American experiences, even where they worked, from the women of Tomebamba. Not all the men returned every year, as Jesus did, in large part because they were still "illegal aliens," as was Jesus until his employer helped him attain resident status after the 1986 immigration reform act. Unhappy with this long-distance abandonment, some of the women had finally gotten the courage at the time of my study to try to make it to New York City—against their husbands' wishes—a journey that entails paying professional smugglers $6,000 to $8,000 (on credit) to help them cross several borders and then land in New York City with no welcoming family member to ease their introduction.

Although Jesus had shuttled like a pendulum between Tomebamba and New York City for more than a decade and had already "made it" financially and legally, he had no intention of ever bringing his family to live with him in Queens, a fact that he did not hide from anyone. He did not need a sociologist to tell him that once his children entered public schools in New York City, returning home would be unlikely; they would become gringos and would never again want to live in a rural village. Perhaps Jesus knew that feeling all too well; giving up his Manhattan job and Queens house (shared with seven men from Tomebamba) did not seem to be an option for the foreseeable future. His dream was to either start a small business one day, perhaps an auto parts store in the nearby town of Checa, or just retire. But in a country without any real welfare assistance, when is enough enough? He knew several migrants who had tried returning permanently to Ecuador, but they usually ended up shuttling to "la YANY" again within a year. A century of immigration research by social scientists notwithstanding, it was not at all clear what the future held for Jesus, Tomebamba, or the rest of Azuay. Thus, I came to think of migration from both regions as more of an emergent transnational social reality, involving migrants and nonmigrants alike, than simply an international movement of labor.

In fact, a growing number of studies in the 1990s uncovered similar kinds of "transnational communities" among a wide range of immigrant, refugee, and activist groups not part of transnational corporations. This has even led to a new -ism to describe the situation, "transnationalism," and multimillion-dollar research projects to study it around the world. Yet we are far from a consensus on what it is or is not, in large part owing precisely to its global and, therefore, extremely diverse incarnations. How can we place the transnational activities of Jesus, a Salvadoran refugee, and a Tibetan monk in the same descriptive category and still have it be meaningful? Another source of pointed discussion comes from closer examinations of historical accounts of past waves of mass "immigration," when many engaged, at least initially (and that is the point), in transnational practices. Immigrants from Poland and southern Italy a century ago attempted to affect political and economic affairs back in their home communities (Thomas and Znanieki 1927; see also Foner 1997); in the end, about a third of the Italian immigrants returned home permanently. In what ways is Jesus like, or not like, a Sicilian peasant artisan working in Manhattan in 1890? Is Jesus a "transmigrant" simply because he is a newcomer, like past first-generation immigrants, or because the fundamental political and economic structures shaping immigration have changed?

While much of the transnationalism literature attempts to uncover and even celebrate the sociopolitical multifocality and cultural hybridity within contemporary diasporas, it generally does not focus on the origins and long-term patterns of such transnational social formations. This is owing, in large part, to the fact that the determinants of many of the migrations leading to increased transnationalism are manifestly evident. That is, though some view transnational communities as a natural consequence of the contemporary globalization of economic production and distribution using advanced technologies, many of the cases used to illustrate transnationalism thus far typically involve immigrant groups from countries that have recently experienced widespread political unrest and even violent repression.

What makes this Ecuadorian transnational migration different from refugee transnationalism is that it is not overdetermined by widespread civil strife and U.S. military involvement. Lacking such obvious "push" factors, does it represent a novel, more sustainable form of transnationalism emerging in response to globalization per se or to more bounded types of foreign market demands? What is unusual about both Azuay and Otavalo is that they were, in fact, integrated into global markets relatively early.

If some migrate in response to a set of unique historically grounded, transnational connections in subnational regions—not just in the urban destination—then we would expect to find a richer diversity of transnational activities and lifestyles, some of which may blur the lines between movements of labor and capital. In that case, contemporary transnational migrations, as part of a more localized process, may have an even greater social and political complexity than past immigrant and refugee flows.

=

The study on which this book is based is an attempt to solve an inductive mystery regarding divergent transnational mobility patterns in two regions and four communities within highland Ecuador. It explores the origins of transnational migrations based on a set of prior transnational connections and socially constructed group identities *(ethnie)* such that a common national and even sociodemographic background (human capital) still led to radically different transnational economic strategies. Rather than attempt to build new global theories, and a general definition, of *transnationalism* by reconceptualizing cases of migration within the existing research literature, this book examines the applicability of existing theories of international migration for understanding the origins of two cases new to the migration literature. It is the kind of opportunity that comes along rarely in international migration research, whereby we are able to evaluate theories with different empirical cases not used to support the original post hoc theoretical formulations. One premise of this book is that, while there may be novel features to these Ecuadorian cases of transnational migration, decades of social research concerning the causes of international migration are still useful at all stages of research. Only after existing theories have been examined in light of study findings can we begin to explore those formulations in need of modification, extension, and new theoretical directions.

Conceived in the early 1990s, this study is loosely modeled on three contemporary classics of international immigration research: Alejandro Portes and R. L. Bach's study of Cuban and Mexican immigrants (1985), Douglas Massey and associates' study of several Mexican sending communities

(Massey et al. 1987), and Sherri Grasmuck and Patricia Pessar's study of sending communities in the Dominican Republic (1991), which foreshadowed the burgeoning transnationalism literature that followed it. All of these studies share three characteristics, which I have incorporated into the present study: first, theoretical concerns are organically built into the study design and analysis; second, they compare more than one sending group or community; finally, they examine migration as a social process embedded in multiple social structures, such as the household, the community, national membership, and the world economy, and at multiple locations and temporal phases of migration systems. I adopted this approach not just for its inherent wisdom, such as its avoidance of overgeneralizations from a single case, but also as a way of "conversing" with these studies.

Theories of migration differ primarily because researchers' questions and methods differ, in that they are themselves shaped by disciplinary cultures. Apart from examining two migrant groups new to the migration literature, this study diverges from past studies in the variety of its research sites and types of transnational economic migration. First, the definition of *transnational economic migration* lies at the center of its comparative research design: though one group sells its labor (Azuay) and the other sells ethnic handicrafts and music (Otavalo), both have similar goals of capital accumulation through transnational mobility. In addition, all four research sites in the study are primarily composed of rural inhabitants (nominally, peasants) from the Ecuadorian Andes whose household economies are based on a combination of subsistence agriculture, cottage industry, and wage labor, though there is variation in the extent to which each is emphasized by village and household. Thus, instead of testing theories or approaches as competitors, in this study I have attempted to incorporate their theoretical and methodological insights where appropriate, recognizing that each has its strengths and weaknesses. The primary reason for this theoretical eclecticism, however, is that this is a study about the causes of two migrations new to the research literature. A dogmatic approach, therefore, would likely lead to methods illuminating only one aspect of transnational migration from Ecuador, which may not be an important one.

This study is comparative at three levels of analysis. First, the study compares historically the two regions that have produced such divergent transnational outcomes in the 1990s. Second, it compares two communities in each region to examine how transnational strategies are embedded, at the most local levels, in historical patterns of migration, social networks, and ethnic identities. Finally, it compares migrants and nonmigrants, and their households, to evaluate the roles of human and social capital in the self-selection process of transnational migration. The essential logic is to examine the similarities and differences of the two ethnic groups and the four villages for clues that might explain divergent migration patterns. However, instead of attempting to isolate one or two key determinants, I explore the "multiple conjunctural" causes of migration operating simultaneously at several levels of analysis (Ragin 1987). For example, the same "variable" of ethnic identity may be socially constructed differently at local, national, and transnational levels but can nevertheless be seen to shape migration at each of those levels. It is the historical configuration or combination of regional characteristics that is being compared in the cases of Azuayan and Otavalan transnational migration. (For further discussion of research design and data collection, see appendix A.)

Data collection includes field research using a combination of participant and informal observations with in-depth interviews with key informants, quantitative household survey data, and secondary historical material. With this triangulation of methods, causal explanations using variables from the survey data are combined with more idiographic accounts of the historical development and ethnographic context of transnational activities. Surveys, and the statistical analyses they allow, are more appropriate for abstract research questions that compare communities and regions. In contrast, qualitative data are useful for understanding rare events, such as the original pioneering efforts of the first migrants from a community, and for describing the sociocultural context and meaning of transnational migration. Study data were collected over the course of three trips to Ecuador, totaling twenty months, and several short trips to New York City. While most of the time was spent taking notes and observing life in the communities and nearby towns, the last six months in Ecuador were spent collecting survey data. With the help of research assistants from the communities, census surveys of the four communities were conducted, with a total of 2,185 adults and 723 households in the final data set. With the addition of secondary historical reports, this combination of multiple research sites and methods allows for stronger findings when different data support a similar conclusion or, alternatively, point to discrepancies or gaps that may be overlooked when only a single source of data is used.

Although each village is discussed in greater detail in later chapters, it is helpful at this point for the reader to get a brief overview of each community. Basic demographic, social, and economic characteristics of the four villages are presented in table 1.1 (see also map 1.1). A striking feature of these communities is that there is more variation in many aspects between the two com-

Table 1.1. Selected Characteristics of Study Research Sites, 1993

Community	Azuay		Otavalo	
	Tomebamba	Quipal	Guanansi	Peguche
Demographic				
n	404	511	112	1,158
Population	670	900	300	2,128
Male population (%)[a]	46.0	49.5	50.0	48.5
Number of households	155	170	60	380
Average household size	4.3	5.2	5.0	5.6
Households speaking some or only Quichua (%)	16.0	0.6	96.0	89.0
Socioeconomic status				
Illiteracy (%)	16.0	5.7	47.7	24.0
Postprimary education (%)	4.0	30.0	2.7	25.0
Average schooling (years)	3.8	6.7	2.2	5.0
Households with dirt floor (%)	12.0	16.0	80.0	37.0
Average age of dwelling (years)	18.5	21.0	14.5	14.5
Use of household for informal economic activity (%)	87.0	66.0	60.0	79.0
Less than one hectare of land (%)	95.0	96.0	75.0	95.0
Participation in communal lands (%)	44.0	10.0	57.0	5.0
Health problems preventing work (%)	3.0	3.7	10.0	13.0
Community infrastructure				
Electricity in home (%)	88.0	94.0	0.0	88.0
Telephone service (%)	2.0	33.0	0.0	1.1

Source: Study data, May 1993.

[a] Includes migrants who still form part of a household, including those abroad at the time of the survey.

munities of a single region, in levels of education, for example, than between the regions themselves. It is at the village level that we can best understand the comparative logic of this research design.

Tomebamba (a pseudonym), with 155 households, is one of the few indigenous ("Indian") communities left in the province of Azuay, though the Quichua language is rapidly dying out. Since the last century, this homoge-

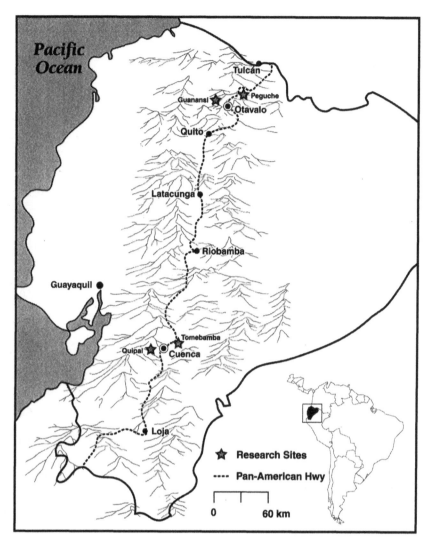

Map 1.1. Ecuador and Research Sites

neous village has been supported by two activities: agriculture and the weaving of Panama hats, which find their way into the global economy through local intermediaries. When the Panama hat trade declined in the 1950s, many residents of Tomebamba began to seasonally migrate to the coast, where work could be found in the banana and sugar plantations. International migration has now replaced domestic migration for the men of the village; the majority of the women stay behind to tend to the family plot and continue to weave straw hats.

Quipal (also a pseudonym), a village of 170 households, also located in Azuay, is divided geographically and ethnically into three nearly equal parts: *blancos* (whites), cholos (mestizos), and *naturales* (indigenous "naturals"). Its economy is oriented toward the nearby urban center of Cuenca. Apart from subsistence agriculture, economic activity is also divided along ethnic lines: the more indigenous population is dedicated to logging and the weaving of straw baskets, while whites (those of Spanish blood) and mestizos engage in the cottage industry of sewing clothes for the urban market of Cuenca and other unskilled and semiskilled wage work. Symbolic of its social and cultural divisions, Quipal lacks a well-defined community center or plaza.

Peguche, an indigenous village of 380 households in the northern province of Imbabura, is one of the most important communities of the Otavalan ethnie. Under colonial captive-labor arrangements *(huasipungo)*, which officially ended as recently as 1964, some Otavalan villages were singled out for weaving factories while other Otavalan villages were incorporated into several large haciendas, providing agricultural labor. As inhabitants of a former center of weaving production under colonial arrangements, Otavalans from Peguche have parlayed their skills into the creation of an entrepreneurial class that produces a variety of handicrafts for local, national, and even foreign markets. Recently, many young men have turned to folkloric performances, locally and abroad, to raise enough capital to enter into the lucrative handicraft trade.

Guanansi, a traditionally agricultural community of sixty households, is located less than a mile from Peguche, though in a much more isolated setting. Until the late 1970s, the village was integrated into a former hacienda, of which, after a successful period of violent uprising, the residents now own part. The legacy of the hacienda has left the village with a substantial tract of community land used for commercial agricultural production. The weaving and selling of sweaters and tapestries are only recent developments. Although still awaiting the introduction of electricity and its first automobile, Guanansi sees its future as imitating the economic success of nearby Peguche.

≡

This book explores the diverse lives and social networks of people in four highland communities who have taken to heart the evangelical gospel of redemption through a specifically global form of capitalism, even as they must overcome a myriad of constantly changing barriers along the way. This kind of comparative endeavor always involves some difficult choices regarding depth versus breadth, and my bias has been to focus primarily on regional and community-level configurations of resources and identities as a significant dimension of the diversity of transnational economic strategies we find within the province of Azuay and the smaller canton of Otavalo. I argue that preexisting configurations of ethnic identities and economic repertoires in the sending communities, shaped by centuries of internal and external negotiation and conflict, play a significant role in who goes or stays and what they will do abroad, even among those with similar levels of human capital.

CHAPTER TWO

Common Context, Divergent Outcomes

> Me vine a la YANY, me vine a trabajar, no importa en que, pero voy a
> ganar. Los dólares vienen, los dólares van, con toda esa plata, yo voy a
> comprar: ropita, casita, y el auto popular. Soy Cholo Boy y me voy a
> trabajar! Tú sabes . . . chulla vida!
> [I come to New York City, I come to work, it doesn't matter in what,
> but I'm going to make money. Dollars come, dollars go, with all this
> money I am going to buy: clothes, house, and the hottest car. I am a
> Cholo Boy and I'm going to work! You know . . . only one life to live!]

Migration has never been a sideshow in the Andean region, crowned by the most populous mountain range on earth, but rather a key feature contributing to its complex and diverse mix of cultures and economies. Two recurring themes are essential to understanding Ecuadorian society: first, a deep social, cultural, and political regionalism; and, second, its historical dependence on one or two export commodities. In addition, the endurance of colonial relations and ideologies well into the twentieth century has meant the late and tenuous development of political participation and economic independence by large sectors of Ecuador's indigenous and rural mestizo populations.

Although many rural peasants and wageworkers are more literate than their parents, they have found that literacy is of little use to them in improving their economic well-being and social status. Thus, a greater awareness of life abroad through mass media and education has produced unrealistic ex-

The epigraphs at the beginning of chapters 2, 3, 4, 5, 6, and 7 are all from "Soy Cholo Boy," recorded in Cuenca in 1992 by the band Utopía. Translations are mine.

pectations that the Ecuadorian economy cannot fulfill. Yet, indigenous groups have not been uniformly affected by macrohistorical processes in Ecuador. This social and economic differentiation among ethnic groups began before the Spanish arrived and continues to shape the social and economic opportunities available to indigenous peasants and urban workers. Contemporary transnational migration from the Ecuadorian Andes can only be understood within the fractured context of ethnic politics and each subnational region's uneven integration into the capitalist world economy.

Appreciation for the diversity of origins and patterns of transnational migration in four rural communities, all in the highlands, begins with an examination of the historical and contemporary features that migrants in all four sites share: a common colonial and national context. Precisely because so much of this common history involves centuries of both controlled and uncontrolled geographic mobility of whole communities and linguistic groups, Ecuador is marked by extreme regionalism in many areas of social life. By exploring this common historical context of development and mobility, we can then ask more finely tuned questions regarding the divergent transnational strategies we see in the province of Azuay and the canton of Otavalo. In this chapter, I also examine theories of migration based on macroeconomic equilibrium ("push-pull") and individual-level "human capital" in light of study findings.

Although Ecuador is one of the smallest countries in South America, its heterogeneous terrain has played an important role in contributing to the deeply regional character of both pre-Colombian and present-day Ecuadorian society, a fact consistently emphasized by specialists on Ecuador (Schodt 1987). Given the natural barriers presented by the Andes, the Ecuadorian mainland, with an area of a little more than one hundred thousand square miles, is customarily divided into three distinct regions: the coastal lowlands (Costa), the Andean highlands (Sierra), and the Amazonian lowlands (Oriente) (see map 1.1). Within present-day Ecuador, the Oriente accounts for almost half of the national territory, and the remainder is divided almost equally between the Andean highland and coastal lowland regions; but only 3 percent of Ecuador's population of eleven million in 1990 lived in the Oriente, the rest of the population being divided evenly between the Costa and the Sierra.

Historical migration patterns within the territory of present-day Ecuador can be divided into two broad periods: The first was a five-hundred-year period of coerced and regulated mobility, with notable exceptions of those able to escape total control, beginning with the Inca regime and lasting well into the postindependence period of the last century; the second comprises the more recent period of the past one hundred years, characterized by increasing individual freedom of mobility and labor. During the first period of coerced migration, two policies by the dominant Incan and Spanish elite are highlighted: (1) the *mitimae,* an Incan institution of forced resettlement within the empire, simultaneously functioning as a form of punishment, resocialization, and political and military control; and (2) the *reducciónes,* the Spanish colonial policy of attempting to concentrate dispersed indigenous peasants into "feudalistic" corporate communities for greater political and religious control and for easier access to their labor. The second period, which more or less encompasses the twentieth century, can be characterized by three trends: (1) a large-scale population shift from the Sierra to the Costa during the first half of this century, owing to successive cacao and banana booms; (2) a government-sponsored program of Amazonian colonization, which produced a limited immigration to that region during the 1970s; and (3) an increasing urbanization of both coastal and highland cities since the 1960s, continuing through the 1990s.

Pre-Colombian Policies: Forced Mobility

Immediately preceding the Spanish Conquest, the inhabitants of Ecuador were in the midst of an Incan social and cultural revolution. Just as the Inca had succeeded in conquering the diverse tribes of the southern Andean region and coast, they turned their attention in the mid-fifteenth century to the northern territory of present-day Ecuador. The Inca met with "fierce resistance from several Ecuadorian tribes, particularly the Cañari, in the region around modern-day Cuenca; the Cara in the Sierra north of Quito [Otavalo]; and the Quitu, occupants of the site of the modern capital, after whom it was to be named" (Rudolf 1991, 5). However, the disparate tribes of Ecuador were no match for the more advanced and well-organized Incan conquerors.

Despite its relatively short duration—less than fifty years—Incan domination of what is now Ecuador had a profound effect on the social organization and agricultural production of the highland regions. A new social grouping was imposed revolving around the *ayllu,* or agricultural community, headed by a *curaca,* or local indigenous leader. J. H. Rowe defines the *ayllu* as "a kinship group, with theoretical endogamy, with descent in the male line [which] owned a definite territory" (1963, 255). Within the ayllu each family was given a small subsistence plot on which to grow food for its own consumption in exchange for work on large tracts owned by the Inca, further divided into state and religious (Sun God) plots. In theory, families did not own the land they worked; rather, allocations were evaluated and redistributed every year according to family size. Nathan Wachtel (1977) has suggested that this Incan economic structure was organized by two complementary principles: reciprocity, which especially characterized local nonmonetary relations, and redistribution, which characterized the hierarchical pattern of tribute to the elite who, in turn, spread the bounty among officers and commoners alike.

When Francisco Pizarro's conquering expedition arrived in 1532, two Inca brothers had just concluded a five-year civil war for accession to the throne. The Quito-based Atahualpa emerged victorious over the Cuzco-based Huáscar after a battle near what is now Riobamba. These preexisting internal divisions within the Incan regime played into the hands of the Spaniards, who recruited both the losing faction and other native groups.

The first significant population movements recorded in present-day Ecuador occurred during the Incan period immediately preceding the Spanish Conquest. However, we should first note that immobility was the norm during this period. The ayllu held a position of central importance in the Incan bureaucratic structure, encompassing both a political and ideological structure and an organization of economic production: its members were forbidden to leave the community without the express consent of the community leaders, and tribute was weighed and levied collectively on each ayllu, requiring a stable tribute-paying population (Wachtel 1977).

Yet the Inca also induced migration and resettlement for economic and strategic reasons. Using the threat of violent measures calculated to instill fear, the Inca were skillful in persuading their new subjects to peacefully pay tribute. When uprisings and revolts did occur in newly subjugated regions, however, one of the most effective tools for control was not annihilation of a community but forced resettlement to another region of the Tahuantinsuyo, the vast Incan empire. Known as *mitimaes,* communities of up to ten thousand were exchanged between one loyal region and another rebellious region. The loyal families sent to the new regions "remained distinctive in speech, dress, and customs and they were directly responsible to the governor; their role consisted of supervising conquered peoples and forestalling any attempt at rebellion" (Wachtel 1977, 80).

Colonial and Early Republican Policies: Controlled Mobility and Immobility

The transition from Incan to Spanish rule in the mid-sixteenth century brought surprisingly few changes to the mass of indigenous subjects. While the Spanish brought new cultural values and practices, they appropriated the preexisting Incan social and political structures pertaining to labor and mobility, maintained within preexisting settlements. Pre-Incan urban settlements, such as Cuenca, Riobamba, and Quito, became important centers for Spanish settlements. It was in the Andean highland region, under the jurisdiction of the Audencia (the regional high court) of Quito after 1563, where Spanish values were most successfully imposed.

The colonial system was theoretically built on a tripartite system of white elites, a small number of mestizo artisans, and the large mass of Indian labor. Lacking the mineral riches found in Mexico and Peru, Ecuador's principal economic interest was land and its productive use. At first, the *encomienda* system provided large estates to white elites and the right to extract labor from the local Indian population. Similar to the Incan system from which it takes its name, the *mita* was another institution used to extract labor from those outside encomienda control by requiring of adult males a year of labor for some public or private Spanish project, typically a textile sweatshop called an *obraje,* once every five years. In reality, the mita developed into a form of debt peonage whereby the *mitayos* incurred more debts than earnings; the debts could then be bought and sold, turning the mita into de facto slavery through debt peonage. An important aspect to this division of labor was the somewhat stronger political position of the mitayos who lived in Indian communities because of their ability to have access to land (Jaramillo Alvarado 1954). Thus, the division of labor among the Indian underclass in the *serrano* (highland) economy during the colonial period can be divided roughly between those agricultural producers held captive in encomienda arrangements and those literally chained to their looms from dawn to dusk.

Toward the end of the eighteenth century, before Ecuadorian independence was won from Spain, the encomienda system was officially abolished. The social and political structures of Ecuadorian society nevertheless remained intact. After independence, the exploitation of the indigenous labor force persisted through a system similar to the colonial mita, called *huasipungo.* This system required that laborers "exchange" four days of work a week for the usufruct rights to a small plot, or *minifundio.* Once again, abuse of the system led to the buying and selling of debt peons, which often lasted a lifetime (Crain 1991).

Although the Spanish did not continue the formal system of mitimae based on entire community exchanges, they instituted their own policies of labor control and resettlement through *reduccíones,* or reduced settlements. Alain Dubly has noted that the creation of such communities, often built on earlier ayllus, was essential for the conquest of territory: the stated objective of the reducciónes was to "group together scattered Indians across the land ... in order to teach them the Christian doctrine and useful crafts [and] accustom them to live 'together and in partnership' in a 'policed harmony'" (Dubly 1990, 186). That is, by "reducing" the indigenous population into villages, the Spanish sought greater control over indigenous peoples' socialization into Hispanic culture and integration into colonial economic production.

The settlement patterns of the Spanish and native populations were structured to be separate yet parallel. Given the dual systems of civil, religious, and cultural policies that the Spanish developed, dispersed indigenous groups living in reducciónes were distinct from Spanish settlements known as *asientos* (seats). Laws restricting Indians from moving off the reducciónes also prohibited Spaniards, mestizos, mulattos, and African descendants from staying in them for more than three days (Dubly 1990). Because Indians working the land and the mines, paying tribute, weaving cloth, and constructing roads and buildings, constituted their most valuable economic resource, owners of nearby encomiendas, along with clergy and royal representatives, tried to protect reducciónes from both internal and external threats to stability. This system of strict control over the mobility of indigenous peasants and peons was especially persistent in the Sierra well after independence, until the more export-oriented Costa began to dominate the national economy at the end of the nineteenth century.

Despite this general historical pattern of the exploitation of indigenous groups across the more populous highlands, important differences in their independence relative to the dominant mestizo society can be noted from valley to valley. For example, the Spanish faced violent resistance to the implementation of reducciónes at times, but often indigenous communities simply ran away to more inaccessible highland areas or those communities perceived to be less egregious in their treatment of Indians (see Powers 1995). Becoming what were known as *foresteros,* these internal refugees accounted for a large part of the population of some regions, such as the current province of Azuay. Ecuador's regional differences developed into an intense rivalry between the liberal, anticlerical Costa and the conservative, Catholic Andean Sierra. These cultural-ideological schisms were exacerbated by divergent economic interests: coastal business elites had long resented what they perceived to be a transfer of wealth to the more stagnant capital of Quito, the traditional seat of colonial power. Although the republican period brought few changes to the mass of Indian laborers, a fight for control over the state apparatus and economy of Ecuador intensified important regional differences among the mestizo elites.

Migration Unbound? Peripheral
Capitalism and Mobile Labor

In Europe, the end of feudalism and the rise of private property marked the beginning of a mass exodus from the countryside to nascent cities. Faced with a similar transition in the 1950s and 1960s, the Ecuadorian variant of a rural peasantry began to leave the Sierra, the stronghold of colonial-era social relations within haciendas, for the less-populated and economically dynamic Costa.* The transformation of Ecuador's domestic migration patterns during the past one hundred years is essentially a story of the slow transition from colonial labor relations, based on the corporate community, to capitalistic relations based on commodified individual labor. Although it was not until 1964 that the political and economic institutions of colonial relations of production were completely abolished with the end of the huasipungo, incorporation of the Ecuadorian economy into global markets during the nineteenth century was already eroding the economic foundations of traditional Sierran society and the state's techniques for controlling the mobility of the community-oriented workforce.

The principal characteristic of the Ecuadorian economy in the modern era of the world economy is its overall continuity with past patterns of external dependence. Apart from agricultural production in the Sierra for domestic consumption, Ecuador has relied on one or two export commodities. Since the late nineteenth century, the export sector has led the Ecuadorian economy and has typically been dominated by a single commodity—first cacao (1850–1940), then bananas (1950–70), and now petroleum. Ecuadorian agricultural exports depend on unstable demand from the world market (Europe and North America) and the vicissitudes of climatic conditions and crop diseases. Although Ecuador was the world's leading producer of cacao at the turn of the century, the loss of the crop to disease and world competition in the 1930s crippled the entire economy. During the 1950s, increasing banana exports held another promise that was thwarted by competition within twenty years.

Ecuador's experience with oil exports offers a prime example of its eco-

---

* There are three primary sources of data regarding the international migration of Ecuadorians before the time of my study: (1) exit and entry data of Ecuadorians to and from Ecuador compiled by Ecuador's National Institute of Statistics and Censuses (INEC); (2) data collected by the U.S. Immigration and Naturalization Service (INS) and the U.S. Bureau of the Census; and (3) data compiled by the City of New York. These data sources are supplemented by information supplied by informants and press accounts in Ecuador and the United States.

nomic dependence on external markets. Ecuadorian oil exports substantially buoyed the Ecuadorian economy during the 1970s and allowed it to join the Organization of Petroleum Exporting Countries (OPEC). Ecuador's net foreign-exchange earnings went from U.S.$43 million in 1971 to U.S.$350 million in just three years (Flores and Merrill 1991, 106). Yet with Ecuador's profound dependence on oil extraction, the slump in oil prices during the 1980s had a devastating impact on the economy and has greatly increased Ecuador's debt burden. Real wages have been cut in half since 1975; in 1994, the minimum monthly wage was around U.S.$70 dollars per month.

The economic decline notwithstanding, the long-term effect of the oil boom of the 1970s was to strengthen the state apparatus and, thus, shift the seat of economic power from Guayaquil to Quito. The overwhelming reliance on oil exports for the national economy has had the effect of stagnating the agricultural and manufacturing sectors, leading to a strong state involvement in both of these sectors. Since 1960, agriculture (as a percentage of gross domestic product) has decreased from 39 percent to 21 percent in 1980 following a precipitous rise in petroleum export, while the manufacturing sector has stagnated since 1950 (ibid., 105). Common reasons given for the poor performance of the manufacturing sector is "a small domestic market, high production costs in relation to the external markets, and underdeveloped human, physical, and financial infrastructure" (ibid.). Consequently, foreign direct investment in Ecuador has been largely confined to the petroleum sector, playing a critical role in locating and developing oil fields. While oil production altered the political and economic balance of power among regions and classes, it has not produced many backward and forward linkages to other sectors of the economy.

In the early 1980s, the period of increased international migration from the highlands, the Ecuadorian economy suffered a series of market and climatological crises. The oil boom of the early seventies collapsed as the price of petroleum declined. Traditional agricultural exports lost some foreign markets to increasing competition abroad. In addition, the recurring climatological cycle in the Pacific known as El Niño caused both floods and droughts in Ecuador's varied topography, severely damaging crops and transportation infrastructure.

Similar to other oil-producing Latin American countries, Ecuador found that its debt began to climb just as foreign exchange was declining. Moreover, foreign lenders grew reluctant to lend hard currency at precisely the time state-owned companies were in need of capital. Ecuador, like several other Latin American countries in the 1980s, was unable to favorably reschedule its foreign debt. What economists called a "financial crisis" was palpably experienced in the streets as consumer prices rose to burdensome levels for most of the population. To counteract these trends, the state instituted austerity measures and currency devaluations; yet unemployment and inflation continued to climb (ibid.). In short, Ecuador experienced an economic crisis that thwarted the developmental expectations of elites and forced most Ecuadorian households to consider new survival strategies, such as part-time or full-time work in the burgeoning informal economy.

Coastal Boom, Amazonian Colonization, and Highland Urbanization

Three distinct, yet chronologically overlapping, trends characterize domestic migration within Ecuador since the late nineteenth century: (1) temporary and permanent migration of *serranos* to coastal plantations; (2) a government-planned colonization of the Amazonian Oriente; and (3) the increasing urbanization of the Sierra and the Costa. From the late nineteenth century until the era of the oil boom in the 1970s, the central feature of domestic migration was temporary and permanent migration from the land-poor highlands to the commercial plantations of the coastal lowlands. Between 1889 and 1926, spurred by the cacao export boom, the share of Ecuador's coastal population rose from 19 to 38 percent (Schodt 1987). The population of the port city of Guayaquil more than doubled during this period as unemployed laborers, originally from the highland region, gravitated toward the city following the decline of cacao exports in the 1920s and the depression of the 1930s (ibid.). A sharp increase in banana exports during the 1950s produced another significant migration from the Sierra, evidenced by a growth rate double that of the region throughout the 1950s; as a result, Guayaquil is now Ecuador's largest city, with 1.5 million inhabitants.

During the 1950s and 1960s, the southern and central Sierra provinces, such as Azuay, Cañar, and Chimborazo, sent more campesinos (peasants) than the northern provinces surrounding Quito, such as Imbabura (where Otavalo is located), to coastal provinces, such as Guayas. In part this was because of their greater proximity to the southern Costa, where most of the plantations were located. Another force underlying migration to this destination was the simultaneous collapse of the Panama hat trade in Azuay.

In response to mounting population pressure and attendant economic burdens, and to develop a strategic national presence in the context of border disputes with Peru, the government began to promote the colonization of the

Amazonian Oriente in the late 1950s. Once again, the south-central provinces supplied an inordinate number of colonists to adjacent Amazonian regions such as Morona Santiago through the 1950s and 1960s. By the late 1970s, however, declining government interest in colonization projects, based on the mixed results of colonists' efforts, dampened resettlement to the Amazon. It became clear that the future of the Amazon lay not in the hands of resource-poor colonists competing with the territorial claims of native Amazonian groups but rather in the extraction of oil.

Migration to urban centers intensified with the oil boom of the 1970s, which gave both the private and public sectors of the national capital renewed economic power. As a result, the province of Pichincha, where Quito is located, urbanized most rapidly, and nearby provinces, such as Imbabura, began to send temporary and permanent migrants to Quito to work in, for example, construction or domestic services. More central regions, such as Chimborazo, simply shifted their migration destination from the Costa to Quito. It was during this intense urbanization period that large squatter settlements sprang up around Quito and Guayaquil.

Urbanization patterns, however, were not uniform throughout the Sierra. In the 1970s, the provinces of Azuay and Cañar were faltering amid migration networks to the Costa and Oriente that were no longer advantageous, while few had social ties to the distant but now expanding Quito labor market. During this period, Azuay's capital, Cuenca, also grew rapidly, increasing its public sector spending.

Social Change and Protest after the 1960s

An important social change in Ecuador accompanied the economic and political push toward modernization during the 1960s and 1970s. By the late 1980s this change was manifest in the widespread and profound perception that Ecuador was unable or unwilling to meet a myriad of rising expectations regarding political reform, ethnic equality, social development, and economic prosperity. Regarding the possible origins of this perception, two noneconomic trends are noteworthy: (1) the impact of uninspired and underfunded social reforms begun in the 1960s and 1970s, which, nevertheless, raised expectations; and (2) a sharp increase in the social and cultural influence of the United States, as Ecuador became better linked to global mass communication and transportation networks. The first trend is the result of domestic policies; but the Ecuadorian state has not been able to fully control the second.

Throughout most of the twentieth century, Ecuador's state treated its indigenous population as second-class citizens, manipulating them for economic production by coercive means. Moreover, even when land policies replaced the feudalistic huasipungo system of debt peonage in 1964, there was little change in the rural landholding structure between 1954 and 1974, with 87 percent of all farms being less than ten hectares (Tartter 1991, 252). Thus, for many rural indigenous groups, upward mobility came at the expense of their indigenous ethnic identity, which throughout the Andes is largely based on dress (including hairstyle) and lifestyle (including place of residence) rather than race or phenotype.

Not until sociologist Osvaldo Hurtado took power in 1979 did the state seriously begin to bring the indigenous population into the national mainstream (Muratorio 1993). Thus, the cultural heritage of indigenous groups, previously invisible and marginal in official Ecuadorian history, has now turned into an ambiguous point of national pride. The state's focus on vague historical events and cultural icons—not on present-day issues regarding Indian civil rights—demonstrates the ambiguity of this ethnic national pride. Not surprisingly, most of President Hurtado's successors sought to reverse concessions to Indians granted by that government. Although estimates of the indigenous population of Ecuador range from 33 to 45 percent of the national total, the state-censored textbook for eighth-graders has the following entry: "The population of Ecuador is composed of 10 percent White, 9 percent indigenous, and 81 percent Mestizo" (Estudios Sociales 1990). That is, according to state propaganda, there are more Ecuadorians of pure European ancestry than of pure indigenous ancestry.

In contrast with the ambiguity toward Indians in official and civil discourses, ethnic awareness and pride "from below" has taken a more acrimonious route as indigenous groups and urban workers have sought a new voice in the national political and cultural arena. As many indigenous activists have pointed out, in many ways the elites' newfound pride in the country's Indian heritage is simply a continuation of earlier elite discourses regarding the "noble Indian" versus the "dirty Indian," whereby certain indigenous groups are identified as worthy of limited respect (see Muratorio 1993). With widespread discontent and greatly improved transportation and communication networks, ethnic groups and unions began to organize on a national level for the first time in the mid-1980s.

Rising worker discontent and periodic uprisings in the mid-1980s, stemming from austerity measures, led to government repression of leftist political dissidents and union organizers during the free-market regime of Febres Cordero. Although his successor, Rodrigo Borja, had advocated an increasing role for national government to alleviate economic problems causing wide-spread discontent, within a month of taking office in 1988 he announced a new package of currency devaluations and austerity measures, perhaps demonstrating the limits of the Ecuadorian leadership's ability to control the country's own economic and political destiny. However, while fundamental structural problems stemming from historical patterns continue to plague the Ecuadorian economy, social and political changes begun in the 1960s have produced new mass social phenomena. Perhaps the most dramatic event to date was the national uprising, in 1990, of Ecuador's diverse indigenous groups, bringing the nation to a standstill (see Siracusa 1996; Sawyer 1997). However, such collective action has produced little immediate change. The national political culture remains populist and personalistic, while the quasi caste system of ethnic relations remains in place.

Real gains were made for Ecuador's urban and rural laborers in education and, to a lesser extent, in public health. Beginning with reforms in the 1960s and financed with state revenues from petroleum exports in the 1970s, ex-penditures in education have greatly expanded. By 1980, allotments for edu-cation expenditures represented one-third of the state's budget. Officially, lit-eracy rates in rural areas have climbed from 45 percent in 1950 to 76 percent in 1982 (Tartter 1991, 255). Although some Indian leaders now have univer-sity degrees (and international funding), the largest impact of increased ed-ucation levels has not been in improving the high schools and universities, which are continually in a state of financial and academic crisis, but rather in raising the aspirations of newly literate groups beyond what the financially troubled state can provide Ecuadorians in the 1980s and 1990s.

Another important, albeit difficult to measure, cause of national discon-tent is the ever increasing inflow of the culture of consumerism from more developed countries, especially the United States. In this regard, while there may be a debate regarding the degree of economic and political influence of the United States in Ecuador, Hollywood is unquestionably the epicenter of the production of mass entertainment for Ecuadorians in the form of films and television programming. In 1979, just as international migration from the Sierra began to rise substantially, 80 percent of films and 57 percent of the television programs shown in Ecuador were from the United States. In con-trast, less sensational media, such as books from the United States, are much less available in Ecuador (Portais 1989, 108). However, these data are dated and do not reflect the increase in Spanish news programs produced by His-panic channels in the United States, such as Univision. Yet the overall effect remains the same today: an imbalance between the Hollywood images of affluence and information concerning the reality of life in the United States. Referring to the practice of Ecuadorian television news programs to include the temperatures of New York and Miami but not of Ecuadorian cities such as Cuenca or Manta, one Ecuadorian observer noted: "For the banker from Quito or the businessman from Guayaquil, the mental distance separating [him from] Miami is shorter than that which separates [him from] Puyo or Zamora [Ecuadorian Amazonian towns]. . . . But the majority of Ecuadorians are not bankers nor wealthy businessmen and it seems evident that there is an even greater danger in continually presenting a cultural model that is completely inaccessible" (ibid., 109).

Thus, Ecuadorians' untempered perception of life in New York or Miami is of a land of overwhelming contrast with Ecuador's humble abilities to meet new desires for consumer goods and individual freedom. Within this economic and social context, international migration represents one of the most important social and economic forces affecting Ecuadorian society. As an indication of its growing significance, in 1992 the president of Ecuador, Sixto Duran-Ballén, proclaimed the third Sunday of every July to be commemorated annually as, "The Day of the Absent Ecuadorian" (*El Universo*, Dec. 28, 1992).

Diversifying Patterns of International Migration after 1950

Because of its incompleteness and the inherent pitfalls of data on undocumented international migration, existing data can only suggest the general contours of Ecuadorian international migration. Despite existing gaps in our understanding of international migration from Ecuador, three broad patterns are clearly discernible from the available information: (1) a modest legal outflow of Ecuadorians from coastal areas seeking U.S. residency, which gained momentum during the 1960s; (2) a sharp increase during the 1980s in clandestine out-migration from diverse areas in Ecuador, but most notably from the southern provinces of Azuay and Cañar; and (3) a heavy tendency for Ecuadorian immigrants to concentrate in the New York metropolitan area, creating a significant ethnic community.

The historical degree of trade and tourism between any two countries is a good indicator of a modest level of mutual immigration, as some people will inevitably build stronger social ties—such as marriage—while abroad, which subsequently become a reason for an individual to emigrate permanently. This is the kind of migration typical between neighboring countries or within culturally homogeneous regions. Therefore, it is inappropriate to attach a specific date to the absolute origins of international migration, except, per-haps, the date in which a previously closed border became open, such as the case of Japan after the arrival of Commodore Matthew C. Perry. Countries with open borders will always have nationals who settle abroad and foreign-ers who immigrate or become permanent residents.

What, then, is the appropriate starting point for a description of interna-tional migration from a single country? At some point these limited migra-tions by "pioneers" may become mass migrations, forming a distinct pattern apart from the seemingly haphazard decisions of individuals who turn a tem-porary excursion into a permanent stay. Although there is no universal defi-nition of *mass migration*, it is generally characterized as the point where out-migration becomes an institutionalized economic strategy across generations and social classes and marked by the development of a dynamic ethnic com-munity in the receiving region or regions. *Mass migration* describes a local so-cial milieu characterized by a metaphorical "migration fever," whereby prior migration by villagers and relatives becomes the principal motivating force and, as such, must be studied from both microsociological and macrosocio-logical perspectives (Petersen 1958). That is, individual reasons for migrating become, in a sense, superfluous to broader social forces. *Mass* also refers to the tendency for this "migration fever," just like a biological virus, to affect a range of social classes. Similarly, universal definitions of *migration and im-migration* are problematic, since both the objective criteria of length of stay and the more subjective intent of the migrant, either to immigrate perma-nently or return home, are extremely varied and ever changing. A common sentiment among most international migrants leaving a variety of countries to create a financial nest egg is that they do not plan to stay abroad—but in-evitably, many do. Thus, many self-proclaimed migrants, who still intend to return home, have resided abroad much longer than some permanent immi-grants or naturalized U.S. citizens. To put it another way, apart from the movements of political refugees, most immigrations start out as "temporary" migrations from the point of view of the migrant. In this sense, instead of making a sharp distinction between migration and immigration a priori, we can envision a spectrum of migration types ranging from tourism to full cit-izenship.

Legal U.S.-Bound Emigration, 1950 to 1980

We are interested here in tracing the development of a mass international migration from Ecuador to the United States. The first significant migration abroad from Ecuador began in the late 1950s and early 1960s, originating from the outward-looking coastal region of Guayaquil. It is not surprising that international migration originated from the port city of Guayaquil because historically, it has had the highest level of contact with other countries, through trade. The economic impact of the banana bust in the early 1960s was most deeply felt in the Costa and those parts of the south-central Sierra region that had been sending migrants to the Costa. In addition, the increase in the U.S. immigration quota for non-European countries in 1965 contributed to the impression that the United States was welcoming those Ecuadorians who could afford the passage abroad. Hence, with a growing economic crisis at home and a newly receptive destination in the First World, immigration to the United States tripled during the 1960s. According to several prominent Ecuadorian leaders who immigrated to New York City more than thirty years ago, Guayaquileños were prominent pioneers in the migrant emigrations of the 1960s and were typically middle class and relatively educated.*

Although we consider mass migration from Ecuador to be a relatively recent phenomenon, the basic characteristics of current out-migrations were already in place by the end of the 1960s—primarily, a labor migration directed toward the United States, especially New York City. The strong preference for the United States on the part of Ecuadorian emigrants is a trend that has intensified since the 1960s. By 1970, nearly two-thirds of all Ecuadorians abroad resided in the United States (CONADE 1989). Legal immigration to the United States increased again during the 1970s, with fifty thousand Ecuadorians attaining permanent residency in that decade. Attesting to the significance of the Ecuadorian community in New York City by the end of the 1970s, an examination of the flow of telephone calls between 1978 and 1982 indicates that New York City was already the epicenter of international telephone communication for Ecuadorians by that period (see map 2.1).

During the 1980s, the level of legal immigration from Ecuador to the United States was only somewhat greater than during the 1970s (56,000), equaling U.S. quota limits plus those who could enter under family reunification provisions. Throughout this decade, the preference by Ecuadorian migrants for the United States as a destination continued to increase, both in absolute numbers and relative to other destinations. According to the 1990 U.S. Census, 143,000 Ecuadorians were living in the United States that year, up from 86,000 in 1980 (U.S. Bureau of the Census 1993, 50).

---

* Perhaps the greatest gap in our understanding of international migration from Ecuador to the United States is information on the migrant pioneers from Guayaquil, which this book does not attempt to investigate.

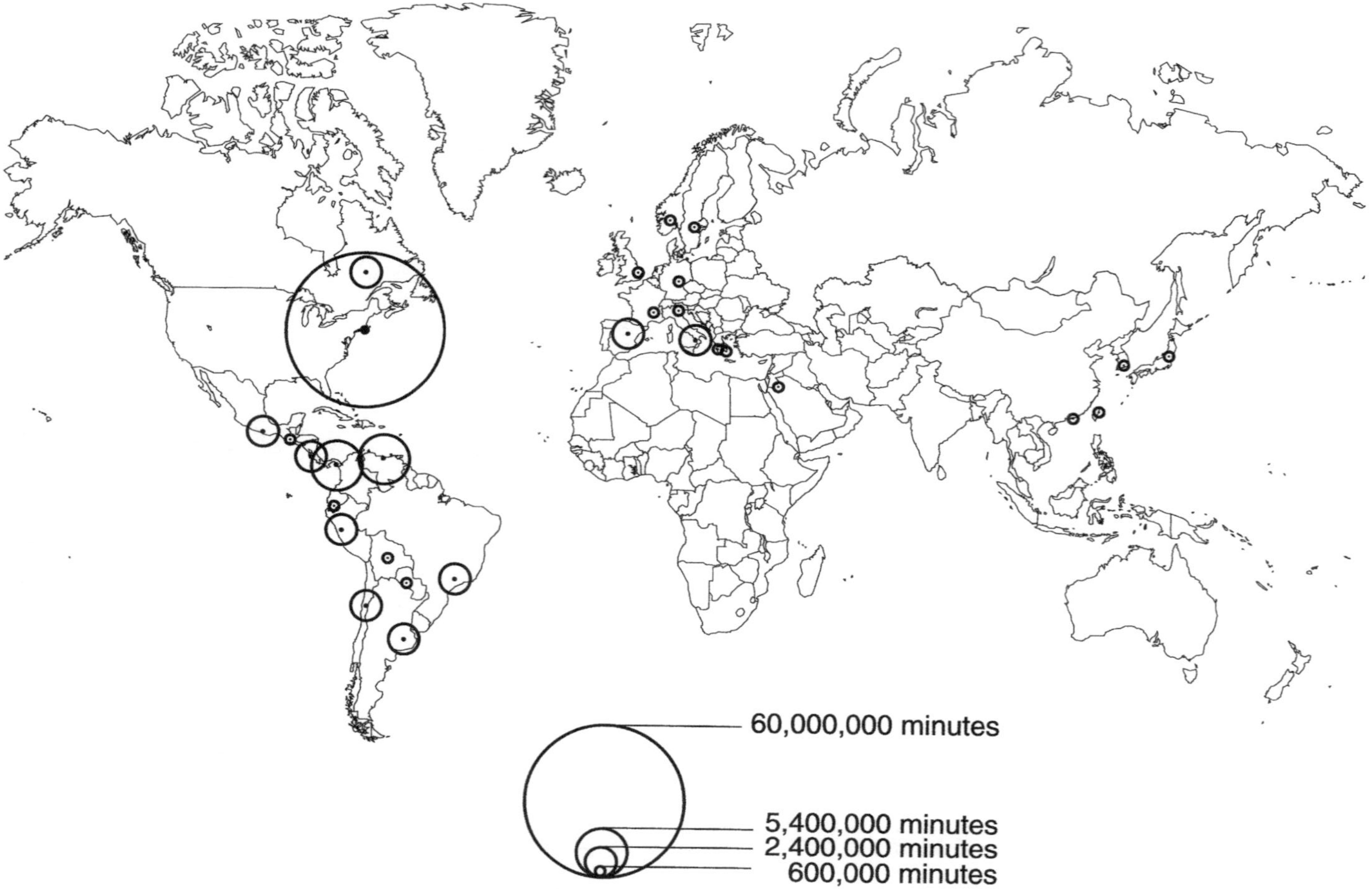

Map 2.1. Telephone Flows by Region. 1978–1982   *Source:* Portais 1989. 106.

60,000,000 minutes

5,400,000 minutes
2,400,000 minutes
600,000 minutes

The Uneven Highland Boom in Undocumented Migration, 1980 to 1990

While the United States remained the favorite destination of Ecuadorian migrants during the 1980s, the social, legal, and regional makeup of international migration flows had shifted by the end of the 1970s. Whereas previous international migration had been predominantly legal, urban, and coastal, new outflows were undocumented and originated directly from both urban and rural areas of the Sierra, especially the south-central provinces of Azuay and Cañar. Since we cannot adequately document illegal border crossings by Ecuadorians by using official data, this central feature of current international migration is best documented quantitatively through estimates of those living abroad. Two specific changes in the geographic and demographic composition of international migration from Ecuador during the 1980s stand out: (1) there has been greater international migration from the Sierra, especially from both the urban and rural areas of the south-central provinces of Azuay and Cañar; and (2) migration to the United States by undocumented migrants can be considered fundamentally a labor migration of mostly male "target earners," or those who intend to stay for a few years in order to save money to invest back home (Piore 1979).

Because Ecuadorian migrants leaving for the United States from Ecuador must do so through the port of Guayaquil and because the majority are traveling with false documents, trying to estimate regional differences in sending levels to the United States requires the use of indirect measurement techniques. One technique is to evaluate mail flows back to specific Ecuadorian regions. Ecuadorian migrants prefer to use private mail couriers, typically part of a travel agency, to send mail and remittances back home, because of their greater security and shorter time to arrival. Computerized statistics provided by Ecuador Travel, a company based in Guayaquil with twelve offices in the New York metro area and numerous offices throughout Ecuador, show that the Azuay-Cañar region receives nearly twice as many letters as metropolitan Guayaquil and surrounding towns and three times as many letters as Quito (see figure 2.1). This surprising difference derives, in part, from the more recent origins of international migration from Cuenca—many families are still divided and, hence, generate more mail and remittances than the more settled families. Nonetheless, these artifactual data provide evidence of a mass migration from the Azuay-Cañar region to New York City.

Also pointing to the uneven nature of international migration from the highlands, the region of Otavalo, in the province of Imbabura, sends large numbers of merchants and musicians abroad. This unique economic strategy, based on an informal growth economy and the social and cultural capi-

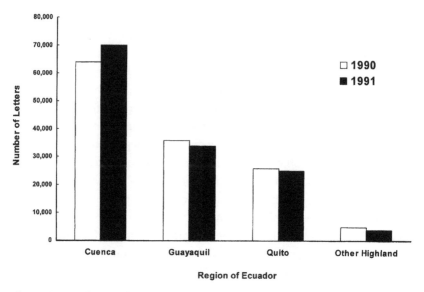

Figure 2.1. Volume of Mail Sent to Various Regions of Ecuador from Ecuador Travel, Inc., 1990–1991   *Source:* Study data.

tal of the Otavaleños, would be impossible to appreciate using national aggregate data.

Ecuadorian census data suggests two basic features of international migration from Ecuador in the late 1980s and the 1990s: net out-migration is increasing for both men and women; and in each year more males than females have left (INEC 1991, 69). Attesting to the labor-oriented nature of the early stages of Ecuadorian transnational migration, most migrants are men between the ages of twenty and fifty. Similarly, Ecuadorian census data on the exit and entrance of Ecuadorians by month also reveal a pattern of high mobility immediately following the Christmas holiday season as migrants return to work (ibid., 5). Another period of high rates of migration occurs during the North American summer. Thus, the aggregate data support, but do not completely verify, a pattern of labor migration composed of so-called target earners (Piore 1979).

There are many ways to cross the border without authorization. Some of these migration strategies are revealed by official data, because they rely on abuse, not avoidance, of the immigration screening system. A common migration strategy is to gain a tourist visa and then overstay the four-month time limit—exit data in 1991 reveal that sixty-three thousand Ecuadorians had traveled to the United States as tourists, the largest category of Ecuadorian migrant (INEC 1991, 36). Others are able to attain visas through the system of preferences allowing the relatives of residents and naturalized citizens to enter the United States. The most common form of chain migration among Ecuadorians, based on social networks of kin, is the use of the Immigration and Naturalization Services's (INS) "second preference," by which entry to the United States is granted to family members of U.S. residents (green-card holders), and the category "spouse of a U.S. citizen" is the second most common preference (City of New York 1992, 61).

The reason that the INS's second preference is so common in comparison with visa preferences granted to U.S. citizens is that Ecuadorians as a group have one of the lowest rates of naturalization. Out of an Ecuadorian cohort admitted to New York City in 1977, fewer than 15 percent had been naturalized by 1989.

Settlement Abroad: The New York Nexus

Since 1965, the year U.S. legislation repealed country-specific immigration quotas, the increasing geographic and economic diversity of immigrant groups from less developed regions has been remarkable—amounting to what is now commonly called the "third wave" of U.S. immigration (Portes and Rumbaut 1996). Nowhere has this been more apparent than in the New York City metropolitan area, where seemingly every country, even the tiniest of Caribbean microstates, has well-developed social and economic networks, often connected to specific sending regions.

Although several researchers have analyzed many of these new immigrant groups arriving in New York City since the 1960s (Sassen-Koob 1981; Marshall 1987; Foner 1987; Papademetriou 1986; Grasmuck and Pessar 1991), Ecuadorians have appeared only as a marginal group, when mentioned at all. However, after forty years of legal immigration and nearly fifteen years of undocumented migration from Ecuador, the Ecuadorian community of New York is now much more visible. Undocumented Ecuadorians in New York City now even outnumber the significant number of undocumented Dominicans and, therefore, are commanding more attention from local government agencies. Using a complex analysis of border crossings, airport data, and the census, the New York Department of City Planning estimates that in 1993, Ecuadorians constituted the number-one undocumented immigrant group in New York, with twenty-seven thousand undocumented Ecuadorians in the state and an equal number living elsewhere in the United States (see figure

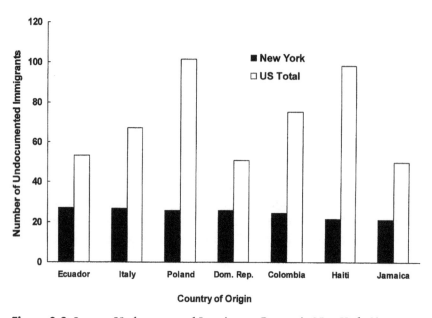

Figure 2.2. Largest Undocumented Immigrant Groups in New York City, 1992 (in thousands)   *Source:* New York City Department of City Planning, quoted in *New York Times,* Sept. 2, 1993, p. B1.

2.2). Figure 2.2 also reveals the concentration of Ecuadorians in New York compared with other immigrant groups.

During the 1980s, Ecuadorian migration to the United States reached critical mass. In 1991, the New York Department of City Planning estimated that there were approximately one hundred thousand documented Ecuadorians in the New York City area—a 100 percent increase since the 1980 U.S. census. If we include nearby communities in New Jersey and the thousands of undocumented immigrants, the number could be well over two hundred thousand. While documented immigration from Ecuador has remained at around five thousand immigrants a year (INS 1988), of which nearly 80 percent go to the New York City area, the size of the New York community indicates a much larger influx, reflecting the substantial increase in undocumented immigrants.

From the perspective of the host society, the Ecuadorian community is difficult to distinguish from other, larger Latin American immigrant groups. Ecuadorians' adaptation to New York City seems to follow the pattern of previous Latin American and Caribbean immigrants; many obtain jobs in the secondary and informal sectors with the assistance of pioneer family members and friends. The similarity with other Latin American groups is further heightened by the fact that many Ecuadorians live in Queens alongside Colombians and Dominicans in the Jackson Heights area, yet they can also be found in large numbers in Manhattan, Brooklyn, the Bronx, and Newark.

However, the Ecuadorian community in New York City reflects the diversity of multiethnic groups found in the distinct geographic and cultural regions of Ecuador: there are currently more than one hundred Ecuadorian clubs and civic associations, many of which have a regional or ethnic association. A striking example is the Chinese-Ecuadorians of New York City Social Club, a community of the descendants of Chinese immigrants to Ecuador who have now themselves moved on to New York City. Several restaurants serving *comida típica* (typical meal) specialize in regional dishes; and community publications and radio programs cater to immigrants from specific provinces. Similarly, the dozen teams in the Ecuadorian American Sport League are identified with specific regions or cities in Ecuador.

After a series of economic busts, reforms, and restructuring, Ecuadorians have been joining the U.S. workforce, either temporarily or permanently, in increasing, though relatively small, numbers since the 1960s. As we have seen, however, human mobility has been intertwined in Ecuador with a profound regionalism and cultural differentiation. A significant development in the migration patterns from Ecuador since 1980 has been a shift to more undocumented, transnational flows from specific regions and communities, especially from the southern province of Azuay.

Similar Individuals, Divergent Outcomes: Assessing Labor Market Theory

Since the codification of economic principles took its cue from nineteenth-century physics, the notion of equilibrium has been applied by economists to a variety of social phenomenon, including international migration. Because migration entails a "flow" from one pole to another, the equilibrium principle seems to fit especially well; as one pole (or side of the equation) develops a need the other pole feels a pressure to meet it. Thus, migration is viewed as a self-regulating mechanism serving to bring the spatially disparate, but essentially harmonious, system back to a state of equilibrium. The microstructures of the equilibrium perspective focus on the rational calculations of immigrants seeking a better life, leaving behind such things as low-income jobs, unemployment, overcrowding, political repression, and natural disasters. These push factors are complemented by pull factors in the receiving society—

jobs, a better social and political environment, a higher living standard—equally affecting a would-be migrant's decision to leave.

The concept of human capital—those traits resulting from an individual's investment in education or training—is employed by economists to explain the variation in immigrants' economic activity and level of attainment in the new country (Becker 1975). Human capital, therefore, becomes a resource that an actor can mobilize toward achieving a goal and also the chief attribute that determines the return on his or her labor. An assumption underlying this last assertion is that employers and employees have perfect information and will act in a rational way, precluding the problem of racial and ethnic discrimination. Thus, any differences observed among immigrants or immigrant groups primarily stem from their different individual attributes and skills. The investment approach within economics recognizes the costs of the trip, the period of settling in, and the emotional stress of leaving loved ones behind (Lucas 1992). Thus younger and somewhat wealthier people are more likely to migrate because they are better able to bear the initial costs of time and money. In short, though there are variations, this approach predicts that the wage differential between two migratory poles is the primary catalyst for migration and that the differences in human capital among potential migrants shape migration patterns.

The survey data indicate both the success of the labor market theory in explaining migration in this case and its limitations, limitations that open the conceptual space for analyses in subsequent chapters. The labor market approach poses an interesting question: do Azuayan and Otavalan migrants have similar or dissimilar levels of human capital in relation to each other and to nonmigrants in their own regions? If we were to find that the individual attributes of migrants in Azuay and Otavalo were largely dissimilar, then this would be a very short book: the variation in migration patterns across the two regions could be largely explained by differences in their age, marital status, education levels, or other individual attributes.

Because the individual attributes of migrants in all four communities are, in fact, roughly similar, most survey findings at that level of analysis have been relegated to appendix B. As the research literature predicts, migrants in all four research sites are more likely to be better educated than their nonmigrant counterparts. They are typically young men who are either single or recently married. Logistic regressions by community, not included in this book, reveal a similar pattern of individual sociodemographic attributes being highly determinative of the onset of transnational migration. It is safe to say that in none of the communities does the poorest migrate; rather, it is the healthiest, the best prepared, and the most ambitious who are most likely to be working in New York City or traveling through Europe on a selling trip. The only significant community difference is that Otavalans from Peguche are more likely to be engaged in handicraft production and to own small workshops in which other laborers are employed. However, this occupation and class position back home cannot be easily separated from the type of migration abroad and features of its strategic organization. Though the individuals who migrate from Azuay and Otavalo come from the same nation-state and have similar levels of human capital, their transnational strategies for economic and social mobility are (seemingly) widely divergent. Before ending this chapter, it is enlightening to examine the extent of this divergence, because it best illustrates the primary mystery to be explored in subsequent chapters.

Once a person decides to migrate abroad, the most immediate issue is not the crossing of a physical border but rather the crossing of a political border. In table 2.1, we see that the majority of villagers from Quipal and Tomebamba made their most recent trip as undocumented or falsely documented aliens. The more rapid development of transnational migration in Tomebamba during the early 1980s is reflected in its higher levels of documented migrations. However, while Tomebamba's migrant population now includes several U.S. residents, or green-card holders, they too first migrated as undocumented migrants. In contrast, migrants from the Otavalan villages rarely migrate illegally, though most of their economic activities abroad are illegal owing to restrictions on those traveling with tourist visas. Most of the undocumented trips reported by Otavalans were to other South American countries, where visas are not required, but by bypassing checkpoints the migrants are sometimes able to avoid paying tariffs.

By examining whether the border was crossed over land or by air, we can roughly tell what percentage of the migrants from Azuay are crossing the Mexican border surreptitiously and what percentage are using false documents, allowing for direct air travel. Each of these undocumented methods carries its own set of risks and drawbacks. In Quipal, a village where most migrants are still undocumented, nearly an equal number are crossing the border by air and by land. Because of the higher prevalence of U.S. residents (36.6%) in the Tomebamba diaspora, nearly 80 percent of this migrant population is currently traveling by air, including both the documented and falsely documented. Among the Otavalan villages, the journey route signifies a different situation; namely, whether the journey is to South America or to the more distant developed countries of Europe and North America.

Perhaps one of the most striking features of the two types of economic migration originating from Azuay and Otavalo are the destinations of the migrants. The Azuayan villages exhibit a propensity to concentrate in one country, while the Otavalans prefer to disperse in search of untapped markets for their goods and music: 97 percent of Azuayans leave for the United States; migrants from Peguche, in contrast, were traveling to at least twenty-three countries in 1993, and the number has continued to grow. In addition, Guanansi has never sent a migrant to the United States, and only 13.7 percent of Peguche's 257 migrants are traveling to the United States. This is a direct result of the state policies of the receiving countries. At the time of this study, most European countries did not require an Ecuadorian, ostensibly traveling as a tourist, to enter with a visa; the United States does. So many from Peguche were traveling to Europe (40%) that that destination was more common than other South American countries (34.4%). However, given the saturation of the European market by Otavalan musicians and street vendors in recent years, not just from Peguche, the preferred destination was the United States, with its untapped urban markets and affluent citizens.

The most varied characteristic of mobility patterns from these four villages is the type of economic activity pursued abroad. Table 2.1 also shows that hardly any of the Otavalan migrants enter foreign labor markets; in contrast, all of the Azuayan migrants enter the labor market of their host country, primarily finding work in the informal sector (see the section of table 2.1 entitled "Employment Sector Abroad"). Given the fundamental difference between the Azuayan and Otavalan villages in the type of migration (labor versus entrepreneurial), it is not surprising that this salient feature colors nearly every aspect of the migration, including characteristics of the journey.

For example, the duration of the last trip abroad by migrants in the four communities, shown in table 2.2, shows similar regional differences stemming from the type of migration. Since most of the Azuayan migrants were abroad at the time of the survey, the duration of their last trip was the time between their departure and the survey in May 1993. In contrast, most of the Otavalan migrants were back home during the survey, making the duration of their last trip a valid measure of their total time abroad. Given the recent rapid development of transnational migration in Quipal, nearly 60 percent of the migrants had been abroad less than one year, including 27 percent leaving in the three-month period immediately preceding the household survey (table 2.2). In contrast, fully 10 percent of the migrants from Tomebamba had made trips lasting more than five years, reflecting its earlier development.

As shown in table 2.3, 81.5 percent of the migrants from Quipal have made just one trip, while 55.8 percent in Tomebamba have made one trip. Stated

Table 2.1. Characteristics of Migrants' Last Trip Abroad, by Village, 1993 (percentage)

Characteristics of the Trip	Quipal	Tomebamba	Guanansi	Peguche
n	43	111	16	257
Documents				
Tourist or resident visa	6.5	36.6	80.0	85.2
Undocumented	93.5	63.4	20.0	14.8
Journey method				
Over land	52.4	21.3	54.5	35.3
By air	47.6	78.7	45.5	64.7
Destination				
Canada	0.0	0.0	0.0	4.7
Caribbean	0.0	0.0	0.0	1.9
Europe	2.1	0.0	28.6	39.8
Mexico and Central America	0.0	0.0	0.0	5.5
South America	0.0	0.9	71.4	34.4
United States	97.9	99.1	0.0	13.7
Number of countries	2	2	4	23
Employment sector abroad				
Self-employed[a]	0.0	0.0	100.0	97.8
Formal sector[b]	0.0	22.8	0.0	2.2
Informal sector[c]	100.0	77.2	0.0	0.0

Source: Study data, 1993.

[a] Self-employment includes selling traditional crafts and performing folkloric music on the streets.

[b] This category is an estimate based on those wage laborers who are U.S. residents, including professionals.

[c] This category is an estimate based on those wage laborers who are not U.S. residents.

differently, nearly 45 percent of Tomebamba's migrants are repeat migrants, making a trip home and then returning to the United States once again. It is this type of circular migration that leads us to label it *transnational.* Transnational migrants from the Otavalan communities rarely extend their migrations beyond one year, with almost half in Peguche and 57 percent in Guanansi going abroad for less than three months (table 2.2). This accounts for the large number of Otavalans who were home during the household survey in April, just before the mid-spring journey abroad, when selling and making music on the streets is more comfortable and profitable than during the winter months in the cold climates of Europe and North America. In table 2.3,

Table 2.2. Duration of Migrants' Last Trip Abroad, by Village, 1993 (percentage)

Duration of the Trip	Quipal	Tomebamba	Guanansi	Peguche
n	43	111	16	257
Mean duration (years)	2.7	3.0	1.1	1.3
Median duration (years)	1.0	2.0	1.0	1.0
< 1 year	59.1	29.4	92.9	85.1
0–3 months	27.3	1.9	57.2	49.8
4–6 months	15.9	2.8	28.6	15.7
6–9 months	6.8	0.0	0.0	8.0
10–12 months	9.1	24.7	7.1	11.6
≤ 2 years	11.6	21.9	7.1	10.0
≤ 3 years	4.6	15.2	0.0	1.2
≤ 4 years	16.3	15.2	0.0	1.6
≤ 5 years	7.0	7.6	0.0	0.0
5+ years	2.3	10.5	0.0	2.0

Source: Study data, 1993.

we see that repeat migration is common among Otavalan migrants. Once an Otavalan has made one trip abroad the likelihood of returning every year is great. Seventeen percent of the migrants from Peguche have made more than six trips abroad, clocking more frequent-flyer miles than the tourists who buy their wares in the Poncho Plaza of Otavalo.

=====

It is significant, in support of the labor market theory, that international migration from Ecuador to the United States during the 1980s and 1990s occurred between two poles characterized by an enormous wage differential: an Ecuadorian in New York City, whether selling his labor or his handicrafts, can earn the equivalent of the Ecuadorian monthly wage in one day, or even a few hours. The recent increase in international migration levels has taken place during a period of currency devaluations and real losses to labor in Ecuador. Yet what is missing is a historical groundedness to such an observation, especially in regard to the political and economic antecedents of these marginal utility differentials residing on opposite sides of a border and maintained by state enforcement. Furthermore, to the extent that such differentials form a pattern among a number of sending and receiving regions it is the deeper logic of such a pattern that must be ultimately explained. In this respect, economist Robert Lucas points out the limitations of traditional labor market theory

Table 2.3. Number of Trips Abroad, by Village, 1993 (percentage)

Number of Trips	Quipal	Tomebamba	Guanansi	Peguche
n	43	111	16	257
Mean	1.3	1.8	4.8	3.4
Median	1.0	1.0	2.0	2.0
1	81.5	55.8	46.2	37.0
2	14.3	21.2	23.1	16.8
3	2.1	15.9	0.0	12.5
4	0.0	5.3	0.0	10.4
5	0.0	0.9	0.0	6.0
6–10	2.1	0.9	23.0	13.3
11–15	0.0	0.0	0.0	2.4
16+	0.0	0.0	7.7	1.2

Source: Study data, 1993.

in explaining the historical causes of international migration: "To say that workers move because the good jobs are elsewhere begs the question of why these jobs are elsewhere. In this sense, economists have relatively little to say about the ultimate causes of migration, as compared to geographers and historians—students of space and time. For if all factors were mobile and [if all workers] pursue the location of highest reward, the system is ultimately indeterminate, and the fixing factors are those of historical incident and of natural locational advantage" (1992, 93).

In addition, the "clean" models of traditional labor market theory tell us little about patterns of international migration or the social structures in which it is embedded, either within or between villages and regions. For example, we cannot assume a priori that labor migration is precluded for Otavalan migrants. The labor market approach is mute regarding the following questions:

- What accounts for these regional and local variations in sending levels and migration development patterns, including the concentration of Azuayans and the dispersion of Otavalans abroad?
- What is the historical context for understanding different economic conditions and strategies among regions and villages?
- Is the social process of migration between these two divergent migration types also disparate or similar?

- Are the two types of transnational mobility found in the two regions a response to similar socioeconomic problems rooted in their home regions or villages?
- In what ways are the impacts of the two migration types on the sending village similar or dissimilar?

The pursuit of these questions structures the remainder of this book.

CHAPTER THREE

The Panama Hat Trail from Azuay

Me acuerdo, difícil, fue de llegar, pagar a coyotes, la migra burlar.
Vendí mis animales, tierrita arada, y hasta los chulqueros yo pedí
prestado. Me dijo un Mexicano como cuate has de hablar, "Cambiaré tu
nombre a 'Mike,' no más, camina, nada, corre, pero ándale m-a-n-o!"
Bendito sea Dios, estoy al otro lado! Soy Cholo Boy y me voy a emigrar!
Tú sabes . . . chulla vida!

[I remember how hard it was to arrive abroad, pay the coyotes, and
thumb our noses at the Border Patrol. I sold my animal, farm, and
borrowed money from the loan sharks. A Mexican told me how to talk,
"Change your name to Mike, run don't walk, get going man!" Blessed be
God, I'm on the other side! I am a Cholo Boy and I'm going to migrate!
You know . . . only one life to live!]

Studies conducted by the New York Department of City Planning continued
to find throughout the 1990s an increasing number of undocumented migrants from Ecuador, most of whom I would contend are from the province
of Azuay. Although Ecuadorians were not on city planners' radar screens in
the 1980s, now they are perhaps the largest group of "illegal aliens" residing
in the metropolitan area. Why did Azuay become the site of a large and mostly
clandestine movement of rural and urban inhabitants to North America, concentrating in New York City?

Before we examine the social antecedents to contemporary migration patterns, it is useful to mine macrosociological theories of international migration for clues in guiding this examination. If past theories prove useful for un-

derstanding the new case of Azuayan migrations to work abroad, then they will be significantly strengthened. If they are found wanting, then we can attempt to identify whether the theories need modification or whether Azuay represents, in fact, a novel type of international migration not conceptualized by past macrosociological-level theory. Indeed, research in the 1980s and 1990s has attempted to conceptualize and research the role of intermediate social networks of family and friends. Similarly, the more recent literature on transnationalism has tended to focus on cases of mass migration established well before 1990, uncovering several unconventional transnational strategies for immigrant adaptation and political activism in both countries of origin and countries of destination; but they have left largely unquestioned causal theories of migration at the macrosociological level. It is important to remember, however, that any theoretical shortcomings may not indicate a "gap" per se but rather may indicate a shift in the causal dimensions of some international (or transnational) flows of labor.

Most recent theorizing of international migration has not privileged one conceptual dimension to the extent that "historical-structural determinants" do all of the work (Massey et al. 1998). Nonetheless, nearly all theories of immigration include a component that places the cases they are examining within the broader "world-system," though there is debate regarding the nature of such a world-system. After all, sociological theories regarding the internationalization of labor, which has been a thread running through analyses of capitalism since Karl Marx, have been very successful in conceptualizing and predicting the widespread contemporary notion of globalization for several decades now. There has also been a close relationship between macrosociological theories of international migration and theories of development. In the 1970s, the paradigm shift in sociology from modernization theories of international development to neo-Marxist and dependency schools, and further influenced by Immanuel Wallerstein's (1974) path-breaking work on world-systems, has had a profound influence on sociological theorizing and research on international migration. Although individual theories on the nature of global capitalism or international migration are varied within this approach, it shares the original Marxist focus on material and structural processes and transformations through time and space.

Contrary to the harmonious depiction of migration and development presented by the conventional economic perspective discussed in the last chapter, the historical-structural perspective is less sanguine regarding the rewards of international migration. Critics of equilibrium theories have asserted that out-migration from "peripheral regions" to developed countries is a feature of global capitalism characterized by permanent disequilibrium, resulting in ever increasing underdevelopment, through a "vicious circle of poverty" (Myrdal 1957). For example, André Gunder Frank's assessment (1970), drawing on the analyses of Karl Marx and Paul Baran, posits that underdevelopment is the result of an active process that drains the periphery of surplus labor and capital within the context of political subordination. International migration is viewed as taking place within the historical context of the dependent relationship between central (core) and peripheral states in the capitalist world economy. Peripheral states provide cheap, abundant labor for the central states within the context of an integrated world labor market, thus creating an "international division of labor" (Sassen-Koob 1978). Accordingly, international migration is seen as taking place within an overarching system, not between autonomous state units (Portes and Walton 1981).

In general, the historical-structural perspective emphasizes the specific labor needs of the advanced core countries and their subsequent efforts to induce immigration appropriate to meeting those needs. For example, to explain the variation of migration patterns found within the same country, several authors have pointed to direct recruitment by North American employers during previous eras as central to the onset of international migration (Massey et al. 1987; Portes and Walton 1981). In particular, current levels of undocumented migration are shown to be associated with subsequently thwarted legal migration flows, of which the Mexican case offers a prime example. While migrant families may be comparatively enriched as a result of migrating, the result is to intensify unequal income distribution and orient would-be migrants toward the needs of the receiving countries (Reichert 1981).

Historically, employer inducements in sending areas lend empirical support to the migration-as-labor argument, which is central to the historical-structural perspective. Yet even within an economic and social climate that is often hostile toward documented and undocumented newcomers alike, the current wave of immigration to the United States is spontaneous and resilient. Furthermore, several empirical studies have shown that it is not the displaced poor who are migrating but rather a somewhat higher strata who own some land and resources, partly because the most destitute seldom have the means to finance a trip abroad (e.g., Portes and Bach 1985, 82). Studies have confirmed that immigrants often possess higher levels of education and skills than nonimmigrants (Massey et al. 1987; for an excellent summary, see Portes and Rumbaut 1996).

Researchers using what may be called a more periphery-centered approach within the general historical-structural framework have found structural features common to peripheral countries with high levels of out-migration. These structural conditions seem to form a pattern of development in the home communities leading to out-migration. Commercialization of agriculture leads to rural unemployment, thus forcing proletarianized rural smallholders to the urban centers. Because national cities are not able to meet the employment demands of this influx, there is a high rate of unemployment and underemployment, giving rise to informal economic activity. This marginalization of more and more workers leads to unequal income distribution, thus limiting the countries' internal market, which results in "disarticulated economies" whereby the dominant export sector has no motivation to raise wages (de Janvry 1982). Finally, this mostly urban surplus labor force is further prompted to migrate to the developed countries by the exposure to modern consumer culture promoted through cultural images transmitted by radio, television, and advertising—a lifestyle that few in the periphery are able to realize (Grasmuck and Pessar 1991). Thus it is the development policies and institutions of the sending country, primarily the reliance on an externally driven export sector, that result in land and labor upheavals and, ultimately, out-migration abroad (Amin 1974, 94).

The two threads running through this sociological literature on migration are (1) the need to conceptualize a social, political, and economic system greater than the two sending and destination countries, and (2) the close relationship between migration and "development," including the intended and unintended consequences of development policies. Indeed, in the case of Azuay, we cannot understand current labor mobility without examining the historical trajectory of the province as it has become more and more integrated into global markets. This trajectory, in turn, cannot be understood apart from the ethnic stratifications and social ideologies that developed in the region as different kinds of migrants settled there.

The Pre-Colombian Period: Conquest and Chaos

As with all of Ecuador's diverse regions, the starting points for understanding Azuay are geography and geology. Located approximately three hundred kilometers south of Quito over mountainous terrain, the province of Azuay includes Ecuador's third largest city, Cuenca (population 330,000), and shares a common social and political history with the neighboring provinces of Cañar and Morona Santiago. The valley of the inter-Andean basin, where Cuenca is located, is 2,530 meters above sea level and is transversed by four rivers that eventually empty into the Amazon region to the east. Unlike other regions, however, the basin is really formed by many crosscutting valleys, none of which is very wide.

In this respect, this southern basin is itself a very diverse region, which contains a range of human settlements at different altitudes and degrees of topographic ruggedness. For example, a variation in altitude of a few hundred meters can determine what crops can be grown, such as corn at lower altitudes and potatoes at higher altitudes. Similarly, although the volcanic soil in southern Ecuador is not as fertile as the more recent volcanic soil in the central and northern valleys, the greatest impediment to large-scale agriculture is the Azuayan valley's rough terrain, which makes irrigation possible only in some areas near river valleys.

Before the Inca arrived in the mid-fifteenth century, the southern highland region was inhabited by the Cañari, whose descendants now live in the mostly rural province of Cañar. Although there is a debate as to whether the Cañari were unified under one regime or were confederated, there is no doubt that they formed a distinct linguistic group that covered an area of approximately ten thousand square kilometers, controlling much of the whole southern region of present-day Ecuador (Espinoza and Achig 1989, 38). Similar to other regions conquered by the Inca, the Cañari had already reached a level of technological development that nearly rivaled that of the Inca, including ceramic making, cloth weaving, working with precious metals, and specialized agriculture. The Cañari traded their metal, cloth, and ceramic handicrafts for salt, cotton, coca, and cinnamon from lowland groups (ibid.).

When the invading Inca did arrive, the Cañari did not submit without a prolonged struggle. Throughout the seventy or so years of Incan domination the Cañari continued to be unruly, requiring the Inca to use the most severe measures to bring their subjects under control. It was the Incan institution of mitimae that undoubtedly had the greatest impact on the region; loyal Quichua and Aymara speakers from the southern and eastern highland regions of the Incan empire in present-day Peru and Bolivia were sent to replace large groups of Cañari, who were, in turn, displaced to those same distant regions of the Incan territory. Even today, the Cañari see this devastating institution—not the Spanish Conquest—as the beginning of their current struggles: "When the Incan Empire began to expand north, we Cañari put up a fierce resistance, which was suffocated by sending part of our people to Cuzco and as many to Quito, and the arrival to our lands of mitimaes that were located in Cojitamba and Chuquipata. Since then, the history of our people has been marked by the permanent search for liberty through various actions"

(CONAIE 1987, 193). Although the complete destruction of the Cañari was not the initial Incan goal of the mitimaes, the cultural and ideological impact of such diverse groups living in neighboring villages was to create the conditions for the slow elimination of a collective cultural memory. Because the mitimaes continued to use the name of their original village, this legacy is still evident today in the names of neighboring villages in the region, which reflect the Cañari, Quichua, and Spanish cultures.

To the further detriment of the Cañari, when civil war broke out between the Incan half-brothers Huáscar and Atahualpa, the Cañari sided with the ill-fated, Cuzco-based Huáscar. In retribution, the site of present-day Cuenca (then called Tomebamba) was destroyed in 1529, and sixty thousand Cañaris were reportedly killed by Atahualpa's army (Hurtado 1980). As these dramatic developments during the Incan regime attest, some of the greatest sociocultural changes in the region occurred immediately preceding the Spaniard's arrival.

The Colonial Period: Social Autonomy and Economic Dependence

Because of their deep resentment of the Inca, the Cañari were the first to ally with the Spanish in their conquest of Incan territory north of Peru, marked by the arrival at Tomebamba of Sebastian Benalcazar in 1533. Just one year later, Quito was founded, and the region of Tomebamba was given over to Diego Sandoval in encomienda. Soon after, other encomiendas, with rights to Indian labor in the form of tribute, were granted in Tomebamba. Just as the Inca before them, the Spaniards found the region to be of great interest because it was strategically located between the important colonial seats of Quito and Lima. Following several Cañari revolts, the Spanish consolidated control of the region by founding the city of Cuenca in 1557 on the site of the Cañari and Incan city of Tomebamba.

The colonial history of this southern region of the Quito Audencia, which developed a unique social milieu during this period, has not enjoyed the level of interest and scholarship that other regions have been given. An exception is Lynn Hirschkind's excellent summary (1980) of the colonial period of Azuay as prologue to her anthropological study of conforming in Cuenca. Apart from the singular sociocultural makeup of the indigenous population, I focus here on two distinctive features of the early Azuay *corregimiento* (a basic colonial administrative unit) that Hirschkind has highlighted: (1) the development of an isolated, self-designated "nobility," which set the economic and social tone of the region for centuries; and (2) the presence of significant numbers of middle-stratum Spaniards and their offspring, who moved into more rural areas among the indigenous population and developed into a relatively independent social grouping. Both of these early social developments contributed, directly and indirectly, to the principal pattern of social life still found today in the region: a conservative, complex social hierarchy based on kinship and closely maintained by ideological, legal, and economic means.

Through administrative structures of local power, the same Spanish elite could control both urban positions of power and the rural economy based on Indian labor. Those elite who owned both urban and rural lands, which often included a *mitayo* grant of Indian labor, were designated *vecinos,* or neighbors; only vecinos could hold local positions of authority. Cuenca had sixty vecinos in 1563, 150 in 1582, and 500 in 1620, of which the elite maintained control by rotating vecino positions among a few families (Hirschkind 1980). As the institution grew, the power of the vecino position waned, but the power of the original vecino families did not. In parallel fashion, the local church authority, which was made a bishopric in 1779, also held vast holdings of land and Indian labor in the region. By sending one son to the priesthood and older unmarried daughters to the convent, the landowning elite held considerable power within the church hierarchy. Thus, both secular and clerical power were limited to relatively few families who began to see themselves as a sort of local nobility. The main ideological feature of this elite was the dual importance of land ownership and residence in the city, the focus of all civilized activities in the urban-centric, Spanish (Greco-Roman) worldview.

Although this concentration of land and power into the hands of a few families may have been somewhat exaggerated because of Cuenca's geographically and politically peripheral position vis-à-vis Quito and Lima, it was not that different, in this regard, from other regions during the colonial period. Nonetheless, the development of a local nobility based on ancestral origins in the original vecino families meant that other Spanish and light-skinned mestizo settlers had to resign themselves to positions of ascribed inferiority with only tenuous control over land and Indian labor.

Stemming from the development an urban-based, local aristocracy, Hirschkind suggests, extreme status consciousness "is one of the all-encompassing, shared systems of cultural meaning that bridges the gulfs between Cuenca's different socio-cultural sectors" (1980, 88). Even today in Cuenca, family wealth, professional status, and community standing are often not enough to make a young "commoner" *(pueblo)* acceptable for marriage within noble circles after surnames and family background are scrutinized.

Thus, though many "common" whites and mestizos became smallholders and even *hacendados* in the countryside, they were left without significant influence in the city. Early chroniclers of the region note the many whites (i.e., Spanish-blooded) and mestizos who inhabited the countryside and small towns surrounding Cuenca. The consequences of a more mestizo, landed peasantry in the region were subtle yet profound, as Hirschkind observes:

> The significance of this demographic pattern is multiple and far-reaching. Whites and some Mestizo peasants were landowners in their own right, though their holdings probably did not rival those of the Cuenca-based *hacendados*. This relatively privileged rural sector was not subject to the taxes and labor conscription methods imposed on Indians. As Whites they were also better able to protect their interests and their lands from encroachments by the powerful and land-hungry. . . . This population could not be dominated by the elite sector in Cuenca in the same way that the elite dominated Indians. . . . In sum, there is much evidence that from the time of the earliest Spanish settlement in the Azuay region, there developed a significant population of small land-holders who were Spaniards and descendants of Spaniards. (1980, 60)

Similarly, even the indigenous population of Azuay enjoyed a somewhat more independent status throughout the colonial period owing to a relatively high level of land ownership.

Two demographic characteristics of the indigenous population, marked by two consecutive periods, shaped this anomalous situation. First, during the first two centuries of the colonial period, with the virtual decimation of the Cañari during the Incan civil war—leaving as few as three thousand Cañari (Espinoza and Achig 1981, 36)—Indians from more northern regions of the Sierra migrated southward to Azuay (Powers 1995). The generally low population density in the more rugged, higher altitudes of Azuay meant that Indians could find sufficient land unclaimed by *haciendas*.

Second, when a large influx of Indians did migrate to Azuay in the eighteenth century, they did so under rare conditions that did not easily permit the capture of their labor. Under pressure to industrialize resulting from Bourbon reforms, Spain had increased the level of tribute required by the colonies. With the economy of the Audencia of Quito already in crisis, indigenous groups, who ultimately bore the burden of tribute, revolted throughout the country; tens of thousands of Indians left their villages in the central Sierra to find unclaimed land to the south in the mountainous areas of Azuay, becoming foresteros. Thus, although by the end of the first decade of the eighteenth century Azuay had become one the most populous departments, most of the indigenous immigrants at the time were smallhold-ers ungoverned by an hacienda. This relative lack of control over the labor force by the elite was noted by outside observers in the 1760s. A judge for the Audencia Real de Quito observed that "there are many who do nothing what-soever, just as there are almost anywhere; the only thing special about here [Azuay] is that one cannot find people to cultivate the land or who want to serve on the estates, which is due to the fact that everyone has his plot of land, though it be small, and since, as I have already said, this region is very fertile; with almost no work the land provides for all needs" (quoted in Hirschkind 1980, 52). A year later in 1765, another visitor made the following observa-tion:

> Thanks to the abundance of produce, the Indians here manage to find greater comfort and rest in their lives, as compared to the bare subsis-tence of those miserable Indians in other parts of the province; but even greater profits from the fertility of the land are enjoyed by another im-mense multitude, those who are here called Mestizos, who, due either to their greater industriousness or to their greater dedication to their work, have taken possession of and divided among themselves a large part of the lands; for this reason noble families are somewhat scarce and due to their poverty and lack of funds, even these few families lack the lustre and splendor of nobles elsewhere. (Ibid., 52–53)

This pattern of land tenure and relative lack of control over the diverse in-digenous population led to an equally unique regional economic structure, which out-migration has only recently begun to alter: a nominally indepen-dent peasantry that had to find supplemental income and an economic elite who demonstrated little entrepreneurial creativity beyond taking profits on imports and exports. The smallholders wove cotton and wool cloth and gath-ered cinchona bark, which was sold for the manufacture of quinine, while the "nobles" attempted to maintain the Spanish ideal of remaining aloof from commerce and industry, except as investors or financiers for a few lucrative exports and imports, namely, those items produced or gathered by the bulk of the peasantry. This left an entrepreneurial vacuum that could only be filled, inadequately, by a middle stratum of local and itinerant mestizo and white *comerciantes* (commercial landowners). Azuay's leading sociologist and econ-omist, Leonardo Espinoza, describes Cuenca's economic structure at the time it was established as a *gobernación* (regional government) in 1771:

> Economic power in the province was exercised by a commercial landowner class, consolidated by means of its intermediary and contra-

band activities in the commercial monopolies of cinchona bark and cane liquor, its collection of Indian tribute, and, additionally, its influential position in the buying and selling of imported manufactured items and of property, especially land. The comparative advantages of obtaining greater earnings in commercial activities rather than in productive activities may help us understand why there was no strong concentration of land ownership in the province. Nevertheless, members of the dominant class made their presence felt as hacendados in their ownership of merely medium-sized extensions of land; their haciendas allowed them to exercise not only economic control, but also political and ideological control over the large mass of Indian peasants, the principal source of the generation of a surplus in the region. (Espinoza 1979, 36)

Was this unproductive *minifundio* structure a result of the ideology of the elite, which outwardly eschewed productive economic activity? Or was the development of a social caste system in the region a response to elite anxiety over their inability to control large areas of the countryside and, hence, produce anything of profitable consequence? Whichever came first, the local caste system of the minifundio structure, the campesinos' inefficient methods, and the general regional disorganization all contributed to Azuay's relatively low productivity during the later colonial period.

The case of spinning and weaving cloth, which began as an activity practiced by both the peasantry and urban women, illustrates the primary social and economic relationships that epitomized the colonial period. Middlemen sold the weavers the wool, cotton, dyes, and soap and also bought the finished cloth, which was then sold to urban merchants who either exported it or resold it to other middlemen (Hirschkind 1980). The peasants were paid a fraction above the costs of the raw material; by the beginning of the eighteenth century, the urban women wove only to satisfy family needs because of the lack of profits. Labor costs were low, and thus Azuay was able to continue selling cloth well after other regions found it unprofitable. Those merchants who traded directly with Lima, through the port of Guayaquil, made the greatest profits, since they could also import *efectos de Castilla* (Spanish dry goods) along with cotton and soap needed to weave, items that could then be resold at usurious prices to peasant-weavers (Hirschkind 1980).*

---

* It is interesting to note in this regard that the first president of Peru, Mariscal José de La Mar, was born in Cuenca and is the namesake of Cuenca's airport.

Unlike the classic highland colonial system of agriculture and labor based on feudalistic labor arrangements, two features dominate the historical economic development of the Azuayan region: (1) the countryside became characterized by extreme minifundio, dependent on—but not completely dominated by—larger haciendas and supplemented by a cottage industry of handicrafts and wage labor and trade, both legal and contraband; and (2) a new class developed—the gentleman elite, who were content to siphon off agricultural surplus through the financing and brokering of local exports and foreign imports, leading to a significant socially intermediate tier of predatory middlemen who were neither rural smallholders nor nobles.

The Republican Period: Incorporation into the World Economy

In the nineteenth century, as Silvia Palomeque (1990) has shown, Azuay experienced fundamental changes in the nature of its relation to the world economy as it was freed from the yoke of royal domination; but, more important, it was the basic continuity in its social structure that impelled and shaped those changes. As a generalized phenomenon, Andrés Guerrero (1991) has noted the nature of change within Ecuador: "In Ecuador . . . basic accumulation is the process of the constitution of the elements of the capitalist mode of production, but not through an historical dissolution and transformation of the strongly structured social structures. These [social structures], located in the inter-Andean alley, which may pass through some transformations, above all conserve themselves and, in any case, slowly liberate some elements" (quoted ibid., 194). Guerrero's general observation could not be more true of Azuay as a specific example. In its autonomy and rigidly bounded social structure, Azuay was more like a state than a province during the colonial period (ibid.). When change occurred in the nineteenth century, the autonomous Azuayan elite and peasantry accommodated the need for a greater external articulation while retaining and even strengthening the social class structure and ideological status quo.

Except for a further entrenchment of the social structure, the principal change to the Azuayan region after independence from Spain was economic, though it was economic change that also would transform the region and further integrate it into distant markets. The lack of royal authority and Azuay's general isolation meant that local elites could consolidate their interests and increase their ideological claims to the region's resources and surplus labor. In the nineteenth century, economic elites introduced the new economic activity of weaving straw hats as a productive activity that did not upset the social structure but rather reinforced it. For several decades, following the decline of the cloth trade, elites had placed little pressure on the Azuayan and Cañari peasantry. Now elites sought to create a completely new cottage industry in which the peasantry could produce a high-quality, low-technology handicraft using inexpensive, though imported, raw materials.

Immigrants from the coastal province of Manabí, where fine Montecristi hats had already gained international fame, had introduced the technique of weaving straw hats with the special palm straw, *paja toquilla,* to Azuay in the 1830s (Domínguez 1991). In 1844, in an uncharacteristic public foray into commerce and industry, perhaps driven by decades of regional economic stagnation, the city councils of Cuenca and nearby Azogues decreed that children be taught hat weaving in addition to their academic studies, built the infrastructure needed for finishing and storing the hats, imported the straw, and brought in skilled teachers from Jipijapa in Manabí. Local prisoners, including the indigent, were forced to weave hats, which were, in turn, offered free to peasants in exchange for a promise that they, too, would learn the craft (ibid.).

In promoting the new industry, local officials noted the low cost of the straw and other materials needed and that, "most importantly, it is an occupation in which all hands can be put to work, including men and women, elderly and children" (ibid., 36). With such a concerted push by the elite and the quick popularity of the hats in sunny Azuay itself, the introduction was a huge success—to the extent that peasants and urban poor were soon weaving hats in nearly every corner of Azuay and Cañar. With the internal demand satisfied, the hats began to be exported for sale to gold miners passing through Panama during the California gold rush of the 1850s (hence the name, *Panama hat*); the value of straw hat exports from Ecuador jumped from 117,008 pesos in 1843 to 830,040 in 1855 (Palomeque 1990).

Like many historical social changes in Azuay, although the weaving of straw hats—planned and instituted by local elites—did not pose a threat to the prevailing social order or ideology, it did begin a radical transformation that would articulate the region into a labor-intensive industrial economy, closely linked to the global markets. Although the cottage industry of hat weaving was similar to that of cloth weaving, whereby both raw material and woven product were brokered to the peasantry by middlemen who were, directly or indirectly, employed by urban export "houses," the production and marketing process entailed a greater division of labor on a much larger scale with (as city officials predicted) the participation of both men and women, young and old, each finding his or her production niche. Very young children helped separate and care for the straw; older children began learning to weave; men finished the hat by washing, ironing, blocking, trimming, measuring, sorting, and boxing for export. The brokering system itself employed a hierarchy of *comisionistas*, who broker for the export houses, and independent *perros* (dogs), who sell to the comisionistas after paying the weaver slightly less for the hat than what the comisionista would have paid. Miguel Domínguez (1991) estimates that at the height of the hat trade in the 1940s, as many as 250,000 children and adults from the provinces of Azuay and Cañar were engaged in some activity directly related to making and marketing Panama hats. In 1946, Azuay's weavers had produced 3,648,580 hats, fetching U.S.$4.7 million for Cuenca's exporters (Hirschkind 1980).

Although the peasant-weavers of Azuay enjoyed an unprecedented freedom in comparison with their counterparts living on haciendas or working in urban sweatshops, their ambiguous class position prevented them from making any significant economic or social gains through group mobilization; though thousands were and continue to be exploited at piecework rates below the subsistence level, this common exploitation as a potential source of group action is outweighed by their conservative position as landowners in direct economic competition with their neighbors—a fact fully exploited by the comisionistas and perros. Not surprisingly, hat weaving proved to be highly resistant to unionization. In 1944, Dr. Luis Monsalve Pozo polemically described this situation:

> Thousands of hands, white, smooth, fine hands of women . . . weave the
> illusion of obtaining their bread and water, when in reality the illusion is
> converted into mere centavos for them, but for others the conversion is to
> palaces, Cadillacs, villas, tourism, and other things. . . . Weavers are scat-
> tered in the cities and in the country. They do not have a spirit of a uni-
> fied class. They do not recognize their problem; they feel it, they live it,
> but not even from afar do they presume to resolve it. This lack of bond
> among the workers, this lack of class unity, and this original scattering
> of themselves, lost in the Andean brambles . . . have contributed to the
> workers not speaking a word, however angry or admonishing. (Quoted
> in Miller 1986, 159)

Tom Miller observes succinctly, "In a cottage industry such as the weaving of Panama hats, the industry regulates the cottage" (ibid., 159). Indeed, while extraeconomic methods of coercion, such as forcing criminals and the indigent to weave, were not unknown, the Panama hat trade gave the elite a level of economic control over the peasantry unmatched during the colonial period.

The increased internal economic integration of the region, brought about through the cottage industry of hat weaving, paralleled Azuay's new articulation with the world economy. Although still socially and physically isolated from other regions of Ecuador, the economy of nineteenth-century Azuay became increasingly linked to global markets: by 1910, at a time when most of the Ecuadorian Sierra was only exporting surplus agriculture to its neighbors, Cuenca was exporting straw hats to Panama, Jamaica, Mexico, New York, London, Hamburg, Cuba, Chile, Venezuela, Guatemala, Puerto Rico, and Paris (Domínguez 1991). By the beginning of the twentieth century, importers in New York City were the major buyers of Panama hats. These buyers then would export all over the world. Similarly, the export of cascarilla from Azuay during the last half of the same century reinforced the region's dependence on foreign markets. The full impact of this early and nearly complete dependence on foreign trade, built on the exploitation of a rural labor force and controlled by ignorance and ideology, would be felt in 1947, when the booming hat trade collapsed.

Palomeque (1990) links coastal migration with the export of cascarilla during the last half of the nineteenth century; it was during periods of increased exports of cascarilla and, thus, more pressure on the peasant's surplus labor that temporary out-migration to coastal regions first appeared. However, Palomeque argues that coastal migration had more to do with the regional crisis of subsistence, brought about by the specific institutions of increased exploitation of the Azuayan peasantry during periods of external market demand, than with the attraction of coastal wages. Thus, she concludes, while the nineteenth-century integration of Azuay into the world economy through such exports as straw hats and cascarilla was a defining moment for the region, its penetration and impact on Azuay were considerably mediated by local patterns of historically embedded internal and external social relations.

The Collapse of the Panama Hat Trade, 1947 to 1957

The principal antecedent to the current Ecuadorian phenomenon of mass international migration based on the selling of one's labor was the decline after World War II in the Panama hat trade, the cornerstone of the Azuayan economy during the republican period. However, international migration from the region was as much a continuation of regional socioeconomic relations as a break with past economic activities.

A long decade of economic depression in Azuay began with the precipitous drop in 1955, and a continuous decline every year until the mid-1960s, in the export of Panama hats. After World War II, Cuenca's principal buyer of Panama hats, the United States, began to import cheaper "straw" hats from Japan, China, Italy, and the Philippines. These mostly Asian countries enjoyed a lower import tariff as part of postwar reconstruction and used a more mechanized factory method to produce a cheaper hat that resembled the Panama, though without its flexibility and durability (Domínguez 1991). In addition, by the 1960s the use of hats had sharply declined in the United States, symbolized by President John F. Kennedy's hatless march to his inauguration. Attempts to modernize Azuay's hat industry by creating more efficient, centralized factories, which could better control the production process and eliminate the usurious middlemen, proved difficult; the dispersed, independent weavers produced hats according to a time schedule set by agricultural, familial, and religious duties. Even today, after forty years of the Asian revolution that brought about the local decline, hat production and its commercialization use technology that has remained essentially unchanged since the 1840s.

The impact of the hat industry's decline on Azuay and Cañar was immediate and severe, initiating a quiet revolution of economic disarticulation and social disintegration. For many members of the urban elite not directly connected to the hat trade, the ability to exploit the new vulnerability of the rural and urban labor force compensated for any financial losses. It was, instead, those diverse groups engaged in some activity related to the hat trade (which at its height included more than a quarter of the population) that had to seek external remedies to the immediate economic crisis they were experiencing. While the local and national elite did not respond effectively to the Azuayan crisis of the 1950s, two groups—the white and mestizo exporters and the rural peasant-weavers—initiated two different types of migration, which later set the stage for a mass exodus in the 1980s and 1990s. It was during the 1950s that the first Azuayans arrived in New York City, mostly young men of wealthy white and mestizo families directly connected to urban hat export houses. They were looking for ways to capitalize financially on their longstanding connections with U.S. importers—and for adventure (Astudillo and Cordero 1990). Also during the late 1950s, regular jet airline service connected Cuenca to New York City via Guayaquil. It was now as easy for an Azuayan to travel to New York City as to Quito.

While many Latin American elites preferred Europe as a destination, especially Paris, these pioneers to New York City were generally not nobles. This is underscored by the pejorative label, *cholo boys*, given to these nouveau riche jet-setters by the snobbish social elite of Cuenca (ibid.). It is this middle-class group that immigrated to New York in the late 1950s and early 1960s, following the "Panama hat trail," who led the way for other friends and relatives to follow, eventually developing a migration network that included former and current peasant-weavers from the countryside.

Those most affected by the hat crisis of the 1950s were the peasantry. Their first strategy in response to this crisis was to reinitiate seasonal migrations to coastal plantations. These migrations were similar to earlier ones at the end of the nineteenth century in response to the collapse of the cascarilla market. However, now, because of the fragmentation of land in Azuay, minifundio had become *microfundio* through steady population growth, soil erosion, and inheritance customs that divided land equally among offspring, thus making many Azuayan peasants more dependent on the cash economy of selling handicrafts or wage labor than on agricultural produce. This was especially true of those villages and small towns dominated by hat weaving, which are geographically concentrated along a thirty-kilometer corridor between Cuenca and Azogues to the north, the economic centers of the hat export trade. Men and older boys from these villages walked for more than a week down the Andes during harvest season to work in the banana and sugar plantations that now dominate the Costa. Not only was there work to be found on the plantations, but they also generally paid more than Sierran haciendas for agricultural wage labor. Although some became permanent coastal immigrants, thousands of peasant families began a multigenerational tradition of seasonal migration. Some villages located closer to Cuenca also began to send permanent and temporary workers into the city.

While this economic strategy of seasonal migration did entail a temporary absence of some family members for a few months out of the year, the basic family social structure and community culture could still be reproduced. However, this strategy represented two important economic and social changes for migrant communities. First, it meant that formerly independent smallholders were now more proletarianized and alienated from their own labor. Second, as hat weaving and other handicrafts were continued by women, the increasing feminization of this artisanal sector meant that it was assigned an even lower status within the community, thereby cutting off a potential economic strategy for young males.

As the Panama hat crisis dragged on through the 1950s, the whole region fell into an economic depression, exacerbated by Azuay's isolation and lack of infrastructure. Although a road to Quito via Riobamba had opened in 1948 and a road to Guayaquil in 1953 (until that time, pack mules had been used), neither was paved. Furthermore, since Azuay was no longer a major exporter of anything, new transportation links only meant cheaper manufactured imports with which local handicrafts could not compete. Although the national government had exempted all new industry in the region from any taxes for ten years, it was hard to attract capital away from Guayaquil and Quito, owing to the region's isolation and lack of infrastructure, such as sufficient electric power. Nevertheless, as a result of this law and a new, though inadequate, electric plant, the region succeeded in attracting the U.S.-based General Tire Company and a cement plant, both of which began production in the 1960s.

Modernization through Mobilization, 1957 to 1981

Although reconstruction of the region gained momentum during the 1960s through local and national government initiatives, the primary force of change occurred in response to high levels of permanent and temporary out-migration. With funds from a variety of public and private sources, the Center for Economic Reconversion of Azuay, Cañar, and Morona Santiago (CREA) was established in 1960 to chart a course for regional economic development. While CREA succeeded in providing new agricultural and artisanal projects, it could do little to stem the tide of out-migration and even promoted and oversaw colonizing migration to the Amazonian province of Morona Santiago. However, the basic social and economic structure of the region remained intact.

Similarly, other national programs were also counterproductive in hindsight. With a reformist military regime in power, and under pressure from the U.S. Alliance for Progress program, national agrarian reforms were enacted in 1964, designed to end debt peonage and redistribute large hacienda lands into peasant cooperatives. However, the reforms had more of a detrimental effect on the independent Azuayan peasantry who "had no background in cooperative or community organization and were highly individualistic in their work habits" (Hirschkind 1980, 106). The minority who were connected to haciendas were simply given the worst lands without the resources of the hacienda, resulting in the need to migrate to the city or out of the region altogether. Nearly a hundred thousand left the region for either the Costa or the Oriente between 1950 and 1974. As Hirschkind points out, migration had both a positive and negative effect in reactivating the regional economy: though Azuay was losing some of its best human resources, new social and economic ties were being forged with receiving areas, including remittances that enabled relatives of migrants to buy land back home. In sum, the 1960s was a pivotal period for Azuayan society as nascent industrialization was overshadowed by the social and demographic transformation brought about by out-migration and urbanization.

When the national oil boom began in 1973, Cuenca intensified its role as the center of economic and demographic development for the region. In fact, after two decades of economic depression and struggle, Cuencanos became "strong advocates of any project that appeared to conform to the term "development," a concept that, in the past, had gained few advocates among the elite of Cuenca (Hirschkind 1980, 116). Indeed, the 1970s did bring full-scale modernization programs of education and health, hundreds of urban jobs connected to newly opened branches of national ministries, and even a few hundred factory jobs in new industries on the outskirts of the city. Consequently, the population of Cuenca tripled in the twenty-five years leading up to 1980. Cheap urban labor and the rise of a middle class of bureaucrats, fueled by state spending, led to a construction boom that transformed the cityscape of Cuenca.

Yet regional problems still existed and were poorly addressed, especially the social and natural barriers to agricultural production among the rural peasantry. Under the national leadership of a military regime, a new agrarian reform law in 1973 sought to modernize the agricultural sector through more capital inputs and technologies. The impact of this latest round of reforms was, once again, largely negative for the minifundio peasants of Azuay and Cañar, who could not compete with a capital-intensive, agro-industrial sector. The straw hat trade, which had never completely died out as an important source of cash for some rural areas, had made a brief comeback in the mid-1970s, only to go bust once again in 1978 and continue falling through the mid-1980s. In addition, the booming state-led economy based on oil extraction was heating up inflation to record highs. Even though the government raised the state-regulated monthly wage 25 percent, to 1,250 sucres, it was still below subsistence levels for most families in a region that imported not only consumer goods but also basic foodstuffs. In the wake of measures designed to attract foreign capital at the expense of workers (many now fully proletarianized) the military did not tolerate the protests and worker uprisings that followed. In 1977, a worker uprising on the Aztra sugar plantation ended in a massacre of its workers, including several from the Azuay region.

Locally, much of the new development of the 1970s benefited the same families that had always controlled the commercial and financial sectors, which, because of the region's heavy dependence on imported capital, raw materials, industrial equipment, and consumer goods, were the primary growth areas during this period. In addition, there was now more investment capital available to elites through national development banks. The "nobles" were able to apply the old logic of inherent superiority and paternalism to new economic roles in an expanding urban economy; political and economic positions may now have required the façade of a higher academic degree but were still acquired by using kin- and caste-based social networks (Hirschkind 1980). For example, local university faculty positions are often little more than political appointments; elite-based political parties control entire academic and administrative departments as territorial fiefdoms. The result, which has continued into the 1990s, is slow growth stemming from a conservative economic system based on loyalty rather than quality, products that are less than competitive, and continued investment only in areas with quick and secure returns (e.g., imports, banking, furniture making, bottling companies). Part of this slow growth stems from Cuenca's inability vis-à-vis Guayaquil and Quito to attract national and foreign investment. Since reactivating the urban economy, a recalcitrant, ideologically conservative elite has channeled more rhetoric than resources to rural areas since the 1970s.

Nonetheless, given new social and economic linkages with the rest of Ecuador, through better communication and transportation, domestic migration, and economic development, there was a widespread perception by the end of the 1970s that Azuay was finally joining the rest of the world. While the old social order, composed of just fifty or so families, still held sway over the region, their strict ideological control had somewhat weakened in the face of mass education, extraregional contacts, and the rise of a *pueblo rico,* or class of nouveaux riches, who could now credibly vie for economic leadership by using their greater commercial flexibility and competitiveness (Hirschkind 1980). Writing in 1980, at the height of Azuay's period of great expectations, Hirschkind summarizes the feelings of the day:

> The present is seen as a period of transition by Cuencanos. They remember the slowness, the isolation, of twenty years ago. They find themselves experiencing the socio-economic trends of the world at large, its fast pace and rapid rate of change. It seems clear to them that when the transition is finished, Cuenca and Azuay will be "developed" and "modern." The end of the process will bring all the consumer products imaginable, all the services necessary for comfortable living, and their society will be well-organized, efficient, and convenient. In the present industrialization and urbanization processes they see the budding of this future flower. (1980, 118)

Just one year later, oil prices dropped, and Ecuador's economy suffered its worst crisis thus far in terms of debt, inflation, and stagnation; that crisis has persisted into the 1990s. The economic blow was especially tragic for Azuay, which had seemed to be finally shaking the languor sown by the devastation of its straw hat trade.

Mass Migration to New York City, 1981 to 1995

If the 1960s were a transitional decade for the economic development of the region, the 1970s, in hindsight, can be seen as the transitional decade that once again turned Azuay into an international exporter—this time, of people. Results from a 1990 University of Cuenca survey focusing on the regional labor force show that international migration from Azuay and Cañar was already widespread: 45.5 percent of those sampled had at least one family member living in the United States, and 19 percent of these migrants came from rural areas (IDIS 1990).

During a preliminary phase of this study, 329 eleventh- and twelfth-graders were surveyed in three medium-sized Azuayan towns: Paute, Girón, and Gualaceo. Results from the survey support evidence that international migration levels are high and widespread in Azuay. Among the students, fully 47 percent had one or more family members living abroad, most of whom were in the United States, while a full 74 percent had additional family members living abroad. Students' expectations regarding their own plans for migrating out of the country are also high: 44 percent of the students are either definitely planning or considering leaving their country.

Similarly, according to a local press report, about a hundred passports were processed daily by the Azuayan Migration Ministry in 1990, and thirty thousand people, roughly equivalent to 20 percent of Cuenca's population, had left the region during the previous three years (*El Mercurio,* May 30, 1990, 10A). In Cuenca, discussions of family members living in New York City provide an omnipresent subtext to Azuayan daily life. The economic impact of international migration in the region, however, is more than a subtext: the Azuayan branch of the Central Bank estimates that remittances from migrants abroad amount to $120 million per year, making it the largest source of income for the local economy. This is equivalent to sixteen years of straw hat exports, at 1990 levels in Azuay (Serrano 1992).

In one sense, the economic crisis of the 1980s brought about a simple intensification of a trend begun during the past three decades—out-migration as a familial strategy for gaining enough cash to hold on to advances already made or for family formation. Yet, things were also different. Perhaps most important, the economic crisis was national, not just regional, which meant that migration to other regions of Ecuador was now financially risky and unattractive. Temporary migrations to the coast had already become problematic because of the cycle of worker uprisings and violent repression on coastal plantations and in urban barrios. Similarly, languishing Amazonian settlements to the east had been discredited as migratory destinations because of a perceived lack of government services and development support there. Even if these traditional migratory routes had not had so many drawbacks, they would have been, nonetheless, unacceptable routes for Cuenca's new middle class of relatively educated, upwardly mobile "commoners" with high aspirations.

Given this historical context, international migration was not so much a spontaneous answer to the debilitating economic crisis of the early 1980s as a preexisting channel (a migration stream) available to some Azuayans and, therefore, to their immediate social networks. In fact, it was during the 1970s that international migration became a significant phenomenon for whole, albeit limited, sectors of the population based on community and profession, mostly urban workers from Cuenca going to North American destinations, especially New York City (Salamea Cordero 1979, 142).

Apart from a growing tourist and commercial outflow by Cuencano elites to countries all over the world, four occupational sectors stand out as pioneers in this nascent international migration: (1) those urban-based middlemen and exporters connected to Panama hat production and trade, who had left the region in the previous two decades; (2) young, second-generation city dwellers, many originally coming from rural areas also hit by the hat crisis, who could not find sufficient employment after completing high school—or even college—and were now leaving for the United States or Europe in hopes of continuing their education or making use of the preparation they already had; (3) hundreds of goldsmiths who found work with Manhattan jewelers after the price of gold shot up 333 percent in 1973, thus making it more lucrative to export the gold found in the region than to work it for the limited national market (ibid.); and (4) a substantial number of peasants directly leaving the countryside for South American and North American destinations, of whom many were from hat production areas to the north of Cuenca and from more purely agricultural areas to the far south of Cuenca near Girón—both regions sharing a tradition of temporary migration to the Costa since the 1950s. A noteworthy feature of this occupational makeup is the early diversity of the outflow, which includes both a high level of urban students, teachers, professionals, and skilled artisans (including goldsmiths), pointing to a regional brain drain, and a significant number of wageworkers and semi-proletarianized peasants.

Migration Merchants: The Return of the Intermediaries

These pioneering migration networks notwithstanding, the mass region-wide phenomenon of international migration from Azuay, Cañar, and Morona Santiago (largely populated by Azuayan colonists) that developed during the 1980s cannot be completely accounted for by a geometric increase, that is, a simple snowball effect of migrants helping family and neighbors to make the multiple border crossings—especially the high number of rural smallholders migrating to New York City directly from the most rural areas. Unlike other historical international flows of documented and undocumented immigrants, there is no evidence of direct recruitment by North American employers to facilitate the considerable financial and legal obstacles of the journey. Yet in just ten years, the modest international migrations of the 1970s turned into a mass exodus, and Ecuador put itself on the map of global migration flows by becoming one of the largest groups of undocumented immigrants living in New York City.

This sharp increase in international migration, especially from isolated rural areas, can be explained only by the reemergence of a centuries-old institution in the region—the usurious middleman, in this case, an integrated network of *tramitadores,* or facilitators, who provide the range of legal and illegal services needed to make a clandestine trip to the United States. Rather than mediating the hat procurement for export houses, as in the hat trade, tramitadores work, directly or indirectly, for unscrupulous travel agencies, which are themselves participants in larger formal and underground networks of migration merchants.

Although these facilitating networks are international in scope, they begin with a tramitador's sales pitch to the would-be migrant in his or her home village, not unlike the role played by the perros in the straw hat trade. The tramitador offers to arrange all of the national documents needed to leave Ecuador, visas for intermediary countries, all of the physical travel arrangements, and, depending on the type of trip, a falsified U.S. visa or passport. To pay for all of these services, which now run between $6,000 and $10,000—an amount even the wealthiest of Ecuadorians would balk at—the tramitador arranges to have the money lent to the would-be migrant by a *chulquero,* at usurious interest rates of 10–12 percent, compounded monthly, with all land, animals, and possessions of the migrant held as collateral. In addition, numerous local banks and money exchange houses provide the needed financial infrastructure and legal cover for such operations.

Several Ecuadorian press accounts have reported the brisk trade in falsified (altered or forged) U.S. visas, the services of coyotes, and passports:

The office of Migration of Azuay has made a "black list" that includes the names of at least 81 suspected members of a network dedicated to acquiring visas for those interested in travel to the United States illegally. This considerable network of "coyotes" has become untouchable and throws to the wind pressure by officials, due to the silence and unwillingness of migrants to turn them in which impedes their arrest. . . . The activities of the *tramitadores* who "facilitate" the migration of thousands to the United States, principally in Azuay, continues immeasurably, since the fervor to migrate continues. (*Hoy,* July 26, 1994, 8A)

Another article, entitled "A Dream Turned Nightmare," tells of those mostly rural villagers who pay large amounts to tramitadores and corrupt local officials only to be robbed, tricked, or deported; according to this report, during the first six months of 1994 alone, 250 Ecuadorians were deported en route to the United States or other countries (*El Comercio,* July 4, 1994, A8). In addition, it has become clear to even casual observers that what I call "migration merchants," defined here as anyone profiting, legally or illegally, from the commodification of the international migration process, forms a larger system or informal network:

[Mass international migration] is evidence of a total lack of faith in the country and the belief that well-being and progress will never arrive. . . . The coyotes are the first link to numerous travel agencies, where the emigrants receive passports including actual visas to the U.S. and other countries en route, which reveals the corruption that exists at various levels. . . . The Director of Ecuadorian Migration affirms that in these first linkages it is also possible to obtain [Ecuadorian] identity cards and passports, as many false as real, through a bribe to officials at the Civil Registry. (Ibid.)

Local community-based networks of tramitadores and chulqueros, typically, are closely related by kinship, relying on social ties with a high degree of trust and loyalty, thus allowing for clandestine capitalism to operate with fewer costs (both monetary and psychological) related to maintaining the financial and legal security of the covert economic activity. In one medium-sized Azuayan town with high levels of international migration, all of the moneylenders are members of just five families, and these families are further interlocked through marital ties. As an indication of both the high levels of informal financial capital in circulation and the risks of malfeasance inherent in these types of underground economic relations, according to a judge in this same town, informal moneylenders lost more than $600,000 within a six-month period to migrant debtors who simply disappeared after taking several large loans.

It should be emphasized that money lending, as an economic institution with a set of rules and customs, has been a historical feature of the region even before the rural economy was completely monetized. The vicissitudes of small-scale and subsistence farming among the rural smallholders, along with the periodic burden of financing an annual religious festival, have traditionally required the services of moneylenders, who are either coethnic villagers or white-mestizo outsiders and whose rates are officially controlled by the state. For example, in times of crop failure, a loan enabled households not only to buy the few necessary household goods but, most important, to continue the production cycle, which could include temporary coastal migrations and handicraft production.

Although a full historical treatment of money lending as an economic institution in the region is warranted, it is beyond the scope of this study (however, see Carpio 1992, 48–49, for a related discussion). Nonetheless, widespread accounts point to the historical importance of money lending to both the borrower and the lender, forming perhaps the central dyadic socioeconomic relationship between independent peasant and urban elite in Azuay. In times of regional scarcity, loans from "outside" the village, with one of the urban-based *patrons,* often involved usurious practices made possible by the peasant's general position of weakness vis-à-vis the patron.

To illustrate the nature of these relationships we have the following account of its advanced development in the Azuayan town of Gualaceo in the 1940s as a center for such activities catering to the surrounding countryside: "Lending money at high interest rates permitted many families to get rich easily; enriching oneself was greater if one used illicit means such as usury, or if one took advantage of the humble condition of those seeking a loan. In Gualaceo, the Vázquez family was an institution in this respect, not only because of the enormous fortune they accumulated but also the way they operated" (Chacón and Chacón 1991, 59). For example, a priest (from the already wealthy Vázquez family) lent Adolfo Tapia 300 sucres at a time when the legal monthly interest rate was 1 percent. So that the priest would not have to maintain large supplies of corn, Adolfo was to pay only in corn, which was to be calculated every year at the market price but delivered to the priest during a time of scarcity. When a bad season did occur the following year, Adolfo had to buy the corn to be delivered to the priest to cover the year's interest of 30 sucres. When Adolfo arrived at the curate, the priest would not accept any corn not actually grown by Adolfo and, furthermore, could not wait a single day longer for his interest payment of 180 sucres, five times the legal rate. In consideration of the position of the priest, Adolfo did not put up much resistance (ibid., 59–60).

Returning to contemporary human smuggling, with corrupt local officials and a network of professional forgers, the necessary local and national documents are bought by the tramitador. Often the forger's work is so good that U.S. embassy personnel in Quito cannot figure out how they can circumvent infrared detectors and laminate safeguards developed by the 3M company. Next, working with legitimate travel agents, the tramitador makes the travel arrangements, which, broadly speaking, fall into one of two categories: either the direct route to New York City, using a "borrowed" passport or forged visa, which also entails either a significant amount of cultural coaching on how to look and act like a *residente* or the tortuous overland route that includes a sophisticated network of Central American and Mexican contacts, safe houses, and *coyotes* (those who actually lead the migrant across the Rio Grande). Since the Mexican government has made attaining a visa to its country more difficult, sometimes coyotes are also used to get into Mexico through a Guatemalan farm or by boat.

At every step of the way, from the financing of the trip in Ecuador to the dependence on a nefarious international network spanning half a dozen countries, the migrant risks being swindled, jailed, deported, robbed, or subjected to violent abuse, including rape and murder. Not surprisingly, the main task of the tramitador is to gain the trust of the potential client. To understand the tramitador-migrant relationship we need only examine the comisionista-cholo relationship of the straw hat trade, which continues in villages of high migration:

> For hours it seemed virtually every woman—and some men—who lived in the Cantón of Biblián approached Sr. González to sell him their newly woven hats. At his mercy for their weekly pittance, they stood in small bunches, some silent, others chattering, a few solemn, and a couple drunk. I walked around front to get a weaver's-eye view. From their side of the table, González's slender six-foot frame grew another foot. From this vantage point he clearly had the upper hand—in fact, he had the only hand. His eyes, his skin tone, his clothes, his home, his gender, his vocabulary, his height, his wallet—all these gave him every advantage. (Miller 1986, 170)

While the above describes the general system, the particular configuration of financial and human resources brought to bear by each migrant on the problem of getting cross a border is often as unique as the Azuayan villages and barrios. The financing of the trip usually involves a combination of personal savings, free loans by relatives, interest-bearing loans by friends, and usurious loans by chulqueros. Similarly, a catalogue of the techniques used to get across the U.S. border or obtain a tourist visa could fill a medium-sized book. For example, one technique is to form a musical group that can be invited to New York City, often with the help of prominent Ecuadorian accomplices abroad; the group is composed of a few real musicians to which several ersatz musicians are added after paying the U.S.$5,000 price of "invitation." Another method is to borrow a substantial sum of money from a relative already abroad in order to convince the U.S. consul that the "tourist" has no need to work abroad, as evidenced by a healthy bank account. Of course, sometimes those of more humble means, and lacking in useful social contacts, simply start heading north with a few hundred dollars in their pocket and hope for the best. However, these cases are exceptional since it is widely known that the chances of making it across eight national territories physically and financially intact, unaided by professionals or seasoned migrants, are not favorable.

Kin- and community-based migration networks make use of the information and resources circulating within them, thereby making migration paths fairly consistent within a given social network. In this way, the path taken by a successful migrant pioneer gets repeated and revised within his or her network. Sometimes this evolutionary process may induce a pioneer, who has already made several trips and may be a residente or in possession of a green card (work visa), to become an in-network tramitador, coyote, or chulquero whose services are provided for a lower fee or even freely (that is, monetarily speaking, though reciprocity of some sort is assumed). Conversely, it is also quite common for return migrants to lend money to regional intermediaries (of the perro mold), who, in turn, lend at higher rates to professional chulqueros, who, in turn, lend to the new migrant at the highest rate, thus forming a pyramid scheme that requires a constant influx of new migrants to keep capital circulating to the top.

The impact of mass international migration is nothing short of an economic and social transformation for Azuay and Cañar. During the past ten years, international migration has transformed not only the destiny of individual migrants but also the conditions of specific sending communities. In some rural villages near Cuenca, out-migration and subsequent remittances are noticeable by simple observation: primarily the explosive construction of new homes, which are considerably more extravagant than those of other comparably sized towns in Ecuador. International migration from rural areas of the region has been the object of several press reports, including a video documentary, "Tiempo de Mujeres."* The documentary depicts the near total disappearance of males from Santa Rosa, a small village near Cuenca, to New York City. The price of land is so inflated because of competition by migrants in both urban and rural areas that only those who have an income in U.S. dollars can hope to purchase a new plot.

The Azuayan Paradox: Gain and Social Immobility

It was during the colonial period that Azuay found its unique identity in the confluence of indigenous peoples and human resources, or a lack thereof, and a conservative Creole and Spanish elite. This social milieu of urban-oriented "nobles" was supported by an equally uncommon economic system, integrating a region that included large numbers of poor rural whites and relatively independent foresteros of indigenous origin.

In Azuay, we find the seemingly regional paradox of social conservatism in the midst of early capitalist relations, in a region already integrated and dependent on the world economy by the beginning of the nineteenth century. However, far from being a paradox, the two were linked. Given its adversely isolated location and relative lack of natural resources, the region could compete in external markets only by lowering the costs of labor. With a semi-independent peasantry, Azuay's elite was able to avoid the high economic and political costs arising from the direct ownership of its labor. This socioeconomic system could operate only under conditions of extreme ideological and social control, achieved through a multilayered caste system and the conservative socializing role of the Catholic Church. Even today, clergy play an important political and cultural role in the rural areas of Azuay. To be sure, extraeconomic measures could be applied when necessary, such as the forced weaving of hats, but these have been the exception.

The economy of Azuay, from its inception as a Spanish colony, has been oriented toward exports for an international market: first cattle, then cloth, then straw hats, and now its own citizens. The conservative social elite has been able to maintain ideological and economic control over the region in spite of a semi-independent peasantry that includes a significant number of mestizos and whites. This rigid social and economic structure has remained remarkably consistent during each export period and shows no signs of seri-

* Written and directed by Monica Vasquez, Casa de la Cultura, Quito, Ecuador, 1990.

ous weakening during this current phase. In fact, the sight of rural cholos building four-story houses and driving fancy new cars in remote villages after just a few years in the United States provides the primary social morality discourse of the region: gringo dollars will never buy culture, something to which one is born—least of all, in the United States. Nonetheless, the backbone of the regional economy now rests on the continuation of the exodus, which directly provides thousands of jobs to importers, bankers, exchange houses, and public officials.

Does mass international migration from Azuay represent a radical social and economic innovation or a continuation of historical socioeconomic relationships? To answer this question we have only to look at who the key players are in the international migration trade. The historic economic roles played by Azuay's social classes are more entrenched than ever: the basic dynamism of the independent peasantry looking for opportunity, the crucial facilitory role of the predatory middlemen (or migration merchants), and a financial elite reliant on the benefits of a rigid class structure and ideological domination. The combination of these historical socioeconomic relationships and the linkage of local migration merchants to an international network of migration merchants, most notably professional Mexican coyotes, has produced one of the most remarkable mass migrations occurring today in Latin America.

It is in this historical context that the network-building process of international migration is embedded, especially long-distance, risky migrations to New York City by rural peasants; mass migration from Azuay has been fueled not only by the snowball effect of simple community-level migration networks but also by the ability of these networks to make linkages with more institutionalized, though underground, networks of migration merchants. In other words, the considerable resources needed to finance such a large-scale underground mobilization are an illustration of the "strength of weak ties" as conceptualized by Mark Granovetter (1974). Furthermore, while network structures facilitating migration add an important social capital dimension to human capital theories, networks are also embedded in more profound historical processes of political control, cultural ideology, and social institutions.

Azuayan Communities before Transnational Migration

The two research sites of this study represent the sociocultural heterogeneity of Azuay largely resulting largely from past international and internal migrations. Before turning to an examination of contemporary migration from Quipal and Tomebamba in the following chapter, I present below a historical overview of the two communities before contemporary migration abroad became widespread. As will be seen, this historical sociocultural variation between and within villages continues to shape patterns of migration to North America.

Tomebamba

The village of Tomebamba, with 157 households, is located about ten kilometers to the northwest of Cuenca. At the center of the parish is the small town of Checa, mostly populated by mestizos. Tomebamba lies three kilometers from Checa, up a steep, dead-end dirt road, at an altitude of twenty-five hundred to three thousand meters. Unlike the settlement patterns of advanced industrialized countries, throughout the Andes there is generally an inverse relationship between social status and altitude, since the ideal location for agriculture and transportation is a fertile valley. With a climate that fluctuates between fifteen and eighteen degrees centigrade and a moderate annual rainfall, land in Tomebamba is reasonably fertile and is transversed by several small rivers, though land erosion has been significant. Tomebamba, which means "large plateau" in Quichua, is surrounded by a higher ridge, where village members have a large area of communal land. The feeling of isolation in Tomebamba, stemming from its almost hidden geographic location, is reinforced by its indigenous population and their recent past as Quichua speakers, among the few left in Azuay.

Historically, we know little concerning the original formation of the village or its activities during the colonial period. It would be beyond the ability of this study to ascertain, for example, whether the ancestors of the inhabitants of Tomebamba were Cañari who were subsequently socialized into Incan culture or were part of a mitimae contingent from Peru. Significantly, no hacienda was established in the area during the colonial period; thus, the local Indians were largely left to subsistence agriculture (on minifundios) and earning cash by selling agricultural surplus or handicrafts at local markets (*ferias*).

Yet the economic independence of this indigenous village from the hacienda system did not mean complete political or economic autonomy from the regional hierarchy over which the Catholic Church held sway—nor could the people of Tomebamba avoid the hardships of their low social status within the regional ideology. As an example of the unilateral power of the church, when the Bishop of Cuenca formally erected a separate parish in the region in 1909, he changed its name from the ancient Cañari name *Jidcay* to the present *Checa*, in memory of a bishop from Quito. Soon after, in 1922, the parish priest also changed Tomebamba's original name of *Yana-Sacha* (meaning forest of the *yana* tree in Quichua) to its current one, since, to his ears, the former name "sounded very bad" (Monge Zari 1992, 12). Even today, local priests in the region often regard their parish authority as stemming from both a heavenly and an earthly mandate.

From the end of the last century until recently, this homogeneous village was primarily sustained by two activities, agriculture and the weaving of Panama hats. The fact of Tomebamba's early and complete participation in the Panama hat trade indicates three important aspects of its socioeconomic development. First, it underscores the inability of its subsistence agriculture to sustain a growing population. Second, though rural and isolated, for more than one hundred years Tomebamba has been producing handicrafts not for local consumption—or even based on an indigenous design—but for use in northern metropolises. Third, though Tomebamba is composed of nominally independent peasants, the social relations of the production and marketing of Panama hats indicates Tomebamba's severe political and economic subordination to regional elites and their usurious local operatives, whose activities are legitimated by the castelike system of social and ethnic stratification. The mestizo middlemen, or *perros*, still go from house to house in Tomebamba buying hats from the women who continue to weave, generally offering them about 10 percent of the export value of the hat.

As an indication of Tomebamba's dependence on the cash economy even before the decline in the Panama hat trade in the 1950s, some men from the village began to work outside of the community, first as mule drivers and then as liquor smugglers. When the crisis in the Panama hat trade in the 1950s inaugurated a regionwide depression, men from Tomebamba joined the temporary labor migrations to coastal plantations, aided by the completion of a crude road in the 1940s. Nearly all of the able-bodied men and older boys from Tomebamba found seasonal work on banana and sugar plantations, which took about a week to reach on foot (in this respect, it now takes much less time to travel to New York City than it did for previous generations to arrive at coastal plantations). These seasonal migrations to the coast continued until labor unrest on coastal plantations brought violent repression by the government in the 1970s and transnational migration supplanted them in the early 1980s. Some also found temporary work in Cuenca as construction workers or domestic help, though not in significant numbers.

Economic and infrastructural development by regional and national gov-

ernments has been limited and sporadic in Checa, and even more so for remote Tomebamba. In part, this is because many local officials and professionals serving the area still reside in Cuenca and commute to Checa a few
times a week or month to discharge their duties. For example, the first telephone line to Checa arrived in 1983, well after many from the region were already making annual trips to Venezuela and the United States; before 1983, a
telephone call required a trip to Cuenca. A one-room primary school was
founded in 1956 in Tomebamba but was slow to develop until remittances
from abroad in the 1980s allowed for the construction of a schoolhouse and
playground. Health problems must be attended to in Checa on certain days
of the week or in Cuenca. Electricity and running water were introduced in
the late 1970s and still have not been brought to all houses in Tomebamba.
Indoor plumbing is a recent introduction in only a few houses built by migrant families.

Sociocultural practices in Tomebamba reflect the syncretic influences of
Catholicism and pre-Conquest traditions. Although Tomebamba is similar to
neighboring rural villages, the natural sociocultural group is the village itself,
maintained by a practice of marrying within the village group (endogamy).
Indigenous characteristics found in the village before transnational migration in the 1980s included adobe and straw huts, the use of one ponytail by
women instead of the two pigtails favored by local mestizas (cholas), and,
most important, the widespread use of Quichua through the 1970s. In addition, the ancient Andean tradition of eating roasted guinea pig and drinking
chicha (fermented corn) at special celebrations is still common. Perhaps when
compared with other indigenous villages in the Andean highlands, such as
those completely isolated for centuries on large haciendas, Tomebamba
would seem very acculturated in an objective sense (especially now, after fifteen years of international migration). What is significant is that even in the
face of rapid acculturation, Tomebamba continues to be called "Indian" by
urban mestizos in Checa and Cuenca.

This regional socioeconomic stratification and microculture have contributed to the relative lack of an internal class structure in Tomebamba. As
one of the last indigenous villages left in Azuay by the 1970s, Tomebamba's
social and geographic isolation has undoubtedly contributed to its internal
cohesion and feeling of community, further reinforced by kinship and fictive
kinship ties. Most importantly, no "whites" ever settled in the community,
having been kept out by local clergy who could better maintain control without competing ideological claims. Since ethnic identity and economic class
position are highly correlated in Azuay, the ethnic homogeneity of the com-

munity has produced little variation in the objective class position of its members. This lack of class distinction has been further maintained by the availability, until recently, of land of similar quality located on a relatively level plateau.

There are two important features, however, of village life regarding in-group social stratification. First, the most significant stratification in Tomebamba is along gender lines; nearly every economic and social activity in Tomebamba is gender specific. Women are traditionally little more than property for men and are not expected to show any independence within the household or within village affairs. A woman who visits her neighbor while neglecting some minor household chore may elicit a beating by her husband. Second, there is a lively competition between village members for social status, measured above all in the size of one's landholding (though differences are not great), and for desirable marriage partners. The notion of envy and its spiritual and physical side effects on both parties is a well-developed theme in local lore. These stratifications, both between and within villages, have undergone significant structural changes in response to transnational migration, even while they continue to resonate.

Quipal

The village of Quipal, currently composed of 184 households, is located near the small town of Baños, which lies eight kilometers southwest of Cuenca. Quipal's physical setting and settlement pattern make it distinctive from Tomebamba: first, the terrain of Quipal is very hilly, lacking large extensions of level and similar quality land, and, second, the principal road to Quipal from Baños continues through to other settlements in the same parish. Thus, Quipal is less isolated than Tomebamba but also less homogeneous, leading to an ethnic-economic stratification in the distribution of favorable lands.

Unlike Checa, Baños was one of the first rural Spanish parishes and is still the most populous. Spaniards were attracted to nearby silver mines, which ultimately proved unprofitable, and to its thermal springs, thought to have healing powers. Although initially there was plenty of land for agriculture, the rugged topography of the region allowed for only a few small to medium haciendas, or *quintas*. These have served more ideological purposes for their owners than simply creation of actual wealth. This was especially true of those landowning families who continued to live in Cuenca. Yet during the late colonial period, several Spanish families of lower socioeconomic status (far removed from Cuenca's "nobility") settled in the rural areas of the parish, where even they would be accorded respect and economic advantage among the local indigenous population. Thus, those Spaniards who settled in the more rural areas of the parish held the intermediate position in the regional social strata—white yet cholo, landowners yet poor, urban-centric yet rural. With Spanish descendants in Baños, at the center of the parish, and Cañari Indians at its highest and most rural extremes, the parish reproduced Cuencano colonial life.

Similarly, the village of Quipal can be seen as yet another microcosm of colonial Azuayan social relations; it is divided geographically and ethnically into three nearly equal subgroups of blancos, cholos, and naturales, though historically the intermediate group was less significant than it is today. The whites comprise three interrelated kinship groups who traditionally have owned the largest and best extensions of land along the main road.

At the end of a precarious muddy road that veers upward and perpendicular to the main street of Quipal live the indigenous naturales, a label that implies an animal-like existence not far removed from a primitive state of nature. These local indigenous people are said to be the descendants of the Cañari. Although these indigenous inhabitants are not without land, even large plots, their land is on a slope and is of poor quality. Until recently, Indian women were prohibited from wearing the two pigtails indicative of the higher cholo status rather than the traditional single ponytail worn by indios. It should be kept in mind that ethnicity in the Andes is largely defined by dress and lifestyle, not by membership in clearly defined races. These lifestyles, which are directly linked to ethnic identity, have been rigidly enforced and reinforced by scripted roles according to ethnic membership. For example, when a naturale passed a blanco on the road, the proscribed greeting was, "Praise be to Jesus Christ," to which the blanco would respond, "Let it be so, my son (my daughter)." In between these two extremes of blanco and naturale are those families recognized as cholo or mestizo, occupying a position physically and socially situated between these two extremes. Symbolic of its continuing social and cultural divisions, Quipal still lacks a well-defined community center, church, or plaza. Like Tomebamba, gender stratification is also marked and transcends ethnic boundaries.

Until well into the present century, the economic base of Quipal remained almost exclusively subsistence agriculture. Inhabitants grew corn, wheat, beans, quinoa (an Andean grain), leafy vegetables, garlic, onions, and potatoes and also raised sheep, pigs, chickens, cows, and guinea pigs. Many of the indigenous families worked as laborers on the land of the whites, typically as repayment for a debt from a loan made during perennial agricultural shortfalls. Some also worked on a small nearby hacienda, which lacked the total control of its workers characteristic of larger haciendas. Market relations were limited to periodic trips to Cuenca to sell a limited agricultural surplus and to buy salt and rice. Early nonagricultural economic activities by a few indigenous families included the weaving of straw baskets for the regional market, the performance of music during special celebrations, and healing, using local remedies. It should be underscored that, until this point, although whites enjoyed social and economic privileges, their ability to produce a surplus using the same mode of economic production was only marginally better than that of the poorest of the community.

Like independent peasant communities throughout the Andes, as the population of the village grew, increasingly divided plots were unable to sustain new households, even among white families. Hence, during the 1930s, young men hoping to form independent households began to look for ways to supplement subsistence agriculture. Since they were the only group with outside contacts and at least a minimum of resources, a few young white men joined the regional trade of smuggling sugarcane liquor by horseback from remote clandestine distilleries to local distribution centers. Although smugglers ran the risk of being caught and jailed, many were able to greatly increase their incomes. Smugglers generally formed groups of three to five men riding together, typically composed of kin and close friends. Because of the social organization of smuggling and the financial success of the venture, by the 1950s all of the white men and many mestizos from the village were engaged in smuggling. Although young naturales were sometimes contracted to accompany white smugglers as assistants, the general collapse in the previous agricultural system led them to develop alternative economic activities, primarily the felling of trees for lumber and firewood in addition to crude woodworking (men) and basket weaving (women).

In the 1960s, Quipal went through yet another economic transition, from smuggling liquor to a more diversified economic base, above all, the cottage industry of sewing clothes for the urban market. In 1960, a prominent smuggler decided to retire from his illicit activities and began to sew clothes (mostly shirts, pants, and aprons) after having established a contract with a clothing store in Cuenca. The introduction of electricity in the 1950s allowed for the use of electric sewing machines. By 1970, only a couple of smugglers continued their trade, while nearly all the rest of the white and mestizo households were engaged in sewing. Apart from the risk of smuggling, two factors contributed to this transition. First, the original group of young adults to have completed primary schooling were now oriented toward finding an "honorable," nonagricultural job, which sewing and, later, shoe making represented. Second, by this time, several legal distilleries were now operating, producing a better quality liquor and thereby greatly reducing the demand for the contraband liquor.

The cottage industry of sewing followed the basic regional historical pattern of handicrafts whereby the Cuenca retailer would sell the raw material and place the order. The important difference between sewing in Quipal and other regional cottage industries, such as hat weaving, was that the intermediaries who sold the cloth to the household and bought the finished product were also from Quipal and were mostly filling a necessary production niche rather than involving themselves in the usurious activities typical of other professional middlemen. However, by the late 1980s, four small factories were employing up to fifteen tailors and seamstresses, primarily recruiting young (including older children) cholos and blancos, whites, indicating that capitalist class relations had begun to take hold in Quipal, both within and between ethnic groups. Some of the more prominent producers also began to directly market their clothing in the urban markets of Cuenca and even made regular trips to Guayaquil.

During the 1960s, there were also other new economic activities apart from the cottage industry of sewing. Some of the recently educated whites and mestizos began to commute to Cuenca to work in the newly opened General Tire factory, while others found jobs as policemen and soldiers. More importantly, some of the most dispossessed from the indigenous group, the naturales, turned to temporary coastal migration in the same way that peasants from Tomebamba did during this period. Hence, indigenous people in Quipal remained isolated from urban networks even while others from the village were becoming increasingly integrated into urban social and economic networks. In addition, a few mestizo families permanently immigrated to Amazonian settlements as colonists. These economic changes occurring in Quipal from the 1930s to the 1980s brought about relatively few changes in the sociocultural stratification structures of ethnicity and gender. Women were still treated as possessions, not as equals, by fathers and husbands. Similarly, through the 1970s, it was still a grave matter if a cholo or a white wanted to marry a naturale. Marriages were still largely arranged by the parents with a sharp eye toward maintaining ethnic boundaries. Numerous syncretic religious festivals organized around community, or even personal, saints were celebrated separately by the three groups. An important exception was the tendency for those of lower status to ask a white to be the godparent to a baptism or marriage, thus reinforcing reciprocal social and economic relations.

Although these social stratifications were maintained through the 1970s, the declining agricultural mode of production meant that negative social sanctions on the naturales to maintain their proscribed dress and customs were of less economic importance to the community as a whole. By the 1980s, younger naturales, who were also attending primary school, were no longer speaking Quichua or behaving with extreme humility in the presence of whites. These outward changes on the part of Quipal's least acculturated group undercut the ideological assumptions that had kept them as "naturals." Thus, the maintenance of ethnic identities in Quipal became tied less to visceral cultural differences and more to kinship networks. Under a more complex stratification system, it was now access to overlapping social networks that largely determined one's social standing, economic class position, and ability to move in more urban circles. By 1990, even the sons and daughters of cholos who had become policemen or soldiers in the 1960s were now regularly attending high school and even going on to the university in Cuenca.

The province of Azuay has been shaped by a unique culture of straw hat weaving, which has provided a path to New York City. The social institutions surrounding the cottage industry of hat production, especially a sophisticated network of middlemen, financiers, and exporters, have given the region the skills and social resources needed to export people instead of hats. It is now "migration merchants," rather than hat merchants, who dominate the local economy. This common regional drama notwithstanding, the two research sites of Tomebamba and Quipal represent diverse arrangements of ethnic makeup and economic activity, with Tomebamba as a classic hat-weaving community and Quipal engaged in a much wider range of economic activities connected to the nearby city of Cuenca. In the following chapter, we examine how these different community settings affected the migration process as both turned to transnational economic strategies in the 1980s.

CHAPTER FOUR

Azuayan Villages: Tomebamba and Quipal

> Soy Cholo Boy, y me voy a trabajar, en restaurante o factorías, donde
> paguen más. La vida será dura, y me voy a rajar. Después de algunos
> años, envidia me tendrán. Ahora me toca, aprender a cocinar, lavar mis
> camisas y ser muy puntual, media hora para el lunch, y de vuelta a
> camellar. Si trabajo horas extras, el doble me darán. Soy Cholo Boy, y me
> voy a trabajar! Tú sabes . . . chulla vida!
>
> [I am a Cholo Boy, and I'm going to work, in restaurants or factories,
> wherever they pay more. Life will be hard and I will overcome it. After a
> few years, everyone will envy me. For now, I have to learn to cook, wash
> my shirts, and be on time, a half hour for lunch, and then back to work.
> If I work extra hours they pay me double. I am a Cholo Boy, and I'm
> going to work! You know . . . only one life to live!]

When I first submitted a research proposal in 1991 to study migration from Azuay and Otavalo, I had entitled it "The Transnational Village," which I kept as the working title of the project for several years. However, as I analyzed the survey data and reflected on what I had encountered in Ecuador, I realized that the imagery of the transnational village (or community) was precisely the opposite of what I should convey given the reality of the four "communities" in my study. The problem with the concept of a transnational community is that "community," in the sense of bounded social solidarity, is best conceived as a variable within multiple transnational structures rather than a new state attained by formerly "nontransnational communities." Three dynamic and intersecting social dimensions, explored in this chapter, make this so: preexisting social networks, ethnic identities, and gender stratification. An even thornier, but related, question is this: How should we conceptualize what migrates: individuals, households, communities, or networks? How, in turn, do we describe the resulting diversity of transnational social structures—as unbounded traditional communities or as bounded transnational networks?

Understanding transnational households is crucial to understanding the day-to-day drama of migration and social transformations within communities, yet it remains an open question as to whether migration from Azuay should be viewed as community centered or network centered. Even before transnational migration, Tomebamba could be justly called a geographic and social community in every sense of the word, bounded by an identity as uniformly "Indian." Quipal is a community in name only in the social connotation of the concept and is sharply divided by ethnic groups (social networks) living more or less politely together on the side of a mountain. Because regional social networks differ in their access to crucial financial and social resources needed to cross several borders illegally, such as in-network migration merchants who profit from migration, these separate social networks within the same rural village are fundamental to understanding transnational migration patterns. That is not to say that this is simply a social structural story in the new guise of social networks rather than class positions; transnational migration has a cultural and social meaning to people of these communities not easily captured by mapping either individual attributes or preexisting ethnic networks. The dynamism of transnational migration to "la YANY" leads to a slow reconfiguration of many aspects of social relations and cultural ideologies within communities and within the wider region.

Migrant Theories and Moving Targets

Given the different social networks in the region, which only imperfectly map onto a geographical space (i.e., community, neighborhood), past research offers us clues regarding what we might expect to find. Research on international migration since the early 1970s has sought to overcome the limitations of an exclusively macrosociological approach by examining the role of intermediate social structures in the social process of international migration—primarily, the role played by social networks. Most researchers who have conducted close-range examinations of the migration experience in the regions of origin have pointed to the central importance of social networks in augmenting and sustaining migration (Hugo 1981; Lomnitz 1977; Ritchey 1976; Tilly and Brown 1967; Petersen 1958), and it is even implicit in the work of E. G. Ravenstein a century ago (1885). This common feature of migration is stated most forcefully by Charles Tilly: "To put it simply: networks migrate; categories [individual attributes] stay put; and networks create new categories. By and large, the effective units of migration were (and are) neither individuals nor households but sets of people linked by acquaintance, kinship, and work experience who somehow incorporated American destinations into the mobility alternatives they considered when they reached critical decision points in their individual and collective lives" (1990, 84).

Recent research has led the way toward integrating the literature on the social process of migration and its emphasis on network building, with more generalizable findings that can be used to develop theoretical propositions. In these more eclectic formulations, labor demand from core countries provides a necessary but not a sufficient cause for international migration. This research agenda has been pursued primarily through the investigation of the dynamic process of network building, using empirical data collected in both the sending and receiving countries, most notably in works by Sherri Grasmuck and Patricia Pessar (1991) on the Dominican Republic and Douglas Massey and associates on western Mexico (Massey et al.1987). These studies have partly sought to explain how and why international migration often continues long after the structural determinants have subsided. They have reported that migration networks adapt to shifting economic conditions in the core by generating new opportunities that promote migration apart from the original incentives. For example, Massey and associates consider the "core argument" of their study of Mexican migration to be that "migration is a social process with a strong internal momentum that reinforces itself over time" (ibid., 319).

Although this social process approach leads to more nuanced analyses, the treatment of the determinants of the onset of migration remain faithful to the historical-structural model. Massey and associates, while highlighting the role of social networks as an inevitable process, trace the onset of Mexican migration to the United States to historical productive transformations in both Mexico and the United States (ibid.). Alejandro Portes and R. L. Bach have found that the origins of international migration are rooted in "the gradual incorporation of peripheral areas into the world economy, the diffusion of expectations from the centers, and the resulting internal dislocations in these subordinate societies" (1985, 336).

Rather than simply offering an intermediate framework, this approach can also be viewed as an attempt to place migration research within the context of evolutionary changes in the nature of contemporary international migrations: the role of labor as a central concept in migration was more evident in earlier flows, largely based on direct employer (including the U.S. government) inducements, than in the more chaotic undocumented migrations of today. To this extent, there is a dynamic theoretical component to recent research on the social process of international migration; far from remaining static, the macrohistorical conditions of long-distance migrations continue to change, generally having moved from what could be called a core-centered dynamic, whereby mostly rural semiproletarianized workers are directly recruited by employers during periods of absolute labor shortages in the more advanced countries, to a periphery-centered dynamic, whereby problems of capital accumulation in the sending regions produce both the compelling conditions for transnational mobility and a speculative financial climate for facilitating and even recruiting new migrants.

The principal unit of analysis of most social network analyses is not individuals or societies but social relations or ties, which, in turn, form networks. Whereas most social science research uses individual attributes to abstract hypothesized social relationships (e.g., female, Hispanic) social network analysis attempts to empirically characterize social ties and the broader social networks they form as they evolve over time. For example, Mark Granovetter (1974) has shown that because of their closed nature, networks defined by strong social ties, without the counterbalancing effect of weak ties, are inherently weak in gaining access to outside resources. From this social network approach, we can hypothesize that to the extent that the primary group is not able to provide all of the social and physical resources needed for out-migration in a particular setting, weak ties to external resources will play a crucial role in the migration process.

A review article by Douglas Gurak and Fe Caces (1992) outlines three major insights from the sociological literature on social networks, appropriate to the study of migration networks: (1) the strength of weak ties, discussed above; (2) a nonterritorial conceptualization of communities based on networks; and (3) an understanding of social networks in relation to their organizational focus. By studying the personal networks of people living in large metropolitan areas, Barry Wellman (1979) has argued for a nonterritorial conceptualization of community defined as a web of connections among individuals, typically built on many weak but enduring social ties. Of course, this image of a dispersed community built on social networks also describes the new social milieu created by some transnational migration networks.

In this sense, the "migration systems" approach is a logical extension of social networks as communities, that is, extended in space and time (Mabogunje 1970); a migration system can be seen as the largest network of personal networks bounded by common cultural, economic, social, and political content. However, what makes the systems metaphor different from merely a very large network is that it also visualizes material things (commodities, capital) and nonmaterial things (symbols, ideologies) as flowing within a coherent system (Zlotnik 1992). Taking a different approach, S. L. Feld (1981) observes that not all networks are created equally in the sense that they each have a particular organizational focus, which can be social, legal, psychological, or physical goals around which collective action is organized. Thus, it is an obvious fact that there are mature migration networks organized around the goal of facilitating migration. Gurak and Caces ask whether there may, however, be significant differences in the structure of migration networks according to finer distinctions in their organizational focus, such as documented versus undocumented, overland versus by air or ship, and political refugee versus labor migration (1992, 163).

The focus of this set of studies of social networks and migration can be summarized in two questions: (1) How do preexisting social networks, specific to localized sociocultural groups, promote or constrain an individual's migratory activity, including his or her ability to carry it out, the course that it will take abroad, and its sociocultural impact back home? (2) If social networks are to be understood as complex, evolving social phenomena with multiple functions for group members, how is their evolution, maintenance, or devolution related to larger economic, political, and cultural aspects of the social group? Gurak and Caces's review of research on migration networks concludes that in order to advance this area of research we need to systematically investigate and link studies of migration with ethnicity, precisely because it delineates an important preexisting social network (1992). Intranational diversity of immigrant groups in the country of origin, especially ethnic diversity, and its relation to migration patterns remains one of the largest gaps in the empirical and theoretical literatures on international migration.

The reemergence of economic sociology potentially provides an alternative theoretical perspective on international migration, bringing with it a recent tradition of methodological innovation regarding the study of social networks. Primarily resurrected from the foundational works of Max Weber and Emile Durkheim on the intimate relation of economic activity to its wider social environment, this new economic sociology provides an approach for understanding the social structural context and cultural meaning of economic activity. Renewed interest in economic sociology parallels similar attempts in other social science disciplines (e.g., economic anthropology) to conceptualize the social space traditionally left to highly deductive microeconomics. In this sense, both classical and contemporary economic sociology are kindred to the Marxist historical-structural approach in their common opposition to Smithian market analysis, overdeveloped in economic orthodoxy. This commonality is also evident in the historical bent of both approaches.

The singular goal, however, of a sociology of economic life, as expressed by its leading adherents, is to avoid both the undersocialized approach to economic activity typical of conventional economics and the oversocialized approach typical of much sociological (including Marxist) theorizing (Wrong 1961; Granovetter 1985). Instead, economic sociology examines how proximate, intermediate social structures influence the goals of instrumental behavior and how they facilitate or constrain economic activity, defined as the production and distribution of scarce goods and services. A paper by Mark Granovetter on the problem of embeddedness—a concept originally developed by Karl Polanyi (1957), who advocated a substantivist approach to nonmarket economic activity among precapitalist societies—has become a manifesto of the central premises of a new economic sociology. Granovetter's use of social embeddedness implies that, even in advanced capitalist societies, economic activities, institutions, and their outcomes are embedded in, and affected by, the actor's personal relations and by the structure and content of the network of social relationships in which those personal relations are interposed (1985; 1990). There is an obvious overlap between the insights of economic sociology and those of social network analysis, underscored by the pioneering role of Mark Granovetter in both specialized literatures. Hence, Granovetter (1990) has also pointed out structural aspects of embeddedness, largely imported from the findings of social network analysis, including the following: (1) high network density produces greater internal pressure for trust—but also the potential for malfeasance; (2) fragmentation of a network reduces the homogeneity of behavior; and (3) firms need a high degree of trust but cannot be overwhelmed by claims from relatives turning it into a de facto relief agency.

Many international migration researchers have identified crucial aspects of individual migration in relation to migration networks, but few migration researchers have examined migration networks as units of analysis that vary structurally and substantively. Socioeconomic stratification of individual migrants (e.g., by income or education), though important, does not capture the full dynamic complexity of the individual's interpersonal networks nor characteristics of the networks themselves. Although social networks are generally seen to be more dynamic and fluid than social institutions (i.e., family, school, workplace), they do form stable patterns over time.

In contrast to the structural focus of economic sociology, the relational foci of economic sociology, as Granovetter labels it, returns the analytical focus to individual action while explicitly recognizing its linkages with macrosocial structures, such as social networks, social institutions, and ethnic groups. This relational approach returns to the problem of individual economic pursuits, but it rejects a deductive framework for individual behavior, which assumes that instrumental rationality will consistently guide economic activity. People enter into the daily economic activities of their lives with a considerable number of social and cultural preconceptions stemming not only from their socialization into group norms but also from the memory of past dealings with specific individuals and other members of an ethnic group. In other words, economic activity is, in the first instance, a social construction (Berger and Luckmann 1966; Walton 1983; Granovetter 1990). Concepts such as "social capital" (Portes and Sensenbrenner 1993; Coleman 1990; Bourdieu 1986) offer guidelines for understanding intermediate processes linking the individual with his or her immediate social milieu, potentially very useful for developing middle-range theories of international migration. The central insight is that similar economic problems and levels of technological development among groups at time A can produce differential outcomes at time B resulting from characteristics of their embeddedness in social networks and their ability to use both social and individual resources.

The Social Construction of Transnational Migration

We examined the historical context of Azuayan labor migration in chapter 3, including how it developed on the foundations of the earlier Panama hat export trade. We now empirically consider how transnational migration developed in each research site. In other words, our task now is to link the "biography" of the village to the wider regional history, including the development of transnational migration.

The story begins, however, in Cuenca rather than in Tomebamba or Quipal. Often social researchers are so focused on getting "inside" the target group they wish to understand, whether using quantitative or qualitative methods, that they tend to underresearch other groups within the same social milieu. Such "external groups," however, may offer insights into a reference group not able to fully participate in the social phenomenon to be explained or a social setting considered an undesirable option for those we are investigating. That is, we can in part understand the path taken by understanding the one not taken. Most ethnographic studies of rural communities focus on a description in rich detail of the social life of one community or even one or two households. Given the time, resources, and especially goals of this comparative study of four communities in two far-flung regions, that was never a viable option for this research design. My two "home bases" were in the urban centers of Cuenca and Otavalo, where I could better coordinate ongoing research at multiple sites. My main goal for the qualitative part of the study was to locate the initial pioneers or their families to reconstruct the earliest phase of migration (which had occurred not that long ago) and to conduct in-depth interviews with some of those left behind, such as the wives of migrants. In addition, I took daily notes on the many rural and urban settings in which I was circulating. Ironically, it was from my urban base in Cuenca, the geographic and social center of Azuayan life, that I developed a more focused ethnographic study based on participant observation, which I never could have planned for, providing insights into the nearby rural communities that were the ostensible objects of study.

Soon after I arrived in Cuenca to begin the final year of research, a friend invited me to play in a group that needed a keyboard player. I agreed, thinking it might be the only participant observation I could hope to do at night and that it might be useful for comparison with the village life I was getting to know on extended daytime excursions to Tomebamba and Quipal. I was expecting a group of earnest amateurs who played salsa or merengue and were trying to make a few sucres. I soon realized that this group was not like any I had ever played with. The primary goal that first night was not to play music but, rather, to strategize on how to raise enough money to play in Cuba at an international gathering of socialist youth. The group had already played in Cuba and even North Korea, which explained the unique Cuban-Korean decor of the small rehearsal space and why its members addressed one another as *compañero* (comrade). Our first concert, well attended by students from the University of Cuenca, consisted of revolutionary Cuban and Chilean songs, punctuated by shouts from the audience of "La lucha" (the fight) and "La combatividad" (combativeness) led with the clenched fist of a grizzled Cuban female veteran of Central American causes in the 1980s.

As the group took me in, they jokingly changed my last name to the Spanish "Calle" and finally to the indigenous surname "Quille," often with a "doctorcito" in front of it—a process they referred to as "cholofication," as in becoming a cholo. The group, in fact, was as much a gang of close friends as a musical or political group, a type of group known locally as a *jorga*, a group of friends who are like a family. Jorgas typically focus their energies on music or sport, or both. We spent as much time socializing as we did rehearsing.

One activity that bridged working and socializing was the postrehearsal serenading of wives and girlfriends from one of Cuenca's colonial-era cobblestone streets.

I thought I understood life in Cuenca from past extended trips there, which had totaled nearly one year. But I came to realize during my final year of field research that my perceptions had been skewed by the type of social networks I become familiar with, namely, intellectual elites, including local professors and students interested in researching migration. This had placed me squarely in the orbit of the "noble" families and other pretenders to the title who were happy to include an educated North American in their social events. I knew that many of the university departments were dominated by competing leftist factions and that the region as a whole was anything but conservative politically (unlike its social and cultural institutions). A large mural of Ché Guevara was a prominent feature of the university, and many posters of him could be found everywhere. In fact, the Cuban brand of revolution was considered mainstream compared with other, more radical groups such as the Maoists. I now found myself inside a very different world of young "commoner" men who mostly lived in communities on the outskirts of Cuenca and were one generation removed from rural life. A couple of group members were from more middle-class backgrounds, including a father who happened to be a sociologist; one still lived in a rural community. They sang and played traditional Indian and Spanish instruments, including pan flutes of different sizes, the *charango* (a stringed instrument made from the shell of an armadillo), and an assortment of guitars and percussion instruments. They had various day jobs, some more stable than others, depending on their ages. Some were young men still in school, others were in their early thirties and had well-established jobs.

As a group, they were at a crossroads; they had not played together in more than a year and had lost some of their socialist zeal with the recent collapse of the Soviet Union and the worsening economic crisis in Cuba. They were now trying again to play familiar material at international venues, but the effort seemed inspired more by nostalgia than by revolutionary fervor. With *neoliberalismo* on the rise throughout Latin America and *postmodernismo* the rage in intellectual circles, one member confided that the Soviet breakup left him in tears, his world shattered. In the end, we never went to Cuba, and the group changed its name from Grupo Victor Jara to Utopía.

Group members believed that while the Soviet Union was, in the end, a false utopia, the United States still remained responsible for most of the ills of Latin America. However, they were now much more concerned about the im-

mediate future of their own region than ideological rants against foreign op-
pression. In addition to odes to the Cuban revolution, we started incorporating more material containing local social commentary and Andean folkloric
music. They knew I was researching international migration, and it was a
topic of great interest to them. One of the band members had been to New
Jersey for a few months in the mid-1980s, and they all knew someone who
was currently in the United States, in many cases a family member. For them,
international migration to the United States represented a curious mix of opportunity and defeat. Clearly, some of the region's most uneducated and rural
inhabitants seemed to be making a lot of money and flaunting it. But to work
in the United States was to pray at the altar of the dollar and throw away all
of the socialist ideals they had espoused for years. If the Cubans can endure,
they seemed to say, so can we. When conversation turned to migrants from
Azuay in New York City, they did not express rancor and sarcasm toward
them—unlike many I had met from local elite families. For instance, they did
not refer to migrants from rural areas as "cholo boys." After all, members of
elite social networks might consider these young men themselves to be cholos—a term that more often denotes permanent social rank than racial category.

Given their emerging focus on "cultivating their own gardens," we decided
collectively to write a song about international migration from Azuay, but we
had no idea what style or form it should take. Sitting at a restaurant table one
night after rehearsal, I suggested that we write an Andean rap tune, striking a
defiant tone, starting with the title, "Soy Cholo Boy," (I am a cholo boy). Rap
music—including Spanish rap—was currently in vogue in Ecuador, and it
had the right attitude to capture the migration experience of young men who
were, against all odds, wealthy by local standards. They started to play with
the idea by turning it into a game; each person (except me) had to add a line
as we went around the table. One of them took the song home and polished
it up before the next rehearsal, when we added the rhythmic foundation. The
story, told in the first person from the perspective of a migrant, mixes
Quichua, Spanish, and (toward the end) English. *Chulla* is a Quichua word
indicating a single item, especially an item that by definition is a part of a pair
(e.g., one glove). Thus, "chulla vida" roughly translates into "only one life to
live." This attitude (and phrase) is common among migrants as they ratio-
nalize many of the physical, social, and economic risks associated with migration as an adventure of a lifetime.

We recorded "Soy Cholo Boy" in a studio, along with other songs, in December 1992. As the group had intended, the somewhat ambiguous song

caused a local debate on the airwaves regarding whether it glamorized migration or, instead, revealed a bittersweet social reality that few could deny. What was noteworthy about the reaction to the song was how many Azuayans could identify with it because of their own experience of having a family member abroad in "la YANY." Perhaps attesting more to its thematic interest to Azuayans than to its musical appeal, "Soy Cholo Boy" became one of the most popular songs played by radio stations in Cuenca, and the band made plans for a music video.

Apart from giving me a unique type of "cultural capital" among rural villagers in both Azuay and Otavalo, my participation in this musical group gave me insights into why and how those still living in rural communities pursued transnational migration in ways that would be economically and socially difficult for urban wageworkers. Compared with the young man from Tomebamba who has one or two uncles living abroad and whose family already owns some land and animals, the better-educated young mestizo men of Cuenca have nothing to anchor them to the region except the hope that their educational investment will one day pay off; ironically, it is this lack of a financial anchor that can be turned into collateral that makes getting a loan from a migration merchant nearly impossible. Some are lucky enough to get a tourist or student visa or come up with some strategy to skirt U.S. immigration laws, but most will need the aid of professional smugglers and document forgers if they ever hope to work in "la YANY," and that aid was likely to cost more money than they have ever seen. My life in Cuenca among the young men of my group also gave me a glimpse into the alternative for transnational migrants, namely, moving to the city for supposedly better occupational and educational opportunities. I came to understand why many considered that a false dream, a view borne out through the 1990s. There was some economic upward mobility and certainly greater educational opportunities, but true social mobility was largely out of the question. The good jobs, it seemed, always went to the same group of families that had dominated the region for centuries.

To provide an analytical framework in which to organize the description and analysis of the development of transnational migration in Quipal and Tomebamba, we examine it in light of three conceptual migration "problems," or dimensions, universal to the development of mass transnational migration: how transnational migration is pioneered by individuals (the pioneers) using preexisting social resources; how transnational migration then becomes itself a form of transnational social structure that transcends individual agency; and how preexisting local social structures affect both of these processes. These three generalizable dimensions of transnational migration can be summarized as construction, institutionalization, and embeddedness. These should not be confused with elements of a theory, because they do not specify causal relationships; they are, instead, heuristic concepts useful for organizing our analyses of study data and not separable in reality. Although patterns of transnational migration may develop as emergent social structures based on the initial activities of migration pioneers (institutionalization), subsequent migrants may find alternative migration strategies, which, in turn, may become institutionalized.

In addition, to better capture the unfolding nature of migration through networks, we examine two different "migration moments," one corresponding to the onset of international migration within a preexisting occupational or ethnic network and the other corresponding to the onset of international migration within a formal community. In the first migration moment, MM1, the objective opportunity of transnational migration arises for some village members, made available directly or indirectly by the information and resources of regional and national transnational migration pioneers and professional "migration merchants"; the second such moment, MM2, represents the actual onset of transnational migration and its specific pattern of development within each community.

Whereas the survey data is mute concerning MM1, it has much more to say about MM2 and the institutionalization of transnational social structures. The opposite is true of the ethnographic data gained from interviews and observation: although it excels at telling the story of the first regional and village pioneers and how they, in turn, have helped friends and family to cross the border and find jobs, it cannot grasp the scope and pattern of mature transnational migration as a generalized network or village phenomenon.

The First Migration Moment: Networks

In several communities of Azuay, stories circulate about the first pioneer to leave for "la YANY." The local label *pioneer* succinctly describes the social significance of the event: the first to leave is not only opening new adventures and opportunities for himself (the pioneer is typically male) but is also colonizing a social frontier to which many family members and friends will eventually arrive. Yet, none of these migrant pioneer stories tells of individuals so frustrated and, in equal measure, so adventurous that they simply headed north to cross several national borders illegally and hoped for the best. To the contrary, one feature of these stories is that they generally begin with the pioneer's social tie to an Ecuadorian or foreigner who lives in the United States or

Canada. That is, the first few international migrants from a particular social group may be considered pioneers but they are not, strictly speaking, trailblazers. Thus, it is weak ties to others within regional networks, rather than strong internal bonds of solidarity or high levels of human capital, that is the first prerequisite for joining the migration flow. It is for this reason that the first migration moment (MM1) begins not with its own migrant pioneers but rather with a village member's ties to others who have migrated abroad, an opportunity arising from a village's historical integration into regional social and economic institutions.

To the extent that economic institutions in crisis are the first to turn to domestic and international migration, such as the usurious middleman structure of the Panama hat trade, there is considerable overlap between the objective "cause" of transnational migration and its social organization through a preexisting economic network (in crisis). Although the original economic activity may have waned, its social ties form the basis for the development of a commodified migration network and thus a new economic activity. If, indeed, "networks migrate," then preexisting social ties, both strong and weak, will shape the migration process within a region even more than community ties would. Data from the two research sites in Azuay strongly support this hypothesis.

In Tomebamba, a village completely integrated into the Panama hat trade and, therefore, the first network of regional transnational migration pioneers, MM1 occurred relatively early in the regional development of transnational migration. Some of the first rural peasants from Azuay and Cañar to migrate abroad came from the village of Déleg in the early 1970s, some fifteen kilometers to the north of Tomebamba. They, too, were engaged in hat weaving and had been migrating to coastal plantations. Migrant pioneers from Déleg were aided, if not recruited, by urban travel agencies offering underground migration services, including not only the airline ticket but also false documents and information. Thus, Tomebamba was structurally part of the early migration network, supported by professional migration merchants with ties to the Panama hat trade, for nearly ten years before the actual onset of transnational migration (MM2). In contrast, Quipal was poorly integrated into the socioeconomic networks of the Panama hat trade and, therefore, lacked direct contact with the rural middleman and initial migrant pioneers. Instead, Quipal's exposure to transnational migration networks (MM1) came from urban networks. (Recall that Quipal is a community deeply divided by ethnicity and economic activity.)

This type of segmented urban ties to migration networks had two primary implications for MM1 in Quipal: (1) it was exposed to a more diffused phenomenon in the city, where transnational migration did not take off until the 1980s; and (2) the nature of the exposure was more social than economic, with few professional migration merchants taking an interest in recruiting migrants from a village where they knew few villagers and, more importantly, enjoyed little influence or trust. The first person to leave Tomebamba for the United States was, in fact, Jesus, after being persuaded in 1980 by men from nearby Déleg, co-workers on a coastal plantation, who told him about the income he could earn abroad in dollars. More importantly, they provided him with specific information on how the trip could be made through Mexico, using specific coyotes. In this sense, the significance of coastal migration for initiating transnational migration in Tomebamba was not in its mechanical similarity but rather in offering a network of weak ties (co-workers), which expanded the amount of information concerning economic opportunities, new information not found among the strong ties of co-villagers. Many of the plantation workers, including Jesus, had also worked for short periods in Venezuela, where discussions about the United States were frequent. Using a local coyote, who worked with a Mexican network of smugglers, Jesus first went to Chicago, where several male family members (uncles and cousins) later joined him in working at a hotel. After a variety of legal, economic, and health problems, including the deportation of one family member, they all went to New York City to join other Azuayans, forming the primary beachhead for more migrants from Tomebamba.

The initiation of transnational migration (MM2) in Quipal illustrates the fact that networks—not historical communities—migrate. The first person to leave Quipal for the United States was a young woman who married a U.S. Peace Corps volunteer who had been working in Quipal as an agricultural advisor. She left for the United States in 1981. Given the permanent nature and unusual circumstances of her immigration, her role in the village was not that of migration pioneer. In fact, it would be four more years before the next migrant pioneer, Manuel, left for New York City. Manuel, who comes from Quipal's mestizo group identified as cholos-Cuencanos, had married into a family from a neighboring town and moved there with his bride. His father-in-law had already made a trip to New York City and helped Manuel to cross the border in 1985 by contracting a local Mexican smuggler in Tijuana for a few hundred dollars. After a couple of years living in Harlem, Manuel was joined by some of his relatives and friends in Quipal, thus initiating transnational migration as a social phenomenon in Quipal.

However, it was not until the late 1980s and early 1990s that transnational migration from Quipal began to rapidly develop as traditional social structures began to be altered. Yet, unlike Tomebamba, where the migration experience is fairly homogeneous and concentrated, Quipal saw three distinct migration paths: one leading to underground garment factories in New York City, one to a landscaping firm and a toy manufacturer in a small town near Boston, and, in the late 1990s, one to logging companies in the northeastern United States, primarily Pennsylvania. Thus, in Quipal, we must also speak of a second pioneer who has paved the way for an alternative path to Boston and environs. Roberto, who comes from one of the prominent white families of Quipal, had also married into a Baños family and was helped by his wife's relatives to migrate to New York City. However, Roberto soon got tired of the fast pace of city life and was discouraged by the ailing New York economy in the late 1980s. During a visit to Boston he met a local priest who was helping legal and undocumented migrants in various ways. With this encouraging contact, Roberto decided to make the move to a small town near Boston and soon found work as a gardener for a landscaping company.

The job paid relatively well and did not require that he speak much English; he enjoyed the outdoor aspect of the work compared with washing dishes in New York, a job also not fitting Roberto's educational and social status as a white male. Yet, the landscaping job had the significant drawback of being seasonal, leading Roberto to seek work in a nearby toy factory doing odd jobs like sweeping. Roberto's manager was impressed by his performance and soon hired some of Roberto's close relatives. Roberto has now made several trips back to Baños to spend time with his family of five and to personally escort other family members across the Mexican border and on to Boston. Roberto has now become a sort of in-group migration merchant whose services are either free or extremely inexpensive, allowing him to finance trips home and to also bring others to join him, thereby reducing some of the expenses and loneliness abroad. Most of the Boston migrants live in the same five middle-class apartments. Other than a few close friends of Roberto, all of the Boston migrants thus far are related by blood or marriage. At the time of the original survey research none of the Indian members of the community, identified as naturales, had migrated. A follow-up survey conducted in 1994 reveals that one had migrated; by late 1998, my research assistant found that several were now migrating as loggers, the same job they had performed in Azuay. Thus, by the 1990s the three ethnic-based communities-within-a-community became even more entrenched in transnational social structures.

As we have seen from the delayed onset of transnational migration after MM1 in both villages, mere exposure to international migration networks does not guarantee entrance into them (i.e., the transition from MM1 to MM2). Instead, the prerequisite for MM2, the actual initiation of transnational migration from a social group or community, seems to be a stable social tie to a transnational migrant or foreigner who can give trusted information and directly introduce him to the commodified regional migration networks, which are, themselves, integrated into transnational networks of migrants and migration merchants, such as professional Mexican coyotes.

At the time of my original survey research, men from other nearby villages had been already migrating for nearly twenty years, constituting the regional pioneers and forming the primary social and economic context for the initiation of transnational migration in Tomebamba and Quipal. The principal structural feature of MM1 and MM2 in the two communities is the important role of social linkages to outside networks in which transnational migration information and resources circulate. It can, of course, be hypothesized that when those outside networks are part of the commodification process of transnational migration, including increasing integration with transnational networks of migration merchants, emigration will develop rapidly within the community. Thus, information gathered from informants in the two research sites, contextualized with historical data, reveals the concrete social construction of transnational migration. In both villages, it began as an opportunity that was eventually realized through ongoing social relations, albeit with somewhat more distant, nongroup members.

Thus far, the evidence is merely suggestive of the role that segmented networks play in shaping the migration process, because the qualitative data does not capture the actual structure of the migration flows. Unlike ethnographic data, survey data can show us the patterning of transnational migration (MM2) and its embeddedness in preexisting networks and identities (MM1). We also use the survey data to evaluate the determinants and institutionalization of transnational social services at the household and community levels.

Maps 4.1 and 4.2 present data on the onset of transnational migration in households of the two villages. That is, they show the year in which the first migrant left a particular household by its location on a geometrically proportional map of the village. They do not indicate the number of migrants per household. In this case, the null hypothesis would be that household onset of migration would occur more or less randomly throughout the village. A rejection of the null hypothesis would indicate that transnational migration entails a patterned social process.

In both Tomebamba and Quipal, the sociospatial development of transnational migration is nonrandom. Rather, there are distinct groupings, or clus-

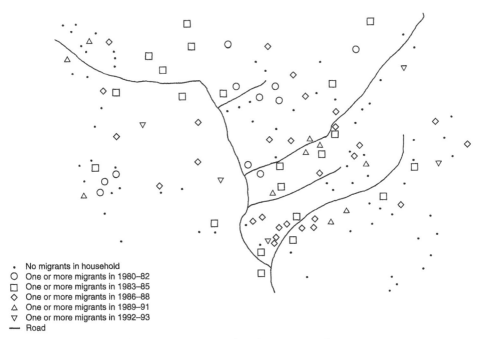

Map 4.1. Household Migration in Tomebamba, by Year of Onset, 1980–1993
Source: Study data.

• No migrants in household
○ One or more migrants in 1980–82
☐ One or more migrants in 1983–85
◇ One or more migrants in 1986–88
△ One or more migrants in 1989–91
▽ One or more migrants in 1992–93
— Road

ters, of migrant households. Furthermore, physical clusters of migrant households also exhibit a temporal grouping regarding the onset of transnational
migration. It seems that one neighbor not only follows another abroad but
also tends to do so within a relatively short period of time, if not simultaneously. Another feature common to both villages is the greater proportion of
migrant households fronting principal village roads, especially near the entrance to the village. To explain these characteristics we need to recall from
previous chapters that because of inheritance customs neighbors tend to be
other extended family members or more distant relatives. Hence, although
the common social competition among neighbors to outdo one another is in
full effect, the difference is that familial solidarity and obligations of reciprocity make it unlikely that one family will remain ahead of others for long:
within a couple of years after migrating, international migrants use their dollars for conspicuous consumption, assuring that other family members will
want to replicate the migrant's success. This pattern is especially clear in the
case of Tomebamba, where villagers occupy roughly similar ethnic and class
positions and community solidarity is high. Another factor contributing to

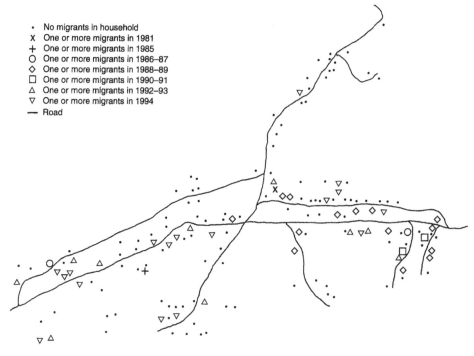

Map 4.2. Household Migration in Quipal, by Year of Onset, 1980–1994
Source: Study data.

the social process of transnational migration from Andean villages is the danger and level of adventure involved in the journey from rural life in Ecuador to finding a job in Manhattan: it is a journey made less bitter with the aid of trusted friends and family as the migrants confront a series of physical, emotional, and financial challenges. To repeat, it is extremely unusual to hear of someone simply heading north without substantial help from family, friends, and professional migration merchants.

The fact that the Ecuadorian homes of migrants cluster along the road is a function of three things, presented in their order of importance: (1) it indicates their somewhat higher household socioeconomic status, in that property fronting a road is generally more desirable, which suggests that the poorest of the poor do not have the economic and social resources necessary to migrate; (2) in villages where telephones are still rare, families living along the main road are in a better position to participate in currents of important transnational migration information flowing within the community and be-

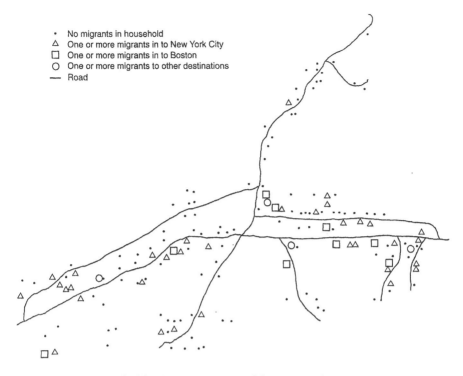

Map 4.3. Household Migration in Quipal, by Destination, 1994
Source: Study data.

tween the village and other external regions; and (3) there is a propensity for migrants to build new houses as close to the village center as possible, including along the main road.

Although there is a similar clustering of the household onset of transnational migration in both villages, the pattern of transnational migration development in Quipal (map 4.2) requires a closer look because its spatial patterning has some distinct features. The most obvious difference between the maps, and thus between the patterns of transnational migration, is the large number of households in the top sector of the map of Quipal not participating in out-migration abroad. Transnational migration is even lacking among almost all households fronting a road in this sector. However, it is along this steep road, perpendicular to the main road, that the naturales live. Recall that the highest levels of domestic migration in the village were found among this same group; only recently, however, did the first member of this group migrate abroad to New York City (1994). Thus, we can conclude that, although

Table 4.1. Migration Financing Method, by Sex and Village, 1993 (percentage)

	Bank	Family Savings	Free Loan	Personal Savings	Migration Merchant	Travel Agent	n
Tomebamba							
Male	0.0	10.0	20.0	4.0	66.0	0.0	50
Female	0.0	10.0	30.0	0.0	60.0	0.0	10
Quipal							
Male	0.0	8.7	34.8	4.3	47.8	4.3	23
Female	10.0	30.0	10.0	0.0	50.0	0.0	10

Source: Adult study data, 1993.

transnational migration from Quipal had been occurring for several years, the preexisting social divisions along ethnic lines excluded the naturales from the emerging migration flows, and they had to develop their own migration strategies and contacts abroad, with the first pioneer within this group leaving in 1994, several years after MM2 in Quipal. In the previous section we noted two distinct migration paths whereby whites were migrating to Boston.

Table 4.2. Migration Financing Method, by Type of Border Crossing and Village, 1993 (percentage)

Number of Migrant Members per Household	By Land	By Air	n
Tomebamba			
Family savings	20.0	80.0	5
Free loan	66.7	33.3	12
Personal savings	0.0	100.0	2
Migration merchant	10.5	89.5	38
Quipal			
Bank	0.0	100.0	1
Family savings	40.0	60.0	5
Free loan	50.0	50.0	8
Personal savings	0.0	100.0	1
Migration merchant	38.5	61.5	13
Travel agent	100.0	0.0	1

Source: Adult study data, 1993.
Note: Cramer $V = .109$***.

Map 4.3 presents the spatial location of household transnational migration according to their migration destination abroad. Thus, survey data support the ethnographic evidence: we can clearly discern a clustering of households by destination—mostly members of the same families.

Presenting the onset of transnational migration over time and space in this graphical manner reveals a nonrandom pattern of transnational migration development, reinforcing our previous observation that transnational migration (1) is an archetypal *social* phenomenon and (2) is best conceptualized as network migration rather than community migration. Logistic regression models support the general observation of the graphical map data on onset of transnational migration (Kyle 1996). The social process of transnational migration also means that there is a logic to migrant selection that transcends personal attributes or economic problems; as Tilly has noted, "networks migrate, categories stay put" (1990, 84). We can examine one aspect of the social process of migration more closely using the survey data.

Tables 4.1 and 4.2 present cross-tabulations of selected characteristics of the financing of the migration, which it will be recalled can cost from U.S.$2,000 to $8,000—an enormous amount for an Azuayan peasant. As can be seen from table 4.1, migration merchants play a significant role in Tomebamba in financing and aiding the would-be migrant (the patterns seem to be similar for men and women). Migrant family members in Quipal are more likely to help wives and daughters cross the border than those in Tomebamba, where most women who wish to migrate have to borrow the money to do so. (These results are corroborated by interviews in both communities and by the ethnographic data presented in the following section.) As we would expect, the use of a migration merchant, who also provides falsified documents, is associated with direct air travel to the United States in both villages (table 4.2). In addition to the tables shown here, survey data reveal that migration from Tomebamba is usually initiated through the use of professional migration merchants, whereas Quipal is less integrated into that network; we see that as migration within a household increases, the use of migration merchants increases as well. In both villages there is a tendency for increasing amounts of aid from family members as the level of household migration increases, either in the form of outright savings or through interest-free, or very low-interest, loans.

In summary, quantitative analyses using survey data have given us a more complete understanding of the institutionalization of transnational migration in Tomebamba and Quipal. Migration abroad has taken on the status of a new, emergent transnational social structure in these villages.

The Second Migration Moment: Transnational Households and Their Communities

Although it may be true that networks migrate, not communities, the human drama of transnational migration plays out within households as sites of social contestation and reproduction and economic production and consumption. A salient feature of the preexisting structures of economic activity in both Azuayan villages is their reliance on the household as the basic economic unit and land as the prerequisite to independent agricultural and artisanal activity for that unit. Every member is expected to contribute to agricultural, artisanal, and domestic activities that benefit the household. Hence, economic decisions are essentially made within the context of the family, often the extended family. Even young adult men continue to contribute to the household economy until they are married rather than viewing their earnings as entirely their own.

Given this household organization of economic production and biological and social reproduction, the most intimate and immediate changes stemming from transnational migration occur at the level of the household, in both its structure and ideology—its political economy. Unlike other forms of mass mobilization whereby community change is effected at the community level (e.g., protest over taxes), the evolution of transnational networks unfolds at the household level. While it may be true that different networks lead to parallel migration flows, transnational households (those with at least one household member living abroad) must contend with a similar set of social, economic (consumption and investment), and legal challenges. The two themes we explore in this regard are economic change and the transformation of gender relations across the two communities.

Because the object of study is economic migration, rather than a refugee flow, the most obvious economic change is the increasing uncoupling of households from the local economy as it becomes a site of speculation, with greater integration with underground labor markets in the United States. Transnational migration distorts local economies in ways that make them conform to its transnational reality, as nonmigrants must conform to the direct or indirect consequences of this new transnational dimension. Local observers describe this process as the "dollarization" of the economy (Carpio 1992) because a prime indicator of the distortion is the use of dollars instead of Ecuadorian sucres. Nearly any time of the day or week one can observe long lines of female peasants (almost entirely *cholas*) queuing up at foreign currency exchange houses in Cuenca ready to cash in U.S. dollars sent from "la

YANY" by family members. Hence, networks may shape who goes and where, but the transformation in local markets connecting all of the networks gives impetus to greater migration levels. As we have seen, for a person to be left out of a particular migration network does not mean that a transnational strategy is beyond reach but only that it will be structured differently, both in Ecuador and at the destination.

The effects of these market distortions more connected to the reality of transnational social structures than local or national trends, such as the dollarization of the economy, are particularly felt in the area of land tenure; in communities such as Tomebamba and Quipal, land is both an economic and sociocultural necessity: in Otavalo, you cannot get married and retain community membership without it. In addition to these use values, land is perceived as the only secure anti-inflationary investment. Thus, returning migrants with dollars, now in a position to outbid even the wealthiest non-migrants for land, pose a social and economic threat to the young adults, especially teenage men; the objective economic threat is often distorted by an even greater perceived threat abated by feelings of relative deprivation. One return migrant in Tomebamba told of how he tried to dissuade a would-be migrant from going because it was becoming harder and harder to find good jobs in New York City, which was in a severe recession at the time (1991). The young man responded that he was simply trying to keep him from enjoying the same success: after all, the migrant had a new two-story house and a truck. There is also the widespread and well-founded belief that when things are bad in the United States they will be even worse in Ecuador. Consequently, following the onset of transnational migration within a range of networks, land prices in both villages have risen sharply, even in relation to regional inflation, making a stint abroad a perceived necessity for young men in many rural areas of Azuay, not just Quipal and Tomebamba.

Transnational migration in Tomebamba and Quipal has entailed a fundamental change in the household mode of production through subsistence agriculture; the centrality of land ownership as an economic strategy is radically diminished even while the desire for more land increases. To be sure, transnational migration is a response, in part, to the trend of preexisting diminishing returns to subsistence agriculture and, especially, local cottage industry. With transnational migration, however, this trend hastens the demise of the logic of a semi-independent household economy by producing new problems. The most basic problem is the loss of household farm labor, requiring the need for paid help to plow, sow, and harvest. The use of paid laborers is much more common among migrant than nonmigrant households in both villages. In the case of Tomebamba, where a majority of the adult men in their prime years have left, the women have been unable and unwilling to maintain agricultural production at earlier levels. Many have turned to raising livestock as a more attractive alternative. In Quipal, the decline of subsistence agriculture had already been noted before the onset of transnational migration as the village became better integrated into urban economic circuits. Many migrant households, however, find it necessary to employ day laborers even on their small plots of land.

Over time, migrant households in Azuay have become a site of consumption and speculative investment rather than economic production. The average remittance per month to the migrant's family back home is $183 for Tomebamba and $376 for Quipal. These remittances are allocated for different expenses, depending on the stage of migration of the household; initially, most money earned abroad goes to paying off the debt incurred to migration merchants and then gradually is channeled toward the provisioning of an urban-style house and all of the electric and electronic goods found in any middle-class American home. Survey data show that the level of ownership of electronic goods, appliances, and automobiles, as well as the size of houses (in numbers of floors), increases in direct proportion to the number of migrants in a household.

Before the survey was conducted, interviews in Quipal revealed that some migrant households changed their physical location upon the departure of the first migrant, typically the male head of household. The family of the migrant rejoined his or his wife's parents' household for two reasons: first, during the initial period, where money earned abroad goes to pay off a debt, there is an economic advantage to combining households; and, second, the "virtue" of the wife is ensured during a prolonged period of separation between the male migrant and the female nonmigrant. Survey data confirm my informal observations in Quipal: a much higher percentage of migrant households was living in dwellings with two households (families). This trend was not found in Tomebamba.

One item from the survey taps the possible acceptance by the respondent of a hypothetical foreign son-in-law or daughter-in-law. Greater household migration leads to a somewhat greater acceptance level. In addition, many of the male spouses of the respondents have become themselves Americanized to varying degrees, thus blurring the distinction between *foreign* and *local*.

One of the most important changes in the social organization and accompanying ideology is the change in gender stratification and roles. In these communities, the prevailing view is that men and women are not equal because God intended it that way—that gender inequality is a part of a "natural order." A man's nature is to be adventurous and brave in the face of adversity with a duty as the head of the household to maintain family resources and status; a women's nature is to be docile and weak with a duty to serve her husband as her earthly master. Among the activities that this patriarchy legitimates and facilitates is transnational migration in the manner that it occurs in Azuay. It is evident from interviews that many women would not agree to the migration if the decision were left solely to them. Furthermore, initially, migrant men continue to exert control over their wives' affairs through remittances and through the use of family members and spies. In contrast, the men enjoy a newfound freedom abroad, as suggested in chapter 1 in the person of Jesus (and as "Soy Cholo Boy" accurately portrays).

The turning point into what might be called a second phase is the realization by wives of migrants and single women that their husbands and boyfriends will probably never return permanently, a realization that initiates changes in their relationships to their husbands and boyfriends and to each other. The initial increase in power gained by male migrants over their spouses through economic control begins to diminish over time as women begin to feel strung along. At this point, women are faced with the decision to focus on community development with little support from the men or to join their husbands abroad, with or without their blessing.

These two phases of the political economy of gender within households do not describe all migrant households nor account for community-level variation in their patterning. Although the onset of transnational migration occurred in both villages at about the same time (1980), transnational migration in Tomebamba rapidly increased in comparison with Quipal. With more than ten years of heavy transnational migration behind it, Tomebamba has clearly reached the second phase of gender relations. In contrast, transnational migration from Quipal has only recently taken off and is still largely in the first phase, though there are already complaints by wives left behind. However, the preexisting economic and ethnic diversity of Quipal and the ways that migration developed in that community led to a somewhat different, less acrimonious, pattern of gender relations within transnational social structures. It should be recalled that a good part of the community had already been involved in sewing clothes, an ideal skill to have for the New York City underground labor market in the early 1990s. Both men and women had human capital that could get better returns abroad. Thus, relatively more women from Quipal have been part of this initial wave of migration abroad, and women are more likely to be included in future migrations, as illustrated by the story of Luis and Anita.

Luis and Anita: Mestizos from Quipal

Sewing clothes out of the home to supplement farming production has been a way of life for Luis and his family for three generations. However, the national economic crisis of the 1980s meant that sewing became less and less profitable while the cost of food not grown by the family rose sharply. Luis, along with three other relatives, left for New York City in 1987 after paying more than U.S.$3,000 to a migration merchant to help them make the three-week journey north; they flew, first, to Costa Rica, then took a bus overland to Tijuana and crossed the border with the help of a coyote, finally arriving in New York City by airplane. Because of their contacts with migration pioneers from Quipal and a nearby community, Luis and his cohort were immediately able to get jobs washing dishes in a Manhattan restaurant. Luis shared an apartment in the Bronx with five other friends and relatives from Quipal.

Luis's wife, Anita, and their three children moved back in with her parents to save money until the debt could be paid off. Initially, the psychological trauma of Luis's departure so immobilized Anita that she neglected the family's animals and even her children. Instead of greater personal freedom without her husband's immediate demands, her life is even more restricted; she cannot walk anywhere unaccompanied by a relative without risking unfounded gossip. For the first five years abroad, Luis sent Anita just enough money to maintain the family and to make payments on the debt; he did not want his wife to join him, because he felt it would be difficult to work with three small children at home. During this period Luis's plan was to return to Quipal after he had paid the migration debt and saved a financial nest-egg to start a small business selling imported clothing in Cuenca.

Luis did return in 1991 to fulfill his dream. However, the many personal and bureaucratic hurdles to owning a shop proved insurmountable. After nearly a year back in Ecuador with little real possibility of starting a viable business, and with his savings dwindling, Luis returned to New York City and was quickly able to reenter the underground labor market. On his next trip back to Quipal, with urging from Anita, Luis agreed to take her with him to "la YANY" to work, leaving the children with her parents until they could find a legal way to send for them. With her sewing skills she was able to quickly find work in an "invisible factory" owned by Dominican immigrants. Their eldest son, who is now fourteen, is trying to learn English so that he will easily adapt to life in New York when he joins his parents within a couple of years.

A Village of Women

After several years of high levels of migration by the adult males of Tomebamba, traditional gender roles are sharply changing, leading to changes in the subsequent social process of migration itself. The most important feature of gender relations in Tomebamba, signaling the end of an initial phase, is an increased autonomy for adult women, which is manifested in everyday village relations and, most importantly, in the ability and willingness of single and married women to themselves migrate out of desperation to reunite or start a family. For a women to migrate without a male relative was extremely rare in 1991, but by 1993 several had made the trip, and more planned to follow in the near future. Far from being supported by male relatives, most of these trips were actively discouraged. To understand how wives and mothers of migrants reached this point we need to understand the emotional and material changes they experienced during the first phase.

Most of the adult women of Tomebamba have experienced varying degrees of both physical and emotional abandonment. The migrant men actively conspire to reveal as little information as possible to their wives and other female relatives regarding their activities abroad, including their place of employment and sometimes even their address. This code of silence is rarely breached, leaving women with little information regarding their husbands' and boyfriends' lives in New York City. Many male migrants abroad do not communicate at all unless necessary (e.g., to make some financial arrangement in the home village). Essentially, in several cases, migration has led to a de facto divorce without emotional closure:

> My husband has not returned in five years since the last time he left for the United States. The first two years he would send money and he would be worried about the family; then nothing, he would neither write, nor call; we don't know what he does because he doesn't write. . . . In the last three years he has sent eight hundred dollars, according to him, for the children. What am I going to do with eight hundred dollars? He thinks that we can live on that. Let him come to bring up the children, feed, dress, and send them to school so he can see if it is enough. . . . I have suffered a lot; some people say that he is not coming back because of me, but I have not done anything for him to misbehave so badly. Now, I don't even want him to return; when he comes back, he will not find me. Some,

who are over there, say that he said he wants to take the children there, but I am not going to let him. How can he take them if he has not done anything for them? He wants to take them "with his hands clean" while I am the one who has cared for them, who is making them study, who has fought for them; I will not let him take them away easily. (Orfelia, 40 years old)

The apparent equilibrium that the women maintained in the community during the first phase began to break down as a result of the more physically and emotionally distant relationships with migrant husbands, evident in less frequent letters and phone calls. The women express discontent, resentment, and powerlessness; however, they also developed closer bonds to female neighbors, godmothers, and relatives (their mothers, sisters, sisters-in-law). Women were more apt to leave their homes for social visits, something that was rare when the men were there. Greater flexibility and freedom exists in the various economic and household chores. For example, when the husband is not at home the women start their chores later in the morning. For some women, not having a domineering husband around was not viewed as a completely negative development, and many have adapted to life in a village with few adult men. Many still believe that it is not a permanent state of affairs and it will soon be over, as if the men were all at sea and had to one day come home.

Nonetheless, some women have concluded that life in a village without men is untenable and have decided to migrate out of both desperation and intense curiosity. Some have been able to migrate without men by banding together and pooling information and resources, which are both at considerable levels after a decade of transnational migration. Since the 1980s, some women had already been involved in the money-lending business through the small, low-interest loans they made to neighboring kin and friends. Because the women left behind have been paying off the loans to professional migration merchants, they also have gained a considerable amount of information concerning how to proceed, from borrowing money and obtaining false documents to finding coyotes to guide them across the several Central American and Mexican borders.

The greater the number of years of transnationalism, the more freedom women typically develop in the management of remittances from male family members. In addition to these material prerequisites to migrating, women have also gained an increasing sense of confidence as they essentially have assumed all the former household and community roles previously carried out by men, with the exception of the most heavy labor, such as preparing and plowing the land. Where the participation and contribution of woman was largely invisible before transnational migration, it is now ubiquitous. A novel sight in Tomebamba is women driving their own cars or trucks to town, an unthinkable practice just a few years ago, when women were often beaten for simply leaving their homes.

The combination of desperation caused by prolonged separation and the socioeconomic empowerment of the wives of migrants has led to the surprising phenomenon of females migrating independently to New York City. Remaining women in the village described both successful and unsuccessful attempts by themselves and their neighbors to get to New York City. Although the women have now learned from past mistakes, many were easy targets for con artists, posing as migration merchants, who would supply them with documents. Some of the preparation for traveling abroad includes wearing more "urban" dress and hairstyles rather than the traditional *pollera* and straw hat; but without the hat they felt strange and got headaches. Realistically assessing the dangers involved in traveling over land through Mexico, one women reported that it was not uncommon for women preparing to migrate to visit the doctor in Checa to obtain birth control pills in case they were raped en route.

In sum, the political economy of gender has been altered in response to transnational migration in a way that has empowered women in limited ways but has also left them wondering whether they are indeed better off than they were before widespread migration abroad. For their sons and, now, daughters, international migration is no longer a personal or social economic decision but rather the only way to spend time with their father and to understand the other side of their transnational households. However, for the adult women left behind, the decision to migrate is tortuous because it entails a dilemma regarding their relationships with their husbands or future husbands. This dilemma and frustration is best summed up in the words of one woman:

> My husband has not returned in ten years, but I want to know nothing of him; if we are going to talk about him, I do not want to talk. At first he would send letters and dollars to me every month for five years, always. Then, the following two years he would send dollars but would no longer write. . . . In the beginning I cried, suffering a lot and writing many letters—I still don't know why he never answered them. . . . Three years ago I began to arrange the papers to go, but my family, and above all my

brother [in Queens], asks me, "Why do you want to go? Don't go—something disgraceful could happen to you. Where are you going to leave your children? It's better that you avoid even worse problems. What are you going to do there? You could find him with another [woman] and then you will be even worse off." . . . Now he only writes our children and calls them by telephone. Sometimes they ask him, "Why don't you send money or write to mama?" . . . My son who is already in fourth grade says that one day he will go—he wants to know where his father works and why he doesn't come home. He doesn't want to study. . . . I get so angry because I know he is sending money to my in-laws; recently they told me he sent them 400 dollars. . . . I know that one day he will return, even if he is dead he has to return. I'm not going to bury him; just burn him and throw him away. (Ana, 45 years old)

———

As the periphery-centered approach indicates, macrostructural changes are necessary but not sufficient causes to initiate and sustain transnational migration; this approach suggests that we also need to examine the role of the migration process operating through social networks in selecting who will migrate abroad. Hence, those who have begun to participate in domestic migrations would be especially susceptible to transnational migration, because they not only have an objective reason for seeking external work but also have begun to restructure social life around migration.*

The greatest difference in the social structures of the two villages lies not in their internal stratification but in their participation in external social structures. Tomebamba has been intimately integrated into the classic network of usurious intermediaries for decades. In Quipal, by contrast, there has been a noteworthy lack of such relations, aside from the impositions of the Catholic Church. Ethnicity alone does not explain this objective reality; unlike the indigenous population of Tomebamba, the naturales of Quipal pro-

---

* There is, of course, a significant difference between temporary and permanent domestic migration regarding the implications for transnational migration. Permanent migration, with its break with village life as migrants move to urban areas, may be the first step in leaving the country altogether. However, temporary migration entails a reorientation of social life toward migration (the "migration process") while, most importantly, retaining the financial and social capital that accompanies land ownership, resources needed for an expensive and complex international migration such as the case of the Ecuador-U.S. flow.

vided a labor force for a nearby hacienda and for mestizo and white neighbors. These differences between the two villages, which affect the financial and social resources available to village members, are embedded in the deeper historical logic and economic development patterns of the region.

To explain the rapid development of transnational migration in Tomebamba in contrast with its slower development in Quipal, we must take into account not only the availability of linkages to outside migration networks but also the historical nature of those linkages. Tomebamba provides an example of how integration into broker capitalism in an earlier period (hat weaving) facilitated the transition to transnational migration through a similar social structure of usurious intermediaries (migration merchants). It should be underscored that both the migration merchant and the migrant are taking enormous risks in these transactions, therefore requiring a high level of trust on both sides. Thus, it was social ties to extracommunal networks that allowed for its rapid and near total development in Tomebamba. In the second stage of transnational migration, migrants from Tomebamba can now rely on internal resources and information to a greater degree—though not completely.

In Quipal, it was the lack of this type of socioeconomic tie to professional migration merchants that impeded the initial development of transnational migration—though Quipal villagers had precisely those sewing skills in great demand in New York City. It was not until organic networks in Quipal gained the internal resources and leadership necessary to helping co-villagers migrate that transnational migration took off—nearly ten years after its initial onset. Hence, it was internal social capital within community networks that eventually turned transnational migration into a mass phenomenon and has given it its unique pattern.

Given these different paths to transnational migration, and their evolutionary patterns as they branch in the United States, the effects of transnational migration on migrants and their households have also been varied. Migrants from Quipal have retained more control over the migration process. The Quipal migrants were also better prepared for work abroad, because skills learned in Ecuador could be put to use in the United States. What is most striking in Quipal, in contrast with Tomebamba, is that those households that had sent members to the coast are the very ones that are not included in the transnational migration stream. Neither people, nor the social networks they form, are mechanical. It is a reminder that temporary transnational migration is not simply a more dramatic version of temporary domestic migration—it may be similar, but it requires a new social construction. Transnational migration requires a large amount of financial, social, political, and cultural resources. As we have seen, social networks are more determinative than social class or human capital for understanding the origins and maintenance of transnational migration. Without the inclusion of both villages in the study, we may have been led to conclude that it was coastal migration that was the principal antecedent. Similarly, this analysis of migration from Azuay must be attenuated by the case of Otavalo to the north, to which I now turn.

CHAPTER FIVE

Tourist Trails out of Otavalo

Soy Cholo Boy y me voy a bacilar, con borinquas, cubanas, que buenas que están. Total chulla vida, no hay que desperdiciar, y ven michu michu, mi huarmi no está. (Mujer sexy: Ay! Papito, dame un besito!). Me cuentan, me dicen, hay una enfermedad, que es descono- cida, pero que más da? De algo hay que morir. Me dijo mi papá, poniéndome "el sombrero," lo puedo evitar. Esposa (enojada): Esa cubana me robó mi Manuel, esa boriquena me robó tu corazón! Oye longo desgraciado, te fuiste a trabajar, ahora vienes con cubanas, fieras longas deben ser. Tu guagua cumplió un año, y otro boté perdiendo; (mas dulce) no seas malito cari. . . . Ya bota volviendo!

[I am a Cholo Boy and I'm going to enjoy Puerto Rican and Cuban women and all the nice ones there. There's only one life so you can't waste it, come here, sweetie, my wife isn't here. (Sexy female voice: Ay! Little father, give me a kiss!). They tell me, they say, there is an illness, that is unknown, but what more can it do? You have to die of some- thing. My father told me to wear my "little hat" to avoid it. Wife (angry voice): This Cuban stole my Manuel, this Puerto Rican stole your heart! Listen disgraceful brute, you went [abroad] to work, now you go with Cuban women, probably ugly brutes. Your baby just turned one year, and the other you are throwing away; (sweet voice) don't be bad little sweetheart. . . . Come home!]

Like the southern Ecuadorian province of Azuay, the northern Andean re- gion of Otavalo is well known for its artisanal production among peasant smallholders, known as Otavalans (in Spanish, Otavaleños)—in this case, the weaving of traditional garments and both traditional and nontraditional handicrafts. Yet, in contrast to villagers of Azuay, who travel to North America as laborers, Otavalans have gained an international reputation for their extensive travels abroad as handicraft merchants. In the course of the overseas marketing of their own products and those of other Indian and non-Indian peasant groups, Otavalans have carved out a global market niche for inexpensive handicrafts manufactured by household labor using preindustrial and industrial technologies of scale. The economic success of the Otavalans, so uncommon among other Latin American indigenous groups, belies an internal stratification; not all Otavalans have shared in the prosperity of local industry and international trade: instead, many make up the internal labor force still intimately connected to agricultural production. Yet, the recent and rapid development of exporting Andean music abroad has allowed even the most dispossessed Otavalans an opportunity for an overseas stint and the accumulation of capital for further entrepreneurial activity.

The canton of Otavalo, in the province of Imbabura (see map 1.1), has been described by successive visitors as one of the most strikingly beautiful valleys in South America, situated at ninety-two hundred feet above sea level and just sixty-five miles north of Quito. The valley is framed by two extinct volcanoes, Imbabura (known as Taita, or father) and Cotacachi (known as Mama, or mother), which are married, according to indigenous lore. At the foot of Imbabura lies San Pablo Lake. The physical beauty and fertility of the region has played a significant role in every historical period, ranging from Incan plans to make it a second Cuzco to modern-day tourism, from which the Otavalans have greatly benefited. Unlike Azuay, whose beauty is more complex and farther removed from international transportation routes, Otavalo has been the subject of numerous chronicles by Ecuadorian and international visitors, including a famous pictorial essay by anthropologists John Collier and Anibel Buitrón (1949), entitled *The Awakening Valley.*

At the center of the canton of Otavalo is the town of Otavalo (estimated population eighteen thousand), traditionally populated by local mestizos, though recently the destination of a growing number of Otavalan migrants from the countryside. There are approximately sixty thousand Otavalans inhabiting some seventy-five communities surrounding the town of Otavalo (Meisch 1997, 9). These *parcialidades* range from a small isolated community with a few scattered households to a nucleated village of several hundred households, complete with the traditional Spanish configuration of town plaza and church. The region still is home to some large haciendas, but one of its most distinctive physical features is the division of the land into small plots, demarcated by plants and stones, which can be seen across the valley and up the mountainsides. Some indigenous households enjoy relatively large extensions of land, but most are characterized by minifundio, tiny family plots not large enough to support a family.

Although the topography of the Otavalo canton is not as rugged as that of the much larger province of Azuay, a number of factors make the location of some communities and their lands much more favorable than others, especially altitude; higher altitudes generally mean a more limited variety of crops and less fertile soil, a greater incline to the land, less availability of irrigation, and remoteness from local transportation routes. Hence, those communities located near the flatter trough of the valley have enjoyed the advantages of that location, although also the disadvantages of greater internal and external competition for the same lands. It is the historical importance of land mixed with the differential advantages of physical and social location among Otavalan communities that forms an important backdrop to understanding the gamut of socioeconomic challenges historically facing villages and the village- and household-level solutions that have arisen to meet them.

The Pre-Colombian Period: The "Noble" Past

Like Azuay, the region of Otavalo experienced a profound sociocultural change under Incan domination in the half-century preceding the Spaniards' arrival. The extent of the transformation under Incan rule has been made increasingly evident by new information concerning the pre-Colombian inhabitants of Otavalo, long thought to be the descendants of an indigenous group called the Cara. This belief arose from the misleading and ambiguous accounts of colonial chroniclers and their repetition by subsequent scholars (Espinoza Soriano 1988a). According to Waldemar Espinoza Soriano, before the Inca arrived in the middle of the fifteenth century, the Caranqui language group allegedly inhabited present-day Otavalo. This group shared the present-day province of Imbabura with the Cayambe. There is some evidence of a pre-Inca merchant class, or *mindalá* corps, who specialized in interzonal trading for both economic and political purposes (Salomon 1986; Espinoza Soriano 1988b).

The various northern groups united to put up one of the fiercest rebellions to the Incan invasion, lasting some forty-five years and ending with an infamous massacre of several thousand rebels. After the conquest, the Inca made present-day Otavalo an administrative center and began to construct temples and extend the imperial road through the region.

Adding to the past and current confusion over the ancestry of the Otavalans was the Inca's use of mitimae, or *mitmakuna*, in subduing the locals, whereby distant loyal communities were exchanged with local ones. Although the record clearly indicates that mitimae communities were sent to northern Ecuador, speculation regarding the specific ancestry of the Otavalans has been circumspect:

> Although it is not definitely stated, it seems quite probable that colonists were also transplanted to the highland Caranque [Caranqui] region. It is more probable, since Caranques (also Cayambes in the valley to the south, and Quitus) were transplanted by the Inca conqueror to the islands of Lake Titicaca inhabited by Quichua- and Aymara-speaking people. . . . It would seem that some of the forbears of the valley's Indian population came from Peru. I venture the hypothesis because so many of the Peruvian traits occur in domestic life [of Otavalans], usually the most conservative part of the culture, and because, in spite of unfavorable circumstances, the Quichua language was established. (Parsons 1945, 2–3)

Given the list of "Peruvian traits" Elsie Clews Parsons found in Otavalo in 1940, she concludes that "Peruvian colonization is indicated" (ibid., 174; see also 170–75). Even today, according to Lynn Meisch, the contemporary dress of Otavalan women "is one of the closest in form to that of Inca women's costume worn anywhere in the Andes" (1987, 10). Yet, most researchers have concluded that the Otavalans were the direct descendants of the Cara or Caranqui, whose society, according to anecdotal information and the survival of a few place names, was not substantially altered even in the face of mitimaes and the practice of sending local leaders to be trained in Cuzco (Buitrón n.d.; Salomon 1981; Oberem 1981).

The question of whether Otavalans were the original Caranqui underdogs or part of an invasion contingent of socialized Incan subjects is not merely an academic mystery. Explanations for the Otavalan's distinctive pattern of socioeconomic organization and relation to extralocal authority generally flow from accounts of the pre-Colombian period. For example, according to Frank Salomon, it was the Cara's early strategy in dealing with Inca officials that partly established the fundamental pattern he observed in the late 1960s: "[Under the Inca] there is a parallel to the modern system in this acquiescence to the material demands of large-scale structures as a proxy for social involvement in them. The price of the accommodation in both cases is the yielding up of whatever is produced beyond subsistence, whether to a market as today or to a fully managed economy as under the

Incas. Otavalo has worked hard to remain on the periphery of the political world" (1981, 435).

Similarly, another popular account, often quoted in Ecuador and in tourist guides, attempts to explain both the fierce independence of the Cara and, simultaneously, their ties to Incan nobility: As the story goes, Paccha, the daughter of the last Cara chief killed in battle by the Inca, married the son of the Incan invader Huayna-Capac—and the son from that marriage, Atahualpa, became the last emperor of the Inca (Buitrón n.d.). This story, which is incorrect, provides the perfect legitimating myth in elite discourse for the singling out of the Otavalans, from the early colonial period to the present, as a "race" of Indians who are distinctly Ecuadorian yet also Incan nobility, primitive yet precocious, rural yet clean, Indian yet handsome (for a more complete ethnogenesis of the Otavalan ethnie, see Meisch 1997; also Muratorio 1993). Another possibility is that the Otavalans' contemporary combination of social conservation and economic innovation stems from a mitimae experience: they were selected precisely for their social conformity but torn from traditional economic relations (social networks) firmly embedded in their home regions, spurring a measure of creativity and savvy in the new land.

The main point here concerning the mystery of the origins of the Otavalans is that, lacking more definitive evidence, the Otavalans are just that—a mystery. We should be especially cautious because, according to Salomon, "the only history of Cara territory written before the extinction of the Cara language in the eighteenth century, that of Jesuit Juan de Velasco, sets forth a picture so rich in extravagant but undocumented detail that its portrait of the Cara as empire-building centralizers must be discounted as mostly regional chauvinism" (1981, 433). Facile interpretations of the Otavalan's current economic activity based on the "traditions" of a romanticized aboriginal people must be balanced with the possibility that the Otavalans were part of an Incan settlement plan in the aftermath of the near total extermination of the Caranquis. To complicate matters further, a third possibility is that both accounts are inaccurate to the extent that each teleologically derives a linear story line for a singular subject from a current sociocultural group, shaped by five hundred years of European contact and rule. It is this mystery that reveals the social construction of an Otavalan identity by successive elites, internal and external to the Otavalan group; what is important to us is not so much the validity of these stories, the establishment of which is a task left to historians, but rather the meaning attached to them by various groups, including the Otavalans, in different periods and to what purpose.

The Colonial Period: The Crown Jewel

The colonial period in Otavalo is primarily characterized by the introduction of the Spanish institutions of forced labor, such as the encomienda, and the settlement of Spaniards and mestizos in the region, following a basic pattern found throughout the Peruvian viceroyalty. However, two related features of Otavalo during this period make it noteworthy: (1) the Otavalans' skills as weavers, and their Incan identity, brought them special privileges by the Crown in comparison with other Indian labor, though they were still mercilessly exploited; and, therefore, (2) neither local mestizos nor the Quito elite attained complete ideological control over Otavalans, like the ideological domination of the Azuayan elite over their hinterlands.

Under Incan rule, every adult Otavalan was required to pay tribute in textiles. Because of the lack of mineral riches in the region, the Spaniards quickly took advantage of local weaving abilities, imposing far harsher tribute demands on indigenous communities than those under the Incan system. In theory, Indians were paid a wage so that tribute payments could be made, though typically they simply accumulated debts to the *encomenderos*.

Salomon illuminates the rapid development of "a local craft into an export industry" by highlighting the severe exploitation of Indians in primitive factories, or *obrajes*, but not Spanish innovation (1981, 437). Without diminishing the exploitation of Indian labor, I might note that this observation may be somewhat overstated, considering three important areas of technological advance that came with Spanish rule: (1) the use of the treadle loom and other tools for carding and spinning wool, which greatly increased production over the traditional back-strap loom (Meisch 1987); (2) the introduction of sheep and the expansion of cotton growing in the lowlands, which supplied highland obrajes; and (3) the concentration of labor into one productive setting, a protofactory that has generally been shown to be more efficient—albeit efficient in the control and abuse of a captive labor force.

In one of the first encomiendas, much of the Otavalan labor for weaving was given to the conquistador, Rodrigo Salazar, for a period of two generations. Under the weight of tribute laws, Otavalo quickly began to produce a large share of the viceroyalty's textile needs, including everything from coarse rope to fine handkerchiefs. Yet, the principal export from the region was ordinary cloth for clothing and woolen blankets. When Salazar's encomienda lapsed in 1581 along with other smaller encomiendas at the end of the sixteenth century, Otavalo was assigned unique status as a Crown tributary (Salomon 1981). That is, the Otavalans, very early on, were singled out to become laborers working directly for the Spanish state as royal tributaries. The level of textile production from the Audencia of Quito (a major regional political unit), in general, during the first two centuries of Spanish rule was such that John Phelan describes it as the "sweatshop of South America," providing the primary source of wealth for the Quito elite while clothing much of the mining labor force throughout the viceroyalty (1967, 66, 66–85).

The Otavalan Crown obrajes (one in Otavalo and one begun in Peguche in 1620) represented the apex of a complex and stratified weaving industry in the colonial Andes. At the top of the hierarchy were the Crown obrajes, subject to both the demands and protections that came with that status, including being the first to benefit from successive obraje reforms. In the middle were licensed shops sanctioned by the state, which included both hired and forced labor through the mita system. Obrajes operating under the most exploitative and degrading conditions were the smaller, unlicensed shops, typically owned by powerful local elites such as encomenderos and especially religious orders and even occasionally Indian leaders, or caciques (ibid., 437). When the Otavalo obraje was temporarily put on the market as a leased concession in 1620, it quickly became the most prized obraje in the Audencia of Quito (ibid.).

During the seventeenth century, Otavalo became the centerpiece of the tension between state interests and those of local elites, who were generally content to work Indian laborers to death. San Luis, the once-prosperous royal obraje in Otavalo, had been run so corruptly and inefficiently that Indians were in arrears on their tribute payments by more than one hundred thousand pesos. In 1620, the president of the Audencia of Quito, Dr. Antonio de Morga, instituted a series of remarkable reforms, using the Otavalo region as a test case:

> Among the principal aspects of this program [were provisions that] . . . Indians should be returned to their habitual place of residence. Every native was to be given a house and a small plot adjacent to it. All community lands and individual holdings acquired by the Spaniards even by purchase should be returned. . . . No Spaniard or mestizo may live in an Indian village. . . . Indians of the province were exempt from service in the mita. In order to reduce the cost of local government, each village was to have only one governor, whose principal responsibility is to collect the tribute. A whole group of minor officials called mandones was abolished. (Phelan 1967, 76)

In light of the extent and success of these reform measures (though they were never completely implemented) and the enduring prosperity of the region's inhabitants, Phelan writes, "While many conditions were responsible for the well-being of the province throughout the centuries, the administration of Dr. Antonio de Morga deserves some credit for its modest and realistic efforts to promote the prosperity of that Indian enclave" (ibid.).

When abuses did recur later in the century, new reforms stopped short of abolishing the most horrible unlicensed shops but did, once again, continue to protect the obraje weavers at Otavalo and Peguche, which now employed 498 and 200 workers, respectively. In 1680, for example, the obraje at Peguche was closed on account of labor abuses, specifically the eight-mile radius from which it drew laborers, which left them barely enough time to sleep. Similarly, profits from the San Luis obraje, which had been averaging between ten thousand and twenty thousand pesos annually, was transferred to the village treasury instead of the royal exchequer, which "helped solidify the modest prosperity of Otavalo" (ibid., 79).

With the discontinuation of the encomienda system by the early eighteenth century, Spanish and Creole elites were motivated to buy or seize land, leading to the beginning of latifundism in the Quito Audencia, including the Otavalo region. Yet, roughly similar to Azuay, though under different circumstances, few of the Otavalan villages fell under direct latifundia control, as Salomon describes:

> Otavalo had and still has some sizable *latifundia*, but these did not, as happened farther south in the [central] Andes, convert whole villages into captive colonies of landless debt peons; rather, they have bordered on freehold *parcialidades*, so that *huasipungeros* of the big farm nonetheless remained socially attached to independently landed neighbors. Possibly because Otavalo's relatively gentle climate allows for farming high up on the mountain sides, and consequently permits victims of land-grabbing to resettle, *latifundia* of the Otavalo region have had to rely more on hired labor done part time by *minifundistas* and less on fixed colonies of indebted Indians than those elsewhere. (1981, 439)

Parallel to the rise in latifundia was an increased demand for slavelike mita labor, from which Otavalo was not able to completely escape. In fact, it is against the backdrop of latifundia and mita in the eighteenth century that the following account by Jorge Juan Antonio de Ulloa of the Otavalan's independence and business acumen is so remarkable:

> A multitude of Indians residing in its villages . . . seem to have a natural inclination to weaving; for besides the stuffs made at the common manu-

factories [obrajes], such Indians as are not *Mitayos,* or are independent, and make, on their own account, a variety of goods, as cottons, carpets, pavillons for beds, quilts in damask work, wholly of cotton, either white, blue, or variegated with different colours; but all in great repute, both in the province of Quito and other parts, where they are sold to great advantage. (Quoted in Salomon 1981, 440)

The Republican Period: Finding a Production Niche

The obraje system, which produced cloth and which had become the backbone of the Quito economy, never fully recovered from competition by cheap factory-made imports from Britain, which could now freely enter following Ecuador's independence from Spain (Phelan 1967, 68). In the wake of this decline, a handful of local hacendados and Quito entrepreneurs attempted to compete with industrially produced textiles through a combination of limited mechanization and the de facto slave labor of Indian debt peons, or huasipungeros (a system that did not officially end until 1964). In this sense, the basic obraje organization, as a type of primitive factory, did not come to an end in the nineteenth century. Significant changes did occur, however, in the forms of ideological and physical control over the indigenous labor force and in attempts to innovate and mechanize production in order to compete with the cheap imports. In *Four Years among the Ecuadorians,* the U.S. diplomat, Friedrich Hassaurek, describes his visit in 1863 to the Jijón hacienda near Peguche:

> In the factory of Peguchi coarse woolen goods are made, such as bayetas for ponchos, jergas for the Indians, and shawls for their women . . . cloth for coats, vests, pantaloons, carpets, etc. These goods are exported chiefly to New Granada, as far as Pasto and Popayan [both in present-day Colombia] in the interior, and Barbacoas on the coast. The laborers employed in the factory are almost all Indians. They are concertados, or peones. The factory yields about thirty pieces of cloth per month. (Hassaurek 1967, 151)

Hassaurek also describes, in contrast with the Peguche obraje, a thriving weaving industry in the Indian village of Cotacachi still using traditional methods but specializing in ponchos and silks (both favored among the indigenous population), which did not have any industrialized competition; according to his account, "about six thousand cotton ponchos of all colors are manufactured monthly" (ibid., 175). Just as under the colonial system, this indicates that there may have been considerable space for Indian-led production, and even entrepreneurship, although it was aimed at regional markets rather than the international trade. In other words, the considerable number of local weavers not "employed" by local factories were left to weave not only for internal consumption needs but also to profit from any surplus they were able to produce, either as independent weavers or as Indian-operated "workshops."

In contrast, the strategy of the mestizo elites was faltering during the same period. After Hassaurek's stop in Cotacachi, he next visited a mechanized cotton factory, owned by a mestizo, that was unprofitable because of the high cost of transporting the machinery from Patterson, New Jersey ($40,000). Hassaurek also mentions that when local weavers "saw that it did in an hour what they could do in days or weeks, they thought that it was the invention of the devil" (ibid., 177). Two other haciendas had also introduced machines for weaving and making thread (Salomon 1981, 441). Thus, as Salomon summarizes the late-nineteenth-century economy in Otavalo, "Weavers working outside hacienda workshops could profit by the making of clothes for other Indians, but the technologically fortified vestiges of the *obraje* system [debt peons] still dominated whatever share of the city clothing market that had not fallen to the British" (ibid.).

Another important development in the nineteenth century was "land hunger," which reached a critical period around the turn of the century, when some villages began to experience absolute shortages in cultivable land (ibid.). This desire for land was driven not only by its economic utility but also by its sociocultural significance to the community. As Salomon has underscored, "Land has a double importance: first, it is the only reliable and autonomous way of earning a living; and second, it is the sine qua non of full participation in Indian society, since the alternatives are to abandon the community, become a permanent debtor, or live as a dependent of another household" (ibid., 441). This land hunger was a response to the squeeze by latifundia surrounding parcialidades and by inheritance practices that divided land equally among heirs. Parsons' principal informant, Rosa Lema, for example, explains in 1940 that during previous generations, new households began to claim more and more unincorporated or common lands until there was no more land to be gotten in this way (Parsons 1945).

Thus, the only nonviolent way to gain land was increasingly in the open market, which, in turn, elevated the importance of cash earnings from handicrafts. Salomon's analysis of nascent Otavalan industry and capitalism as being driven by the anxiety of land ownership—having both material and symbolic importance—is similar to Max Weber's explanation of the rise of European industrial capitalism by pointing to early Protestant anxieties over gaining surplus as a sign of divine predestination. In both cases, any surplus gained by a single-minded work ethic was too valuable to be squandered and was thus plowed back into the productive apparatus, leading to high levels of savings and the acceptance of innovations related to production but not to sociocultural norms.

In sum, apart from a long history of "professional" weaving, we can trace the Otavalans' current economic independence and dynamism to developments that took place during the first hundred or so years of the Republic of Ecuador: (1) the local economic space for Indian merchant-weavers created by the devastation of the obraje system in the face of British industrialization; (2) the attempt by elites to tailor Otavalan textile production to a regional market niche rather than introduce a new handicraft; and (3) the early and profound integration of Otavalans into the money economy spurred by land hunger. The foregoing not withstanding, it should be emphasized that the vast majority of Otavalans were still agricultural smallholders, including huasipungeros, and semiautonomous laborers well into the twentieth century, though weaving on the traditional back-strap (or "poncho") loom for domestic use was widespread across villages.

Until now, we have largely focused on the socioeconomic history of Otavalo. However, it is especially appropriate in the case of the Otavalans to highlight their historical relations to authority structures, including their unique relationship to Spanish and mestizo elites and their symbolic identity and currency among the wider society in which they are embedded. In the context of the caste-like Andean social structure inherited from the colonial period, where the dominant society continues to impute subhuman qualities to indios, it is especially important to consider the role of politically motivated elites in the reinforcement, if not creation, of the Otavalan identity as the exception that proves the rule. As Blanca Muratorio points out (1993), the national reputation of the Otavalans was already well established by Hassaurek's time. Hassaurek observed that "there is a general belief in Quito that the Indians of Otavalo . . . are handsomer and cleaner than those of Pichincha, Latacunga, etc., but I have been unable to discover the slightest foundation for such an opinion. . . . As far as cleanliness is concerned, the difference, if it exists, is imperceptible to the foreign eye. The only thing in which the Otavalo Indian excels is his long hair, which [he] . . . but very seldom combs" (1967, 157–58).

Muratorio (1993) has shown that this preexisting reputation was further enhanced and embellished by nationalist elites in the late nineteenth century, whom she calls the "image makers," in their attempt to represent the face of Ecuador at the fourth centenary of Columbus's discovery, held in Madrid in 1892. By analyzing internal documents of the Ecuadorian Organizing Committee, she uncovers a rare glimpse into the elite's strategic representation of ethnicity in their attempt to construct a legitimating myth based on the "master fiction" of *mestizaje*, or a nation of mixed bloods (ibid., 24).

The coastal merchant elites (who were in the midst of the cacao export boom) attempted to take their place at the table of "civilized" nations by demonstrating the noble and aristocratic past of the Ecuadorian mestizaje through a presentation of its Inca and Cara origins, thus choosing Otavalans to represent the progressive element of the present and future (ibid.):* "In contrast to the historic Incas, the image of the Otavaleños is designed to represent the future. Within the nineteenth-century scheme of progress, the Otavaleños symbolize for the authors what all Indians might and should become if the process of civilizing them is allowed to take its 'natural' course. That positive perception of the Otavaleños, which makes of them the 'mould image' of highland Indians to this day, was fashioned very early on" (ibid., 28).

The stated reasons given by the organizing committee for choosing the Otavalans summarize their cumulative image to that point and foreshadow the congealed version of their contemporary business reputation:

> By contrast [to the Amazonian "savages"], despite the fact that the Otavalo Indians are not "pure," according to Mr. Pallares, they remain "outstanding" for their "correct features," their "above-average height" and "their vigorous forms," characteristics that they allegedly have "preserved" from their "Caras" ancestors. In addition, they are "intelligent, hard working, sober, of good manners and accustomed to neatness, order and cleanliness." Most important, however, the Otavalans have "special abilities" such as their "San Juan dances." . . . The small fee that would be charged for this entertainment, may "even help to pay for all the expenses incurred in transporting and housing the Indians themselves." (Ibid., 25)

In analyzing the elites' rationale for singling out the Otavalans, Muratorio observes that it was precisely their economic and political marketability, within the ideological context of liberal democracy and laissez-faire economics, that

---

* Muratorio was unable to confirm whether the Otavalans were actually sent to Madrid, where they were to live in "primitive dwellings" in the Parque de Madrid and exhibit their "unique talents."

reinforced all of the elements that went into their collective reputation (ibid., 30). By highlighting these "marketable" qualities in their "noble" primitives, nationalist "image makers" underscored the "natural order" of the economy while obscuring the social inequalities upon which it was based (ibid.).

Although it would still take a few decades for the Otavalan enclave economy to hit its stride through direct international marketing, we see that some of the central features of the current economic resurgence were already in place by the early years of the twentieth century: namely, an independent productive apparatus partially linked to the cash economy and an ethnic identity intimately tied to a centuries-old business reputation (i.e., that they were "businesslike"). In addition, like Azuay during the same period, peasants were hemmed in by an absolute shortage of land and its inflationary effects.

Transnational Migration from Otavalo, 1917 to 1995

We now turn directly to the remarkable development of Otavalan cottage industry, in the span of less than eight decades, into what Salomon, almost twenty years ago, called the "farmer-weaver complex" and which now, in the mid-1990s, is rapidly becoming a more urbanized "merchant-weaver complex," though still intimately connected to regional subsistence agriculture. Rather than exploring every facet of contemporary Otavalan life, the topic of numerous anthropological studies, I present some of the most significant features of its development into global marketing as a type of transnational migration, the topic of this book.

Andean Tweed: The Transition to Specialty Textiles, 1917 to 1949

Elsie Clews Parsons, in her classic ethnography of Peguche based on several months of field research in 1940 and 1941, mentions in a footnote what for most Otavalo observers is taken to be the beginning of the modern era of the Otavalans' contemporary economic strategy of producing low-cost specialty textiles: she describes her interview with Señor Uribe, the son-in-law of the owners of hacienda Cusín near Otavalo (which still exists today): "He told me that at his marriage in 1917 his prospective mother-in-law had presented him with a poncho beautifully woven by José Cajas [from Quinchuquí], and it occurred to him to set up José Cajas with a Spanish loom, supply samples of casimir to be copied, and afford the weaver a Quito market" (1945, 25 n. 67, emphasis added). Collier and Buitrón add that "[Señor Uribe] was delighted. Now he would not have to send all the way to London for material for his suits. He told his friends. They, too, ordered cloth. The original weaver shared his orders with a friend, and the foundation of a new enterprise was laid" (1949, 160).

José passed his skills—and his "Quito market"—on to his descendants, who were still prominent merchant-weavers in the village of Quinchuquí in the 1960s (Salomon 1981). When Parsons visited Don José, the weaver's son, Antonio, whom he had taught to weave tweed, was in Colombia for one year to "give instruction in weaving" (ibid., 26). Parsons continues in the body of her text to describe how the use of the Spanish loom to weave casimir (tweed) probably spread to neighboring Peguche through the marriage of José Cajas's grandnephew to a women from Peguche, where the newlyweds finally settled.

The importance of this subtle vignette can only be appreciated from the vantage point of having seen, in later decades, the enduring success of the strategy hit upon by Señor Uribe and José Cajas; instead of trying to compete with cheap and consistent factory-made "daily wear," Otavalan commercial weavers would specialize in duplicating specialty fabrics, such as imported tweed, which they could undersell, while taking advantage of any low-technology innovations that would improve production without disturbing the organization of a household-based means of production. As Salomon has forcefully demonstrated, however, the introduction of this strategy alone does not account for its rapid implementation and diffusion among Otavalans; it must also be placed in the context of the need to gain cash for attaining scarce land (Salomon 1981, 441).

What emerges from Parsons' ethnography is a picture of an indigenous group in the throes of a transition from a marginalized agricultural-handicraft economy to a modernizing enclave economy exhibiting the classic entrepreneurial spirit of fearlessness and practical innovation in production and marketing. Still, many of the social changes that are today widespread were just beginning in the early 1940s:

> A few enterprising Peguche weavers and traders even go to Quito, by train or bus. But this adventuring is quite recent, and one gets the impression that the valley folk are not travelsome. The most enterprising person in all Peguche, Rosita Lema, had never been across the valley to Cotacachi. About the world at large Rosita and others of Peguche have little or no knowledge. . . . Colombia and Venezuela are known by name, but Mexico and North America are wholly unknown, and, curiously enough, Peru. (Parsons 1945, 13)

In explaining this naiveté, "worldly-wise as are Peguche folk in some ways," Parsons highlights the near total lack of formal education in the region until that time:

Once I was asked if the sun rose and set in my "land." . . . How should they know about the sun in the outer world? The Church has a reason for teaching them about heaven and hell but not about the sun, and until quite recently the state has been indifferent to secular education for Indians. The little ungraded, one-room school at Peguche was opened by the canton only two years ago. In Otavalo the schools are open to Indians but are little used. In the school for girls . . . there was one Indian girl. . . . In the boy's school . . . out of an enrollment of 180 pupils, there were fifteen Indian boys, all in the two lowest grades. (ibid.)

Given these low levels of education, few Otavalans were able to speak, let alone write, fluently in Spanish. Yet, it was clear that several Otavalan families, undoubtedly from the merchant-weaver group, had decided that speaking and writing Spanish would be valuable assets for the economic and political well-being of the household. In this respect, though few Otavalans lived in the city of Otavalo, and those only as servants (ibid., 10), the seeds of a more urban lifestyle and greater educational opportunities had now been planted.

By the mid-1940s, the preexisting patterns of village specialization in handicrafts that had existed for centuries began to take on more of a class structure as those communities undergoing an "industrial revolution" catering to external markets began to rapidly prosper, thereby affording them the ability to buy still more land and looms:

Today nearly all the Indians of the district of Otavalo know how to weave, but the weavers fall into two distinct groups. Some weave only their necessary clothing, but others weave for sale in the market. The first group uses almost exclusively the native loom; the second group, both native and Spanish looms. The first group weaves only ponchos and flannels; the second group, European-style woolen goods, blankets, shawls, heavy cotton goods, fachalinas [Indian shawls], and belts as well. The first group spins by hand, a task only for women, using a spindle made of thin and fragile reed. In the second group, both men and women spin, using a wheel which speeds up the process by at least five times. The first group weaves wool in its natural colors. The second group is familiar with many kinds of dyes. Not all the Indians in the second group weave the same article or spend the same amount of time on the industry. Various communities have developed specializations. In Carabuela, for example, everyone weaves ponchos; in San Juan cotton goods and fachalinas are made; in Peguche, shawls and yard goods for European suits; in Quinchuquí, blankets; in Agato, flannels and yard goods; in La Compañía, ponchos and belts. (Collier and Buitrón 1949, 163)

The list of villages in the second group demonstrates both the degree and pattern of technological diffusion of the Spanish loom among neighboring villages, clearly indicating the slow but inexorable effect of kinship and fictive kinship networks in shaping the diffusion process. More important, some villages, most notably Peguche, were producing for the urban mestizo market, and others were producing textiles used primarily by locals, albeit still exported to other regions of Ecuador. Notably, none of the textile vendors in the weekly market was white (Parsons 1945, 30).

In contrast with the weavers and traders of those villages near Otavalo, such as Peguche, more rural communities with closer ties to the hacienda were notably less independent. From a survey conducted in 1938 in a community near Cayambe, we have the following description:

> Men weave but not every man, and among weavers there is some specialization. Master weavers and dyers are Félix Maldonado and three others.
> . . . Only the Indian loom is used, although Félix Maldonado has the Spanish loom which he first learned to weave [on] when he was growing up on the hacienda. . . . [Félix] has a dyeing oven, and cloth is brought to him to dye. He weaves for a town factory or for White merchants that supply the thread and wool, a very different system from that of Peguche, where middlemen practice as far as it exists is still in Indian hands except possibly for some end transactions in Quito. (Quoted in Parsons 1945, 184)

Similarly, this community, which had been carved out of part of the nearby hacienda only one hundred years earlier, still retained its agricultural economy whereby all inhabitants had small farms and also worked part of the year on the hacienda.

At this time, we also see the formation of a merchant-weaver class within villages, whereby some households began to dedicate an increasing portion of their time to contracting out piecework or buying finished textiles at the Saturday market and then selling them in other weekly markets around Ecuador and in Colombia and Venezuela. Describing the Saturday market, Collier and Buitrón write:

> In one broad plaza almost all the buyers and sellers are Indian. . . .
> Among the crowd there are dealers who buy as many of the ponchos and woolen goods as they can carry. These dealers come to the Otavalo market early in order to choose quietly and avoid too many competitors. By seven o'clock the best ponchos, shawls, and woolen suitings are gone, and

the dealers are already on their way to other markets of the Ecuadorian highlands as far north as Tulcán and as far south as Loja. In the row next to the ponchos there are woolen materials which copy English tweed. These are hand-spun and hand-woven to sell to the white world of big cities—Quito, Bogotá, and even far-off Caracas. (1949, 15)

Indeed, by the late 1940s, itinerant Otavalan traders were marketing both "Indian" and "European" textiles throughout Ecuador and abroad. Otavalan traders were already becoming a fixture in cities throughout Ecuador and along the northern Caribbean coast, where "they stand in the arcades of busy buildings or in the squares, displaying bolts of Indian tweeds to the passing crowds" and exhibiting "initiative and courage in commercial ventures" (ibid., 164–65).

Rosa Lema, Parsons' principal informant, was part of this emerging merchant class. Parsons describes the stream of "visitors" to Rosa's house, who had either been contracted to card and spin yarn or were offering wool at various stages of processing: "Rosa and José farm out a good many little weaving jobs to their less-well-to-do neighbors" (159). Indeed, "[Rosa] and her husband market a not inconsiderable part of the textile output of Peguche" (150). The Lemas' status also afforded them the ability to keep two servants, a married couple, who were treated "more like 'poor relations' than as servants" (163), though the practice was uncommon among other Indian households at that time. Also, it was evident from Rosa's demeanor that she was of higher social status than her neighbors and certainly those from more rural villages;* "Rosita has an embryonic sense of class, and it would not be difficult for her to think of herself as an Inca lady, if she knew anything about the Inca or a class-stratified Indian society" (163).

A feature of this new merchant class, which Rosa Lema epitomized (and she continues to do so today), was the foresight and ability to move in white circles and cultivate urban contacts that would be of use in the future. These circles included not only commercial contacts in Quito or Bogotá and Europeans living in Ecuador but also important members of the Catholic Church hierarchy. It was crucial for the formation of this independent class to have not only economic contacts but also political allies. For example, after a municipal agent took some clothes from Rosa's clothesline in retribution for not

---

* Members of Rosa Lema's family are still prominent traders; in 1993 she was living in an upscale house in Quito complete with servants and was convinced that she had changed the course of Otavalan life by developing transnational ties and trade.

participating in a street construction project, Rosa successfully got her clothes back the following day after visiting the commissioner, who was a *compadre* (godfather) (163).

Perhaps the clearest example of the importance of these extralocal social networks, and the ability to turn a reputation into financial capital, comes from the preface of Parsons' ethnography, in which she explains how Rosa became her principal informant: "Mrs. Guy Bullock, wife of the British Minister to Ecuador, introduced Mr. Gorrell, who in turn introduced Rosita Lema of Peguche" (v). She was also described to Parsons by "a European friend living in Quito" as "the most intelligent Indian living in Ecuador" (169). The precociousness of Parsons' informant lies precisely in her ability to cultivate and maintain white contacts, not merely in the traditional patronage manner but rather in a way more characteristic of what businesspeople refer to as "networking," whereby seemingly superficial contacts greatly expand one's access to information and resources.

Parsons' study provided not only an introduction of Otavalan life to North American readers but also, indirectly, the introduction of the larger world to Otavalans through Rosa Lema. Rosa's fame, after Parsons' study, and her abundant aptitude for seizing an economic and political opportunity led to an event that marked a transition for the indigenous enclave economy: the use of air travel to visit sympathetic foreigners. Based on a conversation with Rosa Lema, who is now in her eighties, Linda D'Amico gives the following account:

> [Rosa] recounted . . . that the first temporary migration was set up by the U.S. Embassy in Quito for herself and Batico Masaquiza, a weaver from Salazaca, in 1949. Because of her relation with anthropologist Elsie Clews Parsons, she had become well acquainted with U.S. Embassy people, who recognized the quality of Peguche textiles, and would purchase fine woolen twills, shawls, and scarves from her workshop. In fact . . . an entourage of 70 people from the U.S. Embassy came to her house in the late 1940s. This paved the way for her subsequent invitation to the White House . . . and then on to 5th Avenue in New York [City] where she exhibited textile handicrafts. Rosa Lema attributes this initial migration as paving the way for other traveling merchants, who thereafter extended their business horizons to the northern hemisphere. (1993, 38–39)

Ultimately, Rosa would make three such "diplomatic" trips to the United States (ibid.). When Rosa Lema was interviewed as part of the current study, she again emphasized to her youthful Otavalan interviewers that it was she who had started the international migrations that so transformed Otavalan society. Parsons' ethnography not only made Rosa famous but also highlighted the tourist features of Otavalo, though tourism to the region was still minimal in the 1940s. This nascent tourist interest in Otavalo was further heightened by the publication of Collier and Buitrón's beautiful photographic tribute to the region, *The Awakening Valley,* cementing international interest in Otavalan culture. Their take on Otavalan society was similar to historical themes that represented the Otavalans as special among other Indian groups, yet with a new twist: while the authors note that the Otavalans were one of the few indigenous groups able to retain independence from hacienda control, their "noble" past is played down in favor of an ahistorical present and an imagined future:

> Ever since the Spanish conquest the Indians have worked in bondage, robbed of their freedom, in a life of hopeless toil. Even today the pattern is little changed. . . . But in the valley of Otavalo there has been an awakening, a miracle of cultural rebirth. The Indians of Otavalo are rising in a wave of vitality that is breaking the bonds of their traditional poverty, making them into a society of prosperous and independent citizens. The rise of the Indians of Otavalo is a unique story. Yet the Indians of the Awakening Valley are not different from other Indians. The success they have achieved could be shared throughout the Andes, for their vitality is born of universal energies. Theirs is a story of simple people, a story of day-by-day strength, skill, joy, and faith. (Collier and Buitrón 1949, 2)

Thus, Otavalans are represented in the form of an ahistorical fable, where economic and social development occurs through the sweat of one's brow and the faith of one's heart, values similar to the fabled Protestant work ethic. Implicit in this fable is the admonition to other Indian groups, indeed, all downtrodden, to stop sleeping and simply wake up. This poetic morality story encapsulates the central public relations narrative used to attract tourists in later decades—tourists eager to witness not just another colorful Indian group selling trinkets but a social miracle, thereby contributing to the miracle; today, just outside the town of Otavalo is a large billboard, placed there by mestizo leaders, welcoming visitors to "El Valle de Amanecer" (The Awakening Valley). Most importantly, the publication of the Collier and Buitrón's *The Awakening Valley* "helped open the door for preferred treatment and development of Otavalo by national and international interests" (D'Amico 1993, 39).

Modernization, Stratification, and the Commodification of "Indigenous" Culture, 1950 to 1972

During the twenty-three years following Rosa Lema's trip to the United States and the publication of books by Parsons and Collier and Buitrón, eco-

nomic and social changes that had occurred in the previous period continued to intensify, especially the growth of a merchant class within the context
of expanding social and educational opportunities. This period of "modernization" was a result of both the internal interests of the new Otavalan merchant class, especially the desire to attain an education, and reforms enacted
by the national government. However, an important change in the production and marketing of indigenous textiles occurred in this period, albeit one
built on earlier patterns: instead of copying English tweed, Otavalans began
to consciously tailor production to the growing tourist market at home and
the desire for native handicrafts abroad. That is, by the end of this period, it
was clear that the Otavalans' principal asset was not their ability to weave and
supply a preexisting demand but rather their broader cultural identity as an
exotic Other, something that could be marketed—in the same sense that the
"image makers" of 1892 had had in mind. Once again, this successful transition was promoted and mentored by outside admirers with the addition, this
time, of foreign aid.

Interest in education on the part of Otavalans had gained much momentum during the 1940s. Parsons noted few Indian students in the early 1940s,
but by the end of the decade Collier and Buitrón could note that the "national
government schools, intended primarily for whites and *mestizos,* are now
crowded with Indian children" (1949, 182). The authors also observed the relationship between education and the "practical" entrepreneurial attitude of
the Otavalans: "In another generation a large group of the younger Indians
will be as well educated as the townsmen, for the Otavalos are practical, and,
as soon as they see one of their fellows benefiting from education, they too
want to read and write. The textile industry shows the rapid spread of a practical idea; from one, then two, then three ambitious weavers, it has come to
involve whole Indian communities within a single generation" (ibid., 194–
95). This pattern continued in the 1950s. By the 1960s, several Otavalans were
entering Quito universities for the first time and traveling abroad under the
auspices of exchange programs, most notably to Cuba.

It was during the 1960s that the Otavalan merchant class began to consolidate previous advances and reorient local handicraft production toward the
expanding tourist market. According to a study conducted by British sociologist Andrew Pearse in 1960, while several hundred Indians connected to the
textile trade had already moved to the city of Otavalo, thus "escaping from the
estamental division of society" (Pearse 1975, 193) or social stratification, he
also found that the local economy was still largely based on "pre-industrial
production" and "busy internal exchange" (ibid., 189). Pearse also notes that

the indigenous economy was anything but stagnant, however, exhibiting in-stead "a dynamic process of attrition as the peasantry desperately looks for new livelihood opportunities and passes into the later stages of resource-ratio decline" (190). In other words, as the average size of landholdings had now been drastically reduced in those villages closest to Otavalo (he found ten "land groups" averaging less than half of a hectare [194]), it became im-perative to insure the survival of the weaving industry. For a handful of com-munities, the cottage industry of weaving was no longer merely a supplement to agriculture; the situation was, rather, the other way around. It was also the only way to earn cash without the complete disruption of the household or-ganization and community culture, at least during this period.

Pearse also gives the following report on the origins and development of the impressive, though still limited, international marketing of local textiles, indicating the extent that such trade had progressed since Rosa Lema's trip in 1949:

> The people of Peguche are weavers of ponchos which had been sold lo-cally but had caught the taste of the national and international market, and a widespread potential demand was discovered. Commercialization in this case was not developed by the townsfolk of Otavalo. The men of Quinchuquí, the neighboring parcialidad, were almost as land-poor as the Peguche people, averaging no more than 0.77 hectares (of which a large part is a hillside) per family, and finding livelihood as travelling butchers, buying, slaughtering, and cutting up pigs for sale in the town markets. Perceiving the existence of a high-class market for hand-woven woolen goods, they began buying textiles from the Peguche people, for sale in the capital, and later in foreign countries, reaching Rio de Janeiro, Santiago, and New York, where their striking peasant dress and pigtails give a distinctive brand to their wares. (195)

It is probably safe to say that Pearse was unaware of the fact that it was in Quinchuquí that José Cajas in 1917 started producing expressly for the "high-class market." Hence, Pearse turns the socially constructed origins of the trade into a more generalized, structural story by pointing to preexisting economic circuits. Of course, of primary interest in his account is the mention of mer-chant migration outside of South America.

Into this dynamic milieu came a series of activities in the 1960s initiated by outsiders and directly beneficial to Otavalan cottage industry. The first im-portant change came in 1964 with land reform and the abolition of the huasipungo system. The effect of these reforms was to make available more land to both hacienda and nonhacienda Otavalans. However, the 1964 reform was as important symbolically as materially to Otavalans, and it "stimulated great social and cultural change in the region" (D'Amico 1993, 42).

Perhaps the most crucial change occurred when international development agencies and private collectors began to directly assist Otavalan weavers and traders. As early as 1954, a Dutch artist, financed by the United Nations, had taught a workshop in interlocking tapestry weaving for forty highland Indians, including Otavalans; tapestry-based textiles now form a major part of the tourist trade (Meisch 1997). When the youthful Peace Corps arrived in the mid-1960s they did not have to grope around for a productive activity to initiate, as is so often the case; they simply attempted to modernize the pre-existing export economy already in full swing. D'Amico gives the following account based on a conversation with Lawrence Carpenter, a former Peace Corps member who later became a noted Andean linguist: "The Peace Corps established a cooperative craft shop and attempted to institute bilingual schools. They counseled weavers on the design preferences of foreign buyers, and encouraged them to experiment with designs. Periodicals of popular western fashions were consciously introduced to demonstrate both the style and technique in knitting as well as weaving" (1993, 42).

By the early 1970s, the Peace Corps was introducing foreign designs to weavers across Ecuador. However, it is the Otavalans who have been able to incorporate the widest variety of designs to best effect, with their eagerness to produce whatever was selling, as evidenced by the following account by Lynn Meisch: "New tapestry designs are added regularly from a variety of inspirations including M. C. Escher, which Peace Corps volunteer John Ortman saw on T-shirts my boyfriend and I were wearing in 1973. He thought the interlocking designs would make good tapestries, asked us to bring him a catalog from the Escher exhibition in Berkeley. . . . Other sources of tapestry designs range from Navajo rugs, to San Pedro de Cajas, Peru, tapestries" (Meisch 1997, 124).

The "Escher designs" refer to the work of the Dutch artist known for his graphical design based on optical illusions regarding time and space—fitting motifs for the imagined primordia of Otavalan society. The Peace Corps volunteers also introduced designs from North and Central American indigenous groups, such as the Pueblo and the Maya. It was also during this period that the famous Hungarian art dealer Olga Fisch employed Otavalans in her workshop, using designs and techniques that her employees would later continue to use as independent producers. Perhaps what best characterized this new phase of the indigenous export economy was not so much the new technologies and designs themselves but rather the general orientation of the productive apparatus toward niche markets and flexible production. Weavers and merchants became keenly aware of not only what would sell but also what would sell *this* year, a trend that would continue to intensify during the next twenty years.

By the late 1960s, merchant-weaver households had substantial "colonies" in foreign cities and were making temporary selling trips as a matter of course. Based on field research in Otavalo during this period, Salomon writes that "textile merchants from Otavalo, neatly dressed in white pants and shirts under gray or blue ponchos, wearing broad-brimmed hats over long braids, travel as far as Argentina, Colombia, Panama, and even Miami in the conduct of a weaving economy" (1981, 420). In addition, Otavalan intermediaries now owned several handicraft shops in Quito. It was evident by this time that an internal class structure was becoming more pronounced even as export weaving was growing throughout the region.

Thus far, I have told the story of the Otavalan export economy largely from the perspective of the merchant elite, those dedicated, either part-time or full-time, to the direct marketing of *artesanía*. Yet, when the story is told in this manner (as is so often the case), we are left with the false perception of a unitary subject of "Otavalans" whose "successful" (i.e., Western) qualities are embodied in the merchant elite and who have overcome the agricultural dead-end in which some of their "poorer" Otavalan coethnics are stilled enmeshed. The remarkable human agency of the merchant-weavers during this period must be balanced by an understanding of the social structure in which it was operating, that is, an examination of the internal socioeconomic stratification of the Otavalan cultural group, especially at the community level. The nature and extent of Otavalan stratification has been closely related to external political and economic structures and, therefore, has changed along with the colonial and national societies; hence, I limit my discussion to Otavalan stratification circa 1970, the period during which agrarian reforms were being implemented.

Otavalan society has historically been community centered; it is at the community level, rather than at the wider ethnic group level, that we find a fair amount of socioeconomic homogeneity and, therefore, individual identity and ideology. In contrast, some seventy-five Otavalan communities have had extremely diverse development paths, although integrated by a common language, culture, and externally maintained group identity. Meisch (1997) notes that until the 1960s brought more mass-produced traditional clothing, local costumes reflected community identity more than an "Otavalan dress."

As Peter Meier observes, "While the Otavaleños have clearly been better off than those peasantries which, for their reproduction, were completely dependent on the landowners, they were by no means an undifferentiated mass of producers" (1981, 20). If we ignore intracommunity variation for now, an Otavalan community during this period could be categorized by two crosscutting dimensions: its relation to the hacienda and its relation to the market. The former was largely determined by law, while the latter, given the general lack of external middlemen, was determined by the specific type of crafts produced in the community. These are qualitative differences that transcend a simple continuum of the communal mix of agriculture and handicrafts, commonly found among all peasant groups.

By the early nineteenth century, the Otavalo region, in general, had an unusually low number of agricultural peons, or *indios propios,* compared with other highland regions (Guerrero 1991, 156). Yet the remaining *indios libres,* who owned their own plots and lived in nominally external communities, were further divided into two more or less distinct categories: those still dependent on the hacienda and those weaving communities who were able to escape such dependent relations (ibid.). Of our two research sites, Guanansi is an example of the former, Peguche an example of the latter.

Under the *yanapa* arrangement, the semiautonomous peasant, or *yanapero,* was given usufruct rights to communal hacienda lands in exchange for a predetermined amount of labor. The yanapa-hacienda relationship was based on prescribed reciprocal activities for both sides of the land tenure structure, not on individual indebtedness. As Andrés Guerrero notes, "The *yanapa* does not imply a worker, it is a collective form of household labor: on Mondays they [the household] would be assigned a certain area to work with a determined type of activity. . . . [They would] generally work Mondays and Tuesdays" (1991, 162–63), though the number of required workdays varied with the agricultural cycle. In exchange, the yanapa household had rights to the use of a plot of hacienda lands for agriculture and grazing as well as access to hacienda water and firewood.

Yet, the yanapa-hacienda relationship was as much social and ideological as it was economic, closely knitted by reciprocity and ritual (ibid.). Traditional festivities such as the *cargo,* or sponsorship of a ritual feast, central to village social status and manhood, incorporated the *hacendado,* or hacienda owner, as the central symbolic source of community authority. Guerrero observes that the incorporation and use of Otavalan symbols and ideology in hacienda life did, however, mean a cultural space largely molded on Otavalan cultural terms (165). However, one effect of such relations was a worldview radically different from that of nonyanapa communities, a worldview shaped by the physical borders of the hacienda and the social universe of the hacendado and the church. Perhaps more important, the common experience of colonial domination among yanapa communities "y los de arriba" (and those socially and geographically higher) shaped each community's perception of themselves and their relation to other communities (ibid.). In this respect, the ritual, often violent fighting (*pucará*) among communities during the regionwide festival of San Juan, in which each community attempts to take a town plaza, is symbolically pregnant with contemporary import.

Even among those communities and households who were historically free from the hacienda system and had increasingly developed independent craft production since the end of huasipungo, there were significant differences in the social relations of production and marketing connected to a particular craft (Meier 1981). In other words, we are now focusing on those large numbers of Otavalans who are neither agricultural yanaperos nor jet-setting comerciantes. Meier elegantly analyzes Otavalan "peasant crafts" as they were organized during the 1970s; he argues that the type of craft, or "branch of production," is not open to all villages equally (1981, 24) because each craft requires access to a particular type of resource (e.g., *totora* reed, homespun yarn, credit) not available to all villages. Some of these inputs require access to land, some to social networks (reciprocal relations), and others to financial markets. Furthermore, Meier argues, some crafts, such as the traditional belts worn by Otavalan women, have a very limited market compared with crafts targeted at tourists, such as knitted sweaters, which have benefited from the pioneering efforts of the middlemen comerciantes opening markets not only in Otavalo or Quito but also in cities across the Western Hemisphere and Europe.

Hence, every craft production in excess of household consumption can be viewed as a combination of source of input (internal or external) and use of middlemen (independent or dependent); building on Meier's analysis, a two-by-two table using these two dimensions produces the typology found in figure 5.1. Notice that producers of woven mats (cell B) are able to retain control over the labor process while taking advantage of the expanding markets provided by the Otavalan middlemen. Yet, with increasing capitalization and mechanization of craft production in the valley, it is increasingly difficult for small producers to compete with large buyers of synthetic fibers and dyes and electric looms.* By the 1970s, it was clear that to survive the increasingly com-

* This list will, no doubt, soon include automated, computerized looms using the highest technology available.

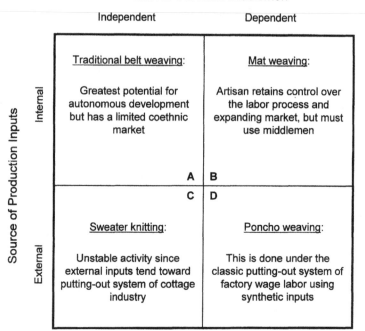

Figure 5.1. Typology of Otavalan Crafts, by Control of Inputs and Marketing
Source: Data from Meier 1981.

petitive environment of Otavalan craft production, households and communities needed more than traditional, or even more modern, weaving skills; they needed access to credit and to foreign markets, two things the historically more independent, "progressive" communities, such as Peguche, Agato, and Quinchuquí (see Buitrón 1947, 49), were readily able to develop.

The Global Bazaar: The Urbanization of Otavalan Life, 1973 to 1995

By any measure, 1973 was a pivotal year for Otavalans and their export weaving industry, which included a new tourist market and a paved road to Quito. Although, as Frank Salomon has observed, in 1973 the Otavalan region "looks like anything but a modern manufacturing center" because of the salience of its "peasant culture" (1981, 420), by the 1990s the sociocultural effects of its manufacturing base were ubiquitous.

The oil boom and the intensification of national modernization programs under the direction of a military administration were in full swing. It was during this period that much of the current infrastructure of Ecuador was built, including the paving of the Pan-American Highway from Quito through Otavalo, which reduced travel time to Quito—and its international airport—to a mere two hours. When Ecuadorian tourism was promoted abroad by government agencies, Otavalans were, and still are, prominently displayed in both national and private travel brochures and guides.

With aid from the Dutch government and with an eye toward capturing the expanding tourist market, the Plaza de Ponchos was constructed on the north side of the town of Otavalo, which included several concrete kiosks in which Otavalan sellers could be semipermanently located. Although the kiosks are rented for a nominal weekly fee, and technically are open to any Otavalan seller, only those households already involved in the merchandising of Otavalan textiles (especially households already located in Otavalo or in villages closest to Otavalo) in 1973 were able to afford the initial fee; those same initial families have tenaciously maintained their control over these prime locations by keeping kiosks manned every week and strategically passing them on to family members (Meisch 1987, 154). As this unabashed tourist market has grown, albeit with some internal trade, as well, hundreds of Otavalan seller-weavers set up temporary kiosks in the surrounding side streets at the Saturday market.

At this point, it should be emphasized that the Otavalan export economy is not a monolithic system with a high degree of regionwide articulation but rather is characterized by a multitude of production patterns and trade networks, each with a merchant-weaver household at its organizational center. Even socially, the prime mechanism that articulates the region is the market economy itself and the demands of gaining and maintaining one's competitive position or niche. The growth of the externally oriented textile economy is driven by dual forces of internal expansion, with more and more Otavalans wanting to weave and trade, and the necessity of industrializing and seeking new markets as the socially acceptable forms of competition among an increasing number of competitors. One of the most striking features of the Saturday market is the generally reserved manner displayed by vendors. Yet, in striking contrast to their nonchalant sales technique is their innovative incorporation of new technologies, which enables them to reap profits through lower production costs and reliable service instead of undercutting their neighbors or cornering the markets. This practice has increased the mechanization of spinning, weaving, and knitting to the extent that one can walk down the streets of Otavalo and hear the drone of industrial weaving machines all day and all night.

Industrialized weaving, using electric power and synthetic fibers, and the increased productive capacity that comes with them have led to a restructuring of gendered household organization and to the necessity of temporary economic migration to new destinations:

> The increasing number of weavers, in contrast to the earlier equilibrium between spinners [women] and weavers [men], has produced a notable supply of textiles, which the weekly market is insufficient for depleting this excess production. It's from this situation that artisans and merchants have seen the necessity of finding new markets and diversifying production, changing patterns of auto-consumption for the satisfaction of an external demand, although to do this they have had to seek undemanding clients in regard to maintaining cultural values and respect for the traditions of the [Otavalan] people. (Jaramillo Cisneros 1987, 14; translation is mine)

This overproduction plays a significant role in motivating more and more Otavalans to seek new markets abroad through domestic and international economic migration. In contrast to the apparent display of camaraderie at the Saturday tourist market, Otavalan merchants jealously guard client contacts and information regarding prime selling locations abroad. One young Otavalan seller commented that what surprised him the most about life in New York City, where a small colony of several hundred Otavalans are constantly shuttling back and forth, was the lack of solidarity and mutual aid among his coethnics (Jonathan Kandell, "Shuttle Capitalism," *Los Angeles Times Magazine,* Nov. 14, 1993, 30).

During the past twenty years, as in every successive period since the initial weaving of "Andean tweed" in 1917, boom periods in the indigenous export economy have produced more pronounced class differences between weavers, workshop owners, and full-time merchants. Yet, the educated Otavalan merchant class has continued to speak for and represent the interests of all Otavalans, even as coethnics supplying much of the labor (but not sharing equitably in the benefits of the booming cottage industry) increasingly perceived the merchants own, often contested, interests. On several occasions the traditional schism between former yanapa communities and the wealthiest merchant-weaver communities has erupted in deadly violence; a notable example is the continuing conflict between cooperatives over the breakup and redistribution of the Quinchuquí hacienda in 1981 (Guerrero 1991), leading to the violent death of an Otavalan in the former yanapa community of La Bolsa in 1994 (Meisch, personal communication).

During a nationwide Indian uprising in 1990, when thousands of indigenous groups sought recognition of their cultural and political identity, many Otavalan merchants were anxious about lost business resulting from the transportation stoppage—"it was simply not good for business" (quoted in D'Amico 1993, 44). Even among merchants, stratification is notable and has begun to lead to more public acrimony between the wealthy merchants and small traders. For example, when the municipal government of Otavalo threatened to relocate several Otavalan "small businessmen" operating on the periphery of the Plaza de Ponchos, traders complained that city officials were "favoring those artisans that earn [U.S.] dollars and have a lot of land, houses, cars, and all of the luxuries" (*La Hora*, March 20, 1993, 16).

Appreciation for the recent economic activity of making "traditional" music at local bars and on the streets of foreign cities cannot be divorced from this context of incipient class relations. Music making is nothing new to the valley: "Imbabura Valley is thought of in Ecuador in a general way as a musical center, but, as far as I know, no records of Indian-played music, instrumental or vocal, have been made" (Parsons 1945, 116). Important Otavalan rituals and feasts have always included musical accompaniment.

In the cultural milieu of the 1960s, when indigenous groups were becoming valorized by national and foreign intellectual sympathizers, the Otavalan dance troupe Rumiñuahi began to participate in the annual parade of Yamor in 1968, an Otavalan celebration that had begun to attract growing numbers of tourists. After an invitation by its First Lady to perform in Mexico, other offers surfaced to dance and play in Ecuador and for the BBC in England, with Conjunto Peguche recording their first album in 1979 (D'Amico 1993, 171).

Yet, similar to the development of the modern weaving industry, the indigenous origins of Otavalan music, which traditionally consists of repetitive, trance-inducing dances called San Juanitos, have been transformed into a more marketable form for export. In the early 1980s, a handful of local musical groups began to incorporate other Andean music and instruments from Bolivia and Peru after groups from those countries visited Otavalo. This new genre, based on a self-conscious, pan-Andean worldview, reached a commercial turning point with the highly successful group Charijayak, an Otavalan group based in Barcelona, Spain. Significantly, most of the group's members had grown up in Spain's Otavalan community. They have taken the pan-Andean genre into the New Age by mixing electric instruments and popular European and North American styles. During their triumphant return to Otavalo in 1987, they were received as local celebrities. Sporting unbraided long hair, European-style clothing, and earrings, they certainly dressed the part (see Meisch 1997). Instantly, they became cultural and economic role models for young Otavalan men. One of Charijayak's members now owns a luxurious private home in Otavalo, which once belonged to a famous poet, where he stays when he is not in Barcelona.

Just as the exporting of tweed from Otavalo presented itself as an opportunity in 1917 during a period of increasing competition for land (Salomon 1981), the performance of folk music presented a similar opportunity in the late 1980s for young men during a period of intense competition in the handicraft trade. The growth in the number of musical groups traveling abroad in just the past five years has been phenomenal; so many are traveling during the summer that the local Otavalan operator of the tour agency, Diceney Tours (probably a misspelling of "Disney"), complained that none were left to play in the local San Juan festival—including her own husband. Although no one can say how many groups are abroad, estimates are in the hundreds. Given the groups' ability to recoup the price of their ticket within a couple of months abroad, local travel agencies often sell them international airline tickets on credit. Thus, music making, unlike the handicraft trade, represents an economic activity requiring little start-up investment, aside from the time it takes to learn a folkloric instrument and form a group. In fact, it is now seen as the only way to gain the capital needed to enter the lucrative and increasingly industrialized handicraft economy. Making music abroad, and all of the adventure that goes with it—including North American and European girlfriends (whom some have married)—has become also a rite of passage for Otavalan men. In this sense, the desire to travel abroad has taken on the characteristic "fever to migrate" found among other groups where more traditional labor migration prevails.

The social and economic changes that have occurred since the opening of the Plaza de Ponchos in 1973, especially greater capitalization of production and the rise of mass transnational migration, has led to a more urbanized society, both demographically and culturally. Thousands of Otavalans have moved into the town of Otavalo in the past ten years, leading to more urbanized lifestyles, although for the most part they have been able to retain their ethnic identity. This move has been a result, in part, of the impossibility of land ownership for many young people in those villages that have been experiencing a land shortage for nearly a decade. However, much of the demographic shift to the city has been a direct outcome of the growth of the handicraft industry, with its need for better infrastructure, including electric power, private telephone lines, shipping companies, and schools. Instead of production punctuated by weekly marketing, both weaving and trading are daily activities. Otavalans now own approximately ninety-four permanent handicraft and textile shops in Otavalo (Meisch 1997), including several shops alongside the tourist restaurants that line the Plaza de Poncho (including an imitation Hard Rock Café). So many Indians have moved to Otavalo that it was the subject of a video documentary in 1993, aired on national Ecuadorian television, entitled, "The Reconquest of Otavalo."

Tensions between the upwardly mobile Otavalans and the downwardly mobile mestizos in Otavalo are visceral: real estate inflation from Otavalan demand is so great that many mestizos whose families have lived in Otavalo for centuries cannot afford to buy a house. There is now the specter of mestizo "indigenous" musical groups playing locally in order to attract dollars and female tourists (see Kandell 1993); during any typical week in Otavalo one can find several European and North American women whose primary purpose in Otavalo is to have an affair with an Otavalan. Many foreign women, some of whom first learn about Otavalans back home, perceive the long-haired Otavalan men to be handsome, noble, exotic, and talented—a fact Otavalan men understand quite well (see also Meisch 1995).

Although there is significant variation in the degree of acculturation, even more rural communities have evolved a mixture of traditional and urban values, directly related to the wide-ranging travels and cultural experiences of some of their inhabitants. One young Otavalan from Peguche who had just returned, sporting jeans and tennis shoes, from a trip to Belgium, pointed to the poster of Bob Marley hanging on his wall (next to one of Madonna) and exclaimed, "He is my God." To improve his English vocabulary, he had placed little labels on various items around his room, identifying the objects in English. He was not alone in his desire to be hip: many late-night Ecuadorian wedding parties now end with pulsating music from Jamaica, North America, and Europe, and groups of teenage boys who have not even traveled yet strut the latest fashions from New York City or Amsterdam.

Education, too, has played a role in orienting Otavalans toward a more urban-centric worldview in a country where *rural* and *peasant* are nearly synonymous with *animal*. This urbanization process, however, can be best characterized as cultural borrowing rather than complete acculturation. In fact, even though the young, wealthier Otavalans are now participating in a postmodern material culture substantially different from that of their grandfathers, their self-conscious pride in their Otavalan identity is probably greater.

In the economic sphere, this ability to urbanize and innovate without losing group identity has allowed some surprising changes in the commodity chain of both local and extralocal indigenous products. Some of the Otavalans' "native" handicrafts are produced by other ethnic groups, including sweaters hand-knitted by Azuayan peasants (the wives of labor migrants to New York City) and balsa figurines carved by Amazonian Indians. Trips abroad include opportunities for Otavalans not only to sell but also to buy indigenous textiles and crafts in countries such as Bolivia, Peru, and Panama, which they then market as their own (most of the time) to unsuspecting tourists back in Otavalo or during selling trips to North America or Europe. In this respect, Otavalans are rapidly becoming the principal brokers of native crafts from Latin America—even supplying handicrafts to tourist destinations lacking colorful indigenous populations; one Otavalan entrepreneur (who speaks Dutch) told me of his ingenious plan to sell Amazonian balsa figurines of tropical parrots to Arubian tourist shops, complete with the label, "Made in Aruba." (Aruba, he explains, is lacking in "colorful natives.")

Hence, we have the basic cultural irony of the economic base of the region—an Andean indigenous group running a global export economy and incorporating the material culture of other native groups into their marketing arsenal, while remaining confident in their own "authentic" cultural identity. To be sure, much of the production of tourist exports—sweaters, handbags, duffel bags, backpacks, blankets, and wall hangings—are produced locally using technology ranging from the ancient back-strap loom to make belts and bracelets to modern weaving machines and synthetic fibers. Nonetheless, the distinction between local and extralocal is blurred in Otavalo because of their willingness to incorporate the most marketable "indigenous" designs and products into their own line of goods. In comparing an authentic Peruvian Indian market frequented by tourists with the Plaza de Poncho in Otavalo, Lynn Meisch writes that "Otavalo is an intentional, authentic tourist market in that most textiles sold are not commercialized versions of traditional Indian weavings which are presented as authentic, but are nontraditional textiles made with the express intent of sale to outsiders. The Otavaleños are production weavers and proud of it, and of their marketing ability" (Meisch 1987, 154, emphasis added).

In other words, the Otavalans' handicrafts are authentically inauthentic. Although many tourists on a ten-day package tour would be unable to tell the difference between the authentic and the inauthentic at the Otavalo Saturday market, Meisch is simply underscoring perhaps the central feature of the Otavalan economy: whether using pre-Incan or twentieth-century methods, production is eminently market driven, even while the Otavalan merchant class and foreign supporters continue to reinvent an "indigenous" Otavalan identity.

This situation has led some Ecuadorian social scientists to decry the seeming loss of an "internal cultural compass" by Otavalan producers and merchants:

> Regarding artisanal designs, the consensus is that they have lost the will to conserve an "identity" in regional weavings. In this sense, the [long-distance] trips of the indigenous merchants sum up the influence exercised by tourism and by those people or missions of "good will" who impose foreign models and tastes into our reality or who introduce the reproduction of artisanal objects from other places, revealing clearly that these people are absolutely unprepared to handle and respect cultural values, such that we have seen the result of this process to be the gradual change in traditional weavings, to the point that they have become simple imitations of things that represent other cultural realities. (Jaramillo Cisneros 1987, 16; translation is mine)

The problem with this observation is that after five hundred years of subjugation by a Eurocentric society, it would be difficult to define the "traditional" in the Otavalan economic sphere. Furthermore, the irony is that though Otavalans' economic production has reached a postmodern zenith in its satisfaction of souvenir shoppers across the developed world, their identity as a sociocultural group could not be stronger, precisely because it is tied, in large part, to their business reputation. It is, in fact, their economic reputation that has always shaped a significant part of the Otavalan internal and external identity and cultural values. Their historical, self-fulfilling reputation of nobility and industry has remained consistent even in the face of urbanization and industrialization. An Iberia Airlines billboard in downtown Quito in the early 1990s depicted an Otavalan in traditional dress carrying a bag of golf clubs under one arm and the caption, "I go to Europe with Iberia—when are you going?"

There is a common thread to the activities of the last two decades, years in which the increasingly postmodern quality of Otavalan cultural life can easily mask, or at least upstage, its internal political economy. In observing the internal stratification process linked to capitalist relations, Salomon asks one of the central questions for Otavalans and their indigenous export economy: "[Can Otavalo] continue to turn large-scale societal conditions to its own advantage without suffering unintended consequences that will gradually take the pace and direction of change out of the reach of its own mechanisms of social policy?" (1981, 443). He continues with the following observations:

> Points of stress are already visible. It may be true that the organization of production in household units sets limits on the scale and complexity of

production, but nothing has prevented some families from developing as adjuncts to the household workshops approaching a factory form of organization. As a result the textile industry has probably increased rather than moderated the inequality of landholdings and standards of living. It is true that the employment of land-poor villagers by other Indians as spinners, weavers, or farm helpers may share out some of the wealth, but the ascendancy of a few entrepreneurially active families in business is conspicuous. If most textile wealth continues to go into the buying up of lands, partible inheritance and the deprecation of greed central to Otavalan ethics may not prevail against the dynamics of private ownership. (Ibid., 444)

To put it another way, without any external economic or political threats on the horizon, the group's only significant threat is self-destruction. If, indeed, during the past twenty years those "points of stress" had developed into widespread, violent class conflict between semiproletarian peasants and an emergent rural bourgeoisie, the social order and, hence, the economic base of the whole region could have been severely threatened, if not shattered, owing to the skittishness of tourists and foreign wholesalers. Meier's analysis of emergent class relations and the tendency toward a putting-out system in the late 1970s—whereby some comerciantes were getting wealthy solely on the exchange value of the crafts, forming colonies in Bogotá and Madrid—certainly would not have given us much cause for hope. Points of stress certainly persist, especially between communities formerly tied to haciendas and those that are not, and these stresses may yet develop into more profound "class" conflict. Thus far, however, this has not occurred. The possibility of a no-win situation of open political conflict within and among Otavalan communities has set a limit on both the degree of coethnic proletarianization and the development of a rural bourgeoisie of factory owners and middlemen.

Furthermore, as we have seen, this limitation has shaped three of the most significant developments during this most recent period. First, the rise of an urban bourgeoisie, living in Otavalo, Quito, or foreign cities, has not only physically separated emergent classes but also uses the ambiguous social cover of traditional mestizo urban bases; within the national society, the move to the cities by indios would, by itself, signal a change in their social and ethnic status to cholo (or mestizo), especially when accompanied by a change to modern dress. In this sense, the rationale for moving to the city, the one given by many merchants, of requiring more advanced infrastructure is the same discourse of legitimation found among urbanites for centuries. The urban craft producer and middleman have the advantage of having more freedom to pick and choose both reciprocal (politically tricky) and commodified social relations with those remaining behind in the rural village.

Second, the significance of incorporating product lines made by other indigenous and mestizo groups within and outside Ecuador becomes clear when seen as an alternative to expanding production on the backs of fellow Otavalans. This strategy, however, has its own drawback, namely, the exposure of the crass nature of cultural commodification: Otavalan middlemen are not just reaping the exchange value of foreign-made crafts, they are also adding to its value by their association with it as "authentic Indians." I do not wish to generalize to all merchants, but when I ask Otavalan vendors whether an item was made by the seller, or even by Otavalans, most claim to have made it themselves or that it was made by a family member back home. Some tourists have taken offense at this practice of passing off "inauthentic" handicrafts—such as Panamanian molas (reverse appliqué designs made by the Cuna indigenous people)—as Otavalan and, hence, have vowed never to return to Otavalo (see Crabb 1993). Yet, this is a relatively minor problem in that wholesalers arriving from Toronto or Tokyo are concerned only about the quality of the product and the reliability of the comerciante to deliver, for which the Otavalan merchants are justifiably reputable.

Third, and most important, the rapid incorporation of music performance as a new export commodity, although understandable in the context of growing intraethnic class relations, should not be viewed as a strategy to reduce class conflict per se. Music making abroad is neither a mechanical evolution of the comerciante's activities nor simply the expression of a cultural rebirth within a postmodern world. Performing music is not as profitable as selling crafts and can be a physically and financially risky venture. Moreover, it is doubtful that so many young men are fanning out across the globe, in their prime working years, for reasons of cultural expression.

Meier's analytical framework is still appropriate, if not more so, today. Returning to figure 5.1, we see that music making, as a "craft," falls into cell C: the only input required is credit for an airline ticket, now nearly routinely granted to young musicians by local travel agencies, and it has the significant advantage of allowing producers (the musicians) independence from middlemen—while still retaining their global markets. Because the travel agencies have a logic of capital accumulation distinct from the handicraft industry, credit for an airline ticket is not the first step toward complete economic dependence on the agency. The significant feature is that nearly all young men identified as Otavalans have at least a chance of traveling abroad as musicians, because the skill is readily attained and the group reputation allows for a high degree of trust on the part of the travel agencies and foreign governments granting visas; mestizos now complain that "all you need to travel is a pony-tail" (D'Amico 1993). Thus, hundreds of young musicians now leaving Otavalo every year are reclaiming the exchange value of their labor and their cultural identity, an extremely fortuitous development.

Thus, by allowing some of the poorest communities to send "representatives" to foreign lands, folkloric music has provided a regionwide escape valve for potential political tensions arising from the consolidation of a merchant class. This strategy entails significant risks. As strictly transnational entrepreneurs (making commercial music locally is seen as a training period, or "paying dues," as it is known by musicians around the world), musicians are especially dependent on the immigration policies of developed countries, now sparking intense national debates. Unlike migration from Azuay, playing music or selling artesanía in the streets everyday are not activities recommended for the undocumented or falsely documented. In addition, transnational music making leads to a type of transnational social structure more linked to foreign cultures than preceding types of craft exports. It remains to be seen whether music will be used as an instrument for creating a more sustainable and inclusive economic base among Otavalan communities. It may, instead, strike a sour note, as its unique sociocultural side effects feed back into the ethnic export economy.

Otavalan Communities before Transnational Migration

The apparent social unity and cultural conservation of the Otavalans belies a deep division in the areas of economic activity, social status, and emerging class structure. Furthermore, this social stratification was present centuries before the present-day transnational migration (Parsons 1945; Buitrón 1947; Salomon 1981). Few studies have seriously considered these within-group differences as integral to the ability of some Otavalans to escape the abject poverty characteristic of most Latin American peasants (for a notable exception, see Guerrero 1991; see also Meisch 1997). It has been only recently, with the emergence of a prosperous class of Otavalan middlemen and large-scale producers who connect even the most remote, illiterate weavers with foreign consumers and wholesalers, that the entire region has become vertically integrated, reinforcing internal hierarchies in a group unified by a common culture and language.

The two communities chosen as research sites, Peguche and Guanansi, are examples of the historical diversity of economic activities and attending social status found in the Otavalan region: Peguche has been involved in weaving for a foreign market for at least five centuries and in direct marketing for several decades; in contrast, Guanansi was economically and socially tied to a large hacienda for most of its history; only recently has it begun to enter the regional export industry.

Peguche

Peguche, an indigenous village currently composed of 393 households, lies approximately five kilometers north of Otavalo on the Pan-American Highway. Although it is one of the more important rural communities making handicrafts for tourists and foreign markets, one could easily bypass its main entrance on the highway, marked by a nondescript bus stop sign. Its small plaza includes a church and only a couple of commercial "stores" catering to tourists, though even these remain very low-key. The community has expanded beyond the original nucleus, forming seven distinct barrios, including a recent addition of several rows of two-story brick houses built with Ecuadorian and foreign aid. Peguche lies in some of the most desirable valley land, apart from the lower hacienda lands.

Peguche was the site of several important political, economic, and technological innovations throughout the colonial period. Perhaps the most important Crown obraje was located at Peguche from the sixteenth- through the eighteenth-centuries. It would be difficult to verify why this community was chosen over others for such a status; it is likely, however, that it was already an important weaving site during the Incan period and may have had members of the independent *mindalá* merchant class. Its location near the settlement of Sarance (Otavalo) and its attractive waterfall and river must have made it especially alluring.

After the noninheritable manufacturing obrajes and agricultural encomiendas were transformed into other forms of debt peonage and inheritable haciendas in the mid-eighteenth century, Peguche households remained beyond hacienda control, though surrounded on three sides by the hacienda Quinchuquí. To be sure, Peguche weavers were forced into concertaje and huasipungo systems of control to extract labor for weaving. However, the continuing economic division of labor in the region by community, whereby some villages were dedicated primarily to weaving and others dedicated primarily to agriculture, had profound socioeconomic repercussions for the development trajectory and ideological stance of Otavalan communities and for specific households within those communities. Although land ownership, with its economic and symbolic importance for agriculture, has always been central for gaining full community membership and social status, Peguche has long been a weaving community first and foremost. Using the local lexicon, the distinction is between *agricultores-artesanos* (e.g., Guanansi) and *artesanos-agricultores* (e.g., Peguche) (Guerrero 1991).

The historical handicraft niche of Peguche has set it apart from those Otavalan communities primarily dedicated to agriculture in three important ways. First, weaving and all its ancillary activities require a particular type of skilled labor, one within an industrializing context. Weaving, whether using the traditional back-strap loom or the wooden Spanish loom, is a multifaceted skill acquired from childhood. Labor is divided by gender, with the principal activity of weaving done only by men. However, weaving for an external market as a full-time activity incorporate all of the available household labor, including the cleaning of the wool by small children (see Parsons 1945). Most important, Peguche weaving households were able to witness both dramatic and subtle increases in production as new technologies of machinery and organization were introduced, turning many Peguche households into both industrious and industrialized cottages. Thus, some Peguche weavers by the beginning of the twentieth century were already beginning to acquire industrialized skills with a high level of household organization and a willingness to innovate. Leo Chávez has correctly noted that commercial weavers see themselves as imbued with the classic entrepreneurial qualities of rationality, honesty, and sobriety: "They think of themselves as innovators, as able to adopt new ideas, behaviors, and technologies when they find it useful" (1985, 166). In contrast, mestizos have been traditionally viewed by Otavalans in Peguche as "lazy" (Parsons 1945, 54).

Second, given the long-standing concentration of commercial activity and the desirability of its fertile valley land, Peguche has experienced some of the earliest and highest levels of competition for land within its community. Parsons reports that there were 122 households in Peguche in 1941; by that time, none of the Peguche household plots was large enough to tax (Parsons 1945, 11). Thus, most of Peguche's households were engaged in direct competition for land with their neighbors; the only way to gain more land was to buy it through income gained from weaving or brokering handicrafts. Although this may not seem noteworthy, it stands in contrast to the more communal nature of the Otavalan communities linked to nearby haciendas. At the time of Parsons' fieldwork in 1940, Otavalans had bought "good hacienda land on Yanaurco, Black Mountain, and the great hill just west of Otavalo" (1945, 8). To be able to buy land, especially from the hacendado, is a source of pride because it underscores the status of the independent Otavalan comerciantes as equals to the mestizos and whites meeting in a rationalized marketplace.

Third, Peguche and other weaving communities differed structurally and ideologically in their relationship to white and mestizo elites (haciendas, state representatives, the church) in comparison with agricultor-artesano communities. Structurally, Peguche was largely free from the total socialization of the hacienda. Although work in the weaving factories was harsh, most weavers from Peguche were considered indios libres or *indios sueltos* (free Indians), in contrast with either the indios propios (owned Indians) or the semi-independent yanaperos attached to haciendas. This socioeconomic status was especially important within and among Otavalan communities, in which a clear pride among the artesano-agricultor households stemmed from such a distinction. This structural position also had important ideological and psychological consequences. Independent elite weavers from Peguche embodied the historical mythic image of Otavalans as clean and noble, an image difficult to claim by more agricultural Otavalans dependent on the haciendas. All of these structural and ideological factors contributed to perhaps the most amazing aspect of Otavalan society: within a national culture deeply stratified by ethnicity, some indigenous Otavalans (artesanos-agricultores) perceived themselves to be the social equals to whites and mestizos of every social stratum (Guerrero 1991, 172–77). Although they were not immune to abuse and prejudice, the external interest and respect they gained as a group for their industriousness and business acumen reinforced this perception.

Structurally, the emerging merchant-weaver class benefited greatly from their ability to deal with mestizos more or less as equals by embedding them in a dense web of external contacts able to help them politically and economically as the need arose. Communities such as Peguche were noted in the 1940s for their uniquely open attitude to the external society and for their self-confidence (Buitrón 1947). Where indios propios and yanaperos were granted their internal community social status directly from the hacendado, independent artesanos-agricultores gained it through a diverse network of mestizo and foreign intermediaries aggressively sought in the "external" society. In this sense, Peguche's close proximity to Otavalo facilitated not only the transportation of woven goods but also the development of social and economic contacts and allies so important to retaining control over the production-to-market process. The best example of the rise of a merchant class actively developing multiple ties with local, national, and international elites is Rosa Lema's activities (Parsons 1945). Recall that it was Rosa Lema, Parsons' principal informant, who first traveled to the United States.

This structural and ideological position was further reinforced as elite weaving families from Peguche and other nonhacienda communities began to form a nascent capitalist class, not only by hiring Otavalan peons to work their land and their looms but also, most importantly, through the development of broker capitalism as middlemen merchants. Unfortunately, it is beyond the scope of this book to fully describe the nature of an emergent capitalist "class" as it is developing in Otavalo. Certainly, it would be wrong to conclude that simple class relations developed around the classic distinction of loom ownership primarily because of the way Andean reciprocal relations and the gendered division of labor often mask such complex economic relationships. Capitalist class relations are more evident, however, with the emergence of full-time middlemen merchants from Peguche and other communities, who reap profits by buying from several small to medium household workshops scattered throughout rural Otavalan communities.

Just as in other indigenous communities, several mestizo families were already settled in Peguche by the time of Parsons' ethnography in 1945, supplying durable goods, sugarcane liquor, and *chicha*, a milder fermented corn liquor (1945, 9). However, unlike other Otavalan communities, mestizo families have not succeeded in marginalizing or squeezing out the indigenous population and have remained to the present-day as petty merchants and taxi drivers. In many ways, the local mestizo families have adapted to Otavalan life, rather than the other way around, historically playing intermediary roles between the "Indian" and "white" societies, as needed by Peguche families.

With the failure of the local mestizo elite to mechanize weaving in the nineteenth century, and with the official end to the huasipungo laws in 1964, Peguche's considerable technological skill and infrastructure and its socioeconomic ties to Otavalo, Quito, and beyond were now unfettered and able to flourish. By this time, technological innovation for greater profits was already an established practice; the Spanish loom had been introduced by the early twentieth century, along with foreign designs, synthetic materials, a wide range of designs, and electric looms. It was also during this period that foreigners began to directly aid Peguche.

By the 1950s and 1960s, many of Peguche's emerging merchant class began to send their children to school in Otavalo; these young students received some of the first high school diplomas granted to Otavalans. Education provided the ideological and social resources needed to maintain an equal footing with other Ecuadorians. It was understood that the marketing of local handicrafts throughout the region and abroad required a formal education in Spanish. By the 1980s, some of Peguche's sons and daughters had not only gone on to universities in Quito, some had even attained advanced degrees in the United States, Europe, and Cuba. Although this elite class has been educated and, therefore, partly socialized into national or Western culture, many have returned to Peguche or Otavalo as the source of their identity. They have also returned to the source of their wealth; even the most educated, such as one sociologist I met, have found that, even if they were able to find work in their professions, selling handicrafts abroad is considerably more lucrative, with less prejudice encountered in the marketplace than in professional societies and institutions. To be sure, some have found permanent professional positions abroad, such as a Peguche linguist at the University of Wisconsin, or have continued their professions in Peguche, such as one documentary filmmaker. Some of this considerable intellectual capital, in what could be described as an intelligentsia, has been channeled into a three-story community house, with the top floor serving as the closest thing to a research institute one could hope to find in a rural community. The institute boasts a computer, advanced software, liaisons with activist and research groups throughout the Andes, a monthly publication, and periodic roundtable discussions.

During the late 1960s and 1970s, foreign groups such as the United States Peace Corps and Protestant missionaries found Peguche, especially its merchants and weavers, to be amenable to their developmental and individualistic ideologies. In spite of (or perhaps because of) inroads made by foreigners into village life, this was also a time of cultural renaissance for Peguche elites searching for an indigenous, pan-Andean identity, with Peguche at its epicenter. One of the most important elements of this self-conscious cultural reawakening was the development of musical and dance groups designed specifically to preserve and encourage traditional expressive forms. There has been a proliferation of "traditional" music groups, but other important traditions, such as the *cargo,* or sponsoring of a community feast, were already disappearing by the 1980s.

Guanansi

Guanansi, a community of sixty households located across the Pan-American Highway from Peguche, is an agricultural peasant village of Otavalans. Although it, too, lies near Otavalo, it is much more difficult to reach than Peguche because it is a few kilometers off the highway (opposite Peguche) at the end of an unpaved, often muddy, road. The village itself is perched on a small hill with no natural irrigation. As of 1993, Guanansi was still without electricity, plumbing, or telephone service.

Although the regional weaving and handicraft booms have largely passed

Guanansi by, its recent history is as remarkable as that of Peguche, in that it, too, is now entering the ethnic export economy, yet without the privileged historical position and resources of Peguche. Some Guanansi men have always known how to weave using the traditional back-strap loom. However, weaving was generally practiced for internal household use and remained secondary in importance to subsistence agriculture. Unlike Peguche, the history of Guanansi can be virtually limited to its symbiotic relationship to a single institution, the hacienda Quinchuquí, which also drew on yanaperos and peones from other neighboring villages.

From at least the eighteenth century through the 1950s, Guanansi had been a corporate community completely enveloped, both physically and socially, by the hacienda Quinchuquí, owned by the Jijón family, owners of the famous Peguche obraje (Guerrero 1991, 159). However, a Guanansi peasant did not have the classic status of a debt peon essentially enslaved to the hacienda; he was, rather, a yanapero, and as such he had at least the illusion of certain rights. Although the yanapero status was based on the official fiction of reciprocity, it was clear that it was not a reciprocity among equals. On the one hand, a Guanansi peasant enjoyed the freedom of owning a plot of land free of onerous debts; on the other hand, the hacienda was the social, economic, and political universe for the community.

As Andrés Guerrero tells the story, by the 1960s, changes in the nature of the yanapa-hacienda relationship, so important internally to community economic and social life, set into motion a series of events that led to a violent confrontation and the independence of Guanansi from the hacienda (1991). Specifically, national political and economic changes, such as the agrarian reforms of the 1960s and the petroleum boom of the 1970s, forced the hacienda to modernize production. After an eight-year failed attempt to transform the hacienda into dairy production, the hacienda returned to agriculture—though now mechanized and less labor intensive (ibid., 170). Yanaperos from communities such as Guanansi continued to use hacienda lands, but there was a slow, almost imperceptible, change in which the hacienda, now no longer profitable, sought autonomy from traditional reciprocal relationships and responsibilities with the yanapa communities. These changes, which created a local political vacuum, also coincided with more bureaucratic state intervention, including significantly more formal education for a new generation growing up under a less traditional social climate. By the late 1970s, it was this younger, more educated generation, imbued with leftist ideologies introduced by outsiders, that now formed a more charismatic authority base, rather than the traditional one so wedded to the hacienda. These young leaders formed a "precooperative" in 1978 with the intention of claiming what they felt were their traditional ancestral lands.

As Guerrero observes, the impact of the breakdown of the yanapa-hacienda relationship was not only economic in a narrow sense: "Without a doubt, these were the strongest social changes in at least the previous one-hundred-and-fifty years. . . . First, [there was] an accentuation of the social differentiation among communities in the lower zone [e.g., Guanansi] and the upper zone [e.g., Peguche], and, second, [there were] structural-economic, cultural, and political transformations within communities" (ibid., 171–72). In large measure, social differentiation was accentuated pre-cisely because the landlord had taken advantage of historical social divisions between "los de abajo y los de arriba" (those from below and those from above); when it became evident that the precooperative formed by yanapa communities was gaining the upper hand in the dispute, the landlord began to sell parcels of hacienda land to merchant-weavers in Peguche, who were enthused at the possibility of buying more land, for which they formed their own Asociación de Compradores (buyers' association). Hence, what had been a conflict between the hacienda and the agricultural precooperative had now spread to conflict between communities with radically different internal structures and worldviews. Violence eventually broke out between those com-munities that claimed a moral right to "ancestral lands" and those that claimed an economic right to buy land on the "open" market as equals to the landlord. Ultimately, after the jailing of precooperative leaders for a period, the precooperative won hacienda lands, which were then divided among community-based cooperatives.

The legacy for Guanansi of the defunct hacienda has been twofold: first, Guanansi has attained a substantial tract of community land used for com-mercial agricultural production, especially wheat; and second, this fact has created a new community social structure. Thus, unlike Peguche, or the Azuayan communities, Guanansi has an active agricultural cooperative, which owns approximately eighty acres of fertile land and a tractor; however, the corporate, communal nature of the village has been altered. In fact, the cooperative has split the small community into two factions: those who are members of the cooperative and those who are not. This fact has produced a fairly contentious environment, with accusations of impropriety on both sides. Each side is led by a youthful, dynamic leader, from the first educated generation.

The experience of a successful uprising and acquisition of hacienda lands gave these young leaders much more contact with the regional and national society than they would have had under the traditional yanapa relationship when the hacienda dominated community life. With a combination of these social skills and the recognition that agriculture is not adequate to ensure economic survival, Guanansi leaders have sought out the aid of foreigners to help them establish their own weaving industry.

Given its longer history of isolation from the burgeoning weaving trade and tourist markets, Guanansi is more self-consciously traditional than Peguche. As one informant told me, "When a child dies we still play the harp and sing—it's not like they do in Peguche. . . . They always hire white bands to play." The discourse of the authentically traditional nature of Guanansi, a discourse used in the "struggle" against the merchant-weavers of Peguche over land, is now used as a selling point for Guanansi-made handicrafts and music.

≡

We can now begin to compare and analyze the macrohistorical development of transnational migration in the two regions of Azuay and Otavalo with an eye toward locating remaining questions in our analysis. During the colonial period, even though both Azuay and Otavalo participated in the "national" economy of the Quito Audencia, the weaving of textiles, they differed in both the degree of participation and the vertical integration of the spinners and weavers to the primary consumer, the Spanish state, representing two extremes: in Azuay, both Indian and mestizo semiautonomous peasants were engaged part-time in handicraft production as a supplement to agriculture; in Otavalo we see the classic obraje system, highly integrated with Crown interests. Just as in Azuay, the cloth trade rapidly declined after independence from Spain, owing to new competition from the flood of cheap imported cloth made in British factories. In both regions, the strong value placed on land ownership and independence reduced the propensity for the development of a weaving proletariat. The long-term consequences, however, for the two regions over the course of the rest of the nineteenth century and into the next could not have been more different; where Azuayan peasants lost economic independence with the introduction of a new nonindustrialized export, the straw hat, by elite families, Otavalans were able to ultimately take control of both weaving production and marketing while benefiting from sympathetic foreigners' aid in modernizing and adapting the industry to new demands by tourists and foreign markets.

Yet, we cannot simply deduce from these different regional histories the experiences of actual transnational migrants. In fact, an interesting question arises at this point: Is the social organization and impact of transnational migration from Otavalan communities similar to that of Azuayan communities, given their similar individual attributes and common national setting, or are they fundamentally different because of the divergent logics and locations of the two migration strategies? The following chapter examines more closely the migration experiences of Peguche and Guanansi.

CHAPTER SIX

Otavalan Villages: Peguche and Guanansi

Soy Cholo Boy, y me voy a regresar. Total después de todo, no me ha ido tan mal. Cuando llegue a mi llacta, yo voy a comprar, la casa, la ropa, y el Trooper manejar. A la Cunshi, y a la Rosa, negocio voy a dar. Lo propio, lo nuestro, vamos a exportar. Ya lo tengo bien pensado, y no me va a fallar. Pues, el cuye McDonald's yo voy a instalar. Soy Cholo Boy y me voy a descansar! Tú sabes . . . chulla vida!

[I am a Cholo Boy, and I'm going to go home. After everything, I didn't do too badly. When I arrive at my farm, I'm going to buy a house, clothes, and a Trooper to drive. To Cunshi and Rosa, a business I will give them. Our own thing we will export. I've thought about it well, and I'm not going to fail. A guinea pig McDonald's I will build. I am a Cholo Boy and I'm going to rest! You know . . . only one life to live! (Eating guinea pigs throughout the Andes is culturally equivalent to eating turkey at Thanksgiving in the United States.)]

On Columbus Day 1993, walking in midtown Manhattan, I noticed two young men crossing the street, duffel bags in tow, with all the features of Otavalans (identical short statures and long ponytails, though no traditional dress). As I began to follow the two young men while thinking of an opening line (they were already being followed by two grinning cops knowingly eyeing their duffel bags), one of the teenagers disappeared into a subway entrance while the other stopped as I approached; he turned out to be from Peguche and knew my fictive kin. Sporting a North Carolina baseball cap and an earring, José accepted my invitation to lunch at a local deli. At nineteen years old, he was on his first selling trip abroad at the request of his father, who had himself traveled all over Europe. His aunt rented an apartment in New York, which he used as home base. José sold handicrafts—produced in his own family's workshop—on the streets (illegally) and played in a pick-up musical group on weekends, mostly for the friendly female contacts it generated. He told me of his earnest intention to one day purchase a state-of-the-art computerized weaving loom. He had gotten the idea from an American girlfriend in Boston he had met while playing music there; he only needed fifty thousand dollars. After six months in the United States, he was about to go home triumphant after selling all of the last shipment and with a plan that would outdo the rest of the merchant community.

As the focus of an enormous body of ethnographic and sociological research, including works generated by foreigners, the local "institute," and Otavalan intellectuals themselves (a list of work on the region would take nearly a full page), the complexities of any attempt to describe what is going on in Otavalo are manifest, often leading to either a one-dimensional romantic vision, in which the educated merchant class single-handedly developed an economic and social miracle, or more acrimonious criticisms of entrepreneurial Otavalans as sellouts more concerned with money than conserving their culture. Any single characterization of the Otavalans, however, overlooks the diversity of the *ethnie* and all its historical complexities. It is also this historical perspective that allows us to appreciate some of the more romantic interpretations, which, nonetheless, communicate important facts about the immediate context of the success of a transnational ethnic economy.

While in Peguche, I was asked to be godfather of a wedding. When I was introduced to the groom's family, a very elderly *tio* got on his knees and attempted to kiss my hand, to the embarrassment of the young adults. He had lived during the slavelike "huasipungo times" (which had ended less than thirty years ago), when both local and foreign whites, especially those who would act as intermediaries, were received with special, ritualized interactions that reinforced the ethnic stratification of the region. It was clear to me early on in my research that with such a long history of interaction with foreigners, especially proactive foreign researchers who have become "players," a contemporary ethnography of Otavalan life, which includes life in several countries around the world by the 1990s, should not be attempted by a relatively novice field researcher such as myself. Professional observers of Otavalan communities who had been there off and on since the 1960s were still struggling to describe the mass transnational migration that had taken off in the late 1980s in villages that had not been part of the original merchant class and to understand its meaning in terms of social and cultural change for Otavalo.

While I did not hope to conduct a formal ethnography of a rapidly changing and self-referential sociocultural milieu in two separate villages, it was crucial to my wider comparative study that I conduct surveys in both communities and, along the way, pick up any insights into how preexisting social networks and class identities shape patterns of transnational mobility and the construction of new transnational social structures. In the many studies carried out in the canton of Otavalo over several decades, formal surveys have been few and far between, and even government census takers entered communities at grave personal risk. The tradition of resistance to any type of census goes back at least to 1777, when Otavalans violently opposed a census under Charles III, leading to a bloody revolt; after being stoned, one official was gutted with a cow horn by local women who then kept his body on display in the plaza for two days (see Stark 1985). I was told by a local anthropologist that a census survey of communities was impossible, had never been done. Yet, times change. I was able to carry out my surveys, though with some initial difficulty, because leaders in both communities now understood that they needed the data for their own goals of attracting outside funding from international agencies. Both communities held formal meetings, apart from many informal discussions, to decide whether to allow my research team, composed of high school–educated young adults from Peguche who were part of a newly created cultural and research center, to go ahead with the survey. As part of the contract I agreed to give them the descriptive results of the surveys before I left Ecuador.

This chapter presents the results of those household surveys and describes some experiences I had that illustrate the central importance of internal and external social networks as an economic resource. I also describe a "migration fever" among young men not unlike that of Azuayan villages. However, given the entrepreneurial aspect of transnational migration from Otavalo and its pattern of dispersion in search of new markets, it would be surprising to find a social process of transnational migration identical to the one found in Azuay. Nonetheless, social networks, ethnic group identities, and the social and cultural capital resulting from them are also important aspects of transnational migration from Otavalo, though the form and function they take conforms to a regional logic. Otavalan transnational migration has led to particular types of transnational social structures as well as other cultural changes in a region that has traditionally resisted acculturation to the dominant mestizo society.

Similar to the hat-weaving communities of Azuay, it was the traditional commercial weaving communities in the Otavalo region that first turned to transnational migration. However, the nature of early transnational migration from Otavalo, as part of the expansion of commercial activities by Otavalan merchants, made it even more selective than labor migration from Azuay, leading to a considerable lag in the onset of transnational migration within and among communities. Although it easily could be overlooked by casual observers, there are two distinct phases in the development of transnational migration from Otavalo. The first phase was almost exclusively limited to elite, Otavalan weavers and merchants who were expanding already successful ventures; the second, more recent, phase now includes a much larger number of Otavalan communities that have not been part of the Otavalan elite, or are part of a younger cohort experiencing tremendous competitive pressures, and are traveling precisely because they do not own a workshop or factory. The second phase of transnational migration in Otavalo has been facilitated to a large extent by the advent of music making as a commercial activity; it requires less skill than handicrafts and comparatively little start-up capital. This is a qualitative distinction in that it implies not just a greater number of migrants but also changes in the political economy and culture of the entire region, both among Otavalans and between Otavalans and mestizos. In addition, this second phase corresponds to mass migration accompanied by the classic migration fever that grips many Azuayan villages and small towns.

The time frames for transnational migration from Peguche and Guanansi, the two research sites, are very different, a reflection of the community histories discussed in chapter 5. Historically, Peguche and Guanansi have been at opposite ends of the socioeconomic spectrum for centuries and are, in several ways, socially distinct. To paraphrase Andrés Guerrero, it has been the uniformity of the Otavalans' blue ponchos (until recently) that has masked internal hierarchies and diverse ideologies among communities identified as "Otavalan" (1991, 190). Yet, changes in the 1980s and 1990s closed this gap somewhat as formerly agricultural communities attempted, for the first time, to join the ethnic export economy. The development of market-driven music making from Peguche both extended the evolving commercial logic and provided a new opportunity for capital accumulation among those households and communities attempting to join the boom in craft production and marketing.

Transnational Dreams: A Tale of Two Communities

Unlike the case of Azuay, transnational migration from Otavalo represents an expansion of a local growth economy as merchants seek out new markets beyond the local indigenous and tourist markets. This overarching fact shapes two salient features of the social process of merchant migration from Otavalo: continual pioneering and greater selectivity during the long first phase of merchant migration abroad. First, there is a continual need to pioneer new destinations (markets) because Otavalan migrants do not share specific information about where to sell or play abroad, even among neighbors in the same village, a fact corroborated by other social scientists who have conducted recent fieldwork. Information percolating through the community is as important to the household economy as the looms used to weave. Information gathering on foreign markets, governments' immigration policies, and who just got back is a constant activity because of the daily, even hourly, updates in such information.

To give a brief example of the proprietary nature of information connected to transnational activities and contacts, when I asked José, the young Otavalan I had met on the streets of Manhattan, why his companion suddenly fled, he explained that he did not know or care, because they had met at the end of the day to take the train back to Queens but were not particularly close. Furthermore, José and his friend never shared information about where the selling had been good—José has a "secret" selling place near a mall in New Jersey. On weekends, the two do play together in a folkloric musical group—not so much for the money as to meet American women.

Back in Ecuador, households hoping to start their own cottage industry with an initial stint abroad seek trusted foreigners as friends, commercial buyers, or fictive kin. In this respect, the local tourist trade takes on an added significance beyond net profits; it is the entrance point into a vast array of external social networks via local visitors, whether tourists, wholesale buyers, or social scientists, though crossing the threshold from the buyer-seller relationship to more nebulous reciprocal relations requires prudence on the part of the Otavalan comerciante. Sometimes these visitors simply provide information regarding their buying preferences or about their own country and hometown, or they are called upon to offer more direct assistance, such as a letter to the U.S. embassy inviting an Otavalan "cultural group." Similarly, in the case of music, there is also a perennial need to form groups, which entails ethnie-wide networking as most musical groups are formed anew each off-season.

Second, the foregoing also means that the social process of transnational migration from Otavalo is more selective, across households and communities, than labor migration from Azuay. Communities such as Peguche have the dual advantage of a longer history of contact with foreigners, including dominance of the selling stalls in the Poncho Plaza, and also a greater ease or facility in making such contacts, in part, helped by somewhat greater levels of formal education. Thus, while a new generation of would-be comerciantes must make their own way, young adults from Peguche have been socialized for such a challenge; these social skills are every bit as important as technical or artistic skills related to handicraft production or playing music. For other communities arriving late to the export economy, such as Guanansi, these are advantages of social and human capital that cannot be overcome by simply borrowing more financial capital to hire a migration merchant, as with Azuayan transnational migration.

Although I had made several short visits to Otavalo over a two-year period, I found few clues to the "backstage" of Otavalan community life in the urban tourist market, which is confined to one plaza in Otavalo and a few side streets. Mary Crabb's (1993) study of tourism in Otavalo confirms and explains this physical and social distance: unlike "ethnic" tourism to other regions, Otavalans sell "native" handicrafts but, for the most part, do not include their own communities as objects of touristic interest. To be sure, one can find excursions to see "native villages," and a weekly air-conditioned tourist bus from Quito rumbles through the streets of Peguche. But considering the large numbers of tourists that flock to the official Saturday market, there is little "ethnic tourism." The reasons for this are multiple, but one stands out: the illusion of the colorful "handicraft" market in Otavalo, where Otavalans in clean, traditional garb placidly vend, may be deflated by the reality of community life buzzing with industrial activity, including electric looms.

Understanding and even describing the origins of transnational migration in Otavalo is a more complex task than in Azuay, but for a revealing reason useful for our regional comparison. It is made complex by the nature of transnational migration itself; instead of the development of an emerging "network of networks" of migrants, such as Ecuadorian labor migrants' concentrating in New York City, Otavalan transnational migration is composed of thousands of kin-based networks that connect a wide range of locales around the world. Not only are there more "doors" through which to enter into transnational migration networks, they are also more difficult to unlock in some ways but not in others. The long tradition, and now even greater need, for incorporating foreigners into local society means that foreign researchers who are not just passing through typically do not have difficulty establishing close relationships with Otavalans; yet, those relationships are often formally deferential, rarely veering from proscribed behavior on both sides. Very soon after arriving in Otavalo to begin several months of survey research there, I was invited by a North American anthropologist to be the *compadre* (godfather) to a wedding of two teenage Otavalans from Peguche; she was the godmother.

The family of the groom had several electric looms to make sweaters and supplemented family labor by hiring weavers and helpers. This, however, was not one of the larger workshops in Peguche but was rather modest; they mostly sold to other merchant relatives who could market their sweaters locally and abroad. The three sons were all young adults having a tough time establishing independent households and workshops. Among the extended family, both real and fictive, there were highly successful merchant-weavers from distinguished families as well as young men who had already traveled abroad making music. The father of the groom, in fact, had spent a short period in the 1970s working for other Otavalans in Spain, where there has developed a small Otavalan colony.

Within days, I was part (a very specific part) of this Peguche family, with obligations and roles to play. As part of the five-day ceremony, the godmother and I, at the specified time, "advised" the *ahijados* (godchildren) on how to treat one another. My first reaction was to remark how warmly we were welcomed into this group, especially in contrast with the reception we received from the poker-faced market vendors. Yet, the reciprocal, almost businesslike nature of my relationship with the family was made clear through the various traditional rituals. At one point, when all of us had been drinking for a couple of days, the mother of the groom approached me, crying; she begged me to look after my new ahijados—specifically, help her sons go to the United States. Even later in the evening, while all of us were dancing to an electrified mestizo band, I began to be physically pulled in opposite directions, with the mother of the groom on one arm and a woman I had met from a poorer, neighboring village on the other, who also wanted me to be the compadre to her son's upcoming wedding; I was now in demand as a compadre. As Anibel Buitrón observed nearly fifty years ago, "Indians rarely go near civil or religious authorities to solve their problems. They always use a white intermediary. To find an intermediary the Indian seeks the most appropriate person and makes him a godfather to a baptism of his child. The godparents of a baptism are always white" (1947, 61). Today, the purpose is similar. However, it is not so much problems in the local society that must be negotiated though as the national societies and market economies of several countries.

With these criteria, other wealthy Otavalan merchants with social ties to buyers in Canada or Chile are now sought in addition to local whites or foreigners. The household survey findings show that 259 baptisms in Peguche had white godparents (27 percent) while in 28 the godparents were foreigners (3 percent). Yet, a significant number of godparents were other Otavalans (family and friends) living in other communities or in Otavalo or Quito (23 percent), a sign that they are probably upwardly mobile. Thus, while *compadrazgo* (godfathership), a vehicle for the active networking by Otavalans, plays a similar role in mediating between the household and the external society, the institution has now been pressed into the service of the handicraft boom. With more and more Otavalan households attempting to join the export trade, sympathetic outsiders who are not just "passing through" are regarded in almost proprietary terms; though we were in New York City, thousands of miles away, the young man from Peguche told me, "Don't tell your compadres that I talked to you or they will be angry [at me]."

With my local credentials firmly established as a compadre, I was able to talk freely with some younger family members and friends who tended to be less formal, including an important member of a well-traveled musical group. I quickly developed a dual identity among the Otavalans I met through the large wedding party: I was a compadre, a title I was now afforded by even distant family members, but I was also a young adult male who had recorded folkloric music in Cuenca and had traveled playing music in the United States and Europe. Just as in Azuay, my identity as a male musician opened some doors and closed others. My ability to have long conversations with Otavalan women, with or without others present, was even more limited than in Azuay. On the other hand, I was able to develop a rapport with several Otavalan musicians who had traveled to North America and Europe and were planning their upcoming trips. Fortunately, apart from the survey research, this was the group in Peguche I was most interested in understanding because they were part of a more recent migration phenomenon akin to the mass labor migration from Azuay.

Pedro, a twenty-six-year-old from Peguche dressed in blue jeans and tennis shoes, had already traveled more widely than most Americans will in a lifetime, and he became my principal informant, though the formality of that term does not convey the friendship we developed. His first trip abroad had been just three years earlier, in 1990, to play "Andean music" (primarily from Peru and Bolivia) in the streets of Holland and to sell handicrafts made at his uncle's workshop, where he has worked as a weaver for several years. Although the trip was successful, the market in many European cities was already saturated by other Otavalans who had come before them. Since Holland and Belgium did not require a visa for entry at that time, they were popular European entry points for Otavalans. Pedro explained that he knew which cities and festivals he wanted to play in the United States but could not tell any of his friends who were part of other musical groups. It seems that there is an inelasticity of demand for Andean music played by indigenous folkloric groups; Pedro told me that it is more profitable to find virgin territory unaccustomed to seeing long-haired "Indians" playing exotic music. The guarding of such market information, which includes both profitability and foreign hospitality, is a real concern, since a lucrative location one year (e.g., in front of the Sheraton in Seattle) can bring a handful of Otavalan groups the following year. Otavalan groups must also "compete" with other Andean musical groups from Bolivia, Chile, or Peru, who are also playing on the streets.

While he is abroad, Pedro's wife, Rosa, remains behind to tend to their two children and the family and communal fields and, most importantly, to help weave the handicrafts that Pedro sells abroad under the guidance of Pedro's uncle. Pedro's selling trips would not have been possible without those at home continuing to produce and send him new shipments of handicrafts as needed. The year after his first trip in Europe, his group decided to try the relatively virgin markets of the United States. Pedro was successful in obtaining a five-year American tourist visa. Other members were not so fortunate and had to seek out other groups returning to Europe. Avoiding New York City, where Otavalans are so conspicuous they have made the front page of the *New York Times,* Pedro and his group flew directly to Los Angeles to try the West Coast. The group played from Seattle down to New Mexico, including participation in the annual "Gathering of Nations Pow-Wow" in Albuquerque. It was not uncommon for the group to make $300 a day from tips and the selling of cassette tapes. The eight-month trip was so successful that upon his return Pedro was able to buy a new car.

In a somewhat bizarre but revealing situation, I mistook one of Pedro's group members who had attended the wedding party for a Peguche local. "Bobby," a Canadian who sported long hair and blended credibly in among his Otavalan companions, had played guitar with Pedro's group for two years, after playing in reggae and folk bands on and off the streets of Canada and the United States. Bobby had "returned" to Peguche with the rest of the group for the off-season, December through March, and had even adopted many aspects of quotidian community life, including bathing in the ice-cold river and having his long hair combed and braided by a female "family" member. According to Bobby, his initial motives for joining the group were financial; Otavalan groups were doing well. From the Otavalans' perspective, Bobby offered not only his considerable talent as a guitar player but also his insider's knowledge of North America, a vast region of untapped potential for Otavalan musicians: Bobby knew the market for street music and could act as a cultural liaison between the group and North American society.

Pedro's trip back to Los Angeles later that year was not so successful. After only one month, the group was caught by the INS selling tapes illegally on the streets of Albuquerque and was deported to Ecuador; Bobby returned to Canada. Now that I was back in the United States, the family turned to me to fix his problems with *la migra* in the United States, especially the return of his passport, which had a five-year stamp to travel to the United States. With help from my brother-in-law, an attorney, we tried for one year, unsuccessfully, to retrieve the passport, which had gotten lost on its way to Quito. To Pedro, this seemed like the end of his dream to save enough money to start his own weaving workshop. It now meant he would have to sell in the less profitable European markets. Others are starting to talk about the untapped opportunities of Asia. Within six months of his deportation, Pedro and a cousin had already set out for a six-week selling trip to Chile.

Although performing folkloric music abroad is a recent activity, for the young adults of Peguche it represents both an economic and cultural continuity with the commercial activities of several generations. In contrast, for the community of Guanansi, there is no such history.

The economic and social development patterns of Peguche and Guanansi differed before present-day international economic migration developed. Buitrón's early assessment of several Otavalan communities in the 1940s clearly shows the socioeconomic diversity of the region. Compare his descriptions of Peguche and La Bolsa, the neighboring yanapa community to Guanansi:

> *Peguche:* Weavers of chalinas, ponchos, and cashmeres [English tweed]. They work their own land (low altitude). . . . They are the wealthiest and most industrious Indians and have most identified with national life and culture. Most speak Spanish and know how to read and write. Some of them continually travel within and outside of the country. They have close contact with the white and mestizo population of Otavalo.

> *La Bolsa:* Weavers of ponchos and chalinas. They work their own land (low altitude). . . . Nearly all are "yanaperos" [tenant farmers] of the hacienda Quinchuquí since they have usufruct rights to its water and land. Very little contact with the white and mestizo population of Otavalo. (1947, 48)

For Buitrón, "progressive" communities such as Peguche were different from their neighbors not just in their level of industrialization but also in their level of contact with the dominant society, leading to a more confident stance vis-à-vis whites (ibid., 61). Because of this divergence, in the narrow area of economic and technological innovation, we can say that a Peguche elite developed specific sociocultural values compatible with the national society, values different from those of its more conservative, agricultural neighbors.

More important the informal economy of growth in Peguche and a handful of other villages has reproduced long-standing social hierarchies not easily reduced to the material terms of loom ownership. The status of truly independent indios libres has given the Otavalan elite from Peguche a range of resources that cannot be purchased on an open market—resources such as a dense web of personal and business contacts outside of the community.

While several social scientists have recognized the diverse socioeconomic levels among Otavalan households and parcialidades, their analyses have been focused primarily on characteristics of land tenure in materialistic terms, such as the size, quality, and altitude of the plots (Buitrón 1947; Salomon 1981). They argue that it has been the lower-altitude, more fertile communities that have been able to afford craft materials needed to be independent weavers. However, it would be difficult to make land the master variable, since some of the poorest communities are the lowest in altitude; however, they were made up of yanaperos working hacienda lands. It is also a circular argument: they have good land because they are wealthy, they are wealthy because they have good land. What is missing is the important historical link to external elites who benefited economically and ideologically from a socially divided region. The social divide is deeper than simply wealthy Otavalans versus poor Otavalans; their historical relationships to regional economic and political elites produced parallel worldviews and social structures hidden beneath a common cultural profile. The differing histories of Peguche and Guanansi have demonstrated this.

The comparative openness of some of Peguche's successful merchant-weavers to potentially beneficial outsiders has formed the basis for the antithesis to a "cycle of poverty"; inordinate attention and interest by foreign researchers and activists have been given to Peguche and its inhabitants precisely because they are, comparatively speaking, militantly cooperative (though not indiscriminately so), whether the foreigner is a Peace Corps worker, an anthropologist, or a Mormon proselyte. Thus, external resources and ideas have more easily flowed to Peguche's alert entrepreneurial comerciantes. Fortunately, as land was becoming more scarce around the turn of the century, a nascent Peguche merchant class was politically and technologically able to find a market niche in specialty woven items and, later, touristic handicrafts, greatly aided by their independence from the hacienda milieu. In this sense, even before the onset of transnational migration, elite merchant-weavers from Peguche were moving beyond mere economic subsistence in the classic peasant sense, with its ambiguous class structure and ideology, and were fully engaged in capital accumulation.

In contrast with Peguche, which has been at the center of political, social, and technological innovations for five centuries; Guanansi has remained very much marginal to the ethnic handicraft economy, though it has recently and dramatically attained independence from the hacienda and, with it, the possibility of joining the export boom of cultural commodities. The Otavalan handicraft industry requires of its independent household producers at least three things: skill, capital, and social networks with links to a range of markets. The skills required for weaving and music making have been gained by a process of technological diffusion; the weaving and selling of sweaters and tapestries are recent introductions to Guanansi by former laborers in Peguche workshops. Thus, skills gained by older boys working for wages in Peguche are now being put to use in independent household workshops in Guanansi. In this way, others from Guanansi are now learning the set of skills needed from family members and co-villagers. These economic ties to Peguche were reinforced through recent intermarriage, a practice that was not allowed by village leaders until recently. In other words, the weaving and handicraft trade practiced in some Otavalan villages for centuries is now being slowly diffused to even the most agricultural villages. However, without electricity Guanansi has not been able to bring the latest industrialized technologies to bear on production and, therefore, has been at a severe disadvantage in the marketplace.

In the case of music, skills are learned by a combination of trial and error, hiring or cajoling an older "master" as teacher, and frequenting the *peña* bars in Otavalo, where folkloric Andean music is played by Otavalans and other visiting Andean musical groups. It is also not uncommon to see teenage boys starting and stopping a cassette tape as they attempt to mimic the preceding musical phrase on their instruments. Learning a musical instrument and the basic commercial repertoire (a limited mix of Otavalan and southern Andean music) is less time-consuming than acquiring the range of complex weaving skills. One young man from Guanansi had begun to learn both the *sampoña* (pan flute) and the charango in hopes of traveling to Italy the following year. His rationale for learning two instruments simultaneously was that group members were more likely to think he had talent if he played two instruments and, therefore, would invite him abroad—the chance of a lifetime.

With sufficient skills and a moderate amount of savings to buy a wooden loom and other materials, a household can join the cottage industry. However, as we have seen in Azuay and in Otavalo, much of the profit is made in the exchanges that occur along the way from "cottage" to First World consumer. In addition, production technology in the region has become more industrialized and, thus, capital-intensive. Guanansi households, still awaiting electricity and reliant on middlemen to market their crafts, were in desperate need of an infusion of capital for infrastructure. Their current roles as either agricultural or workshop laborers were unacceptable to the people of the village, since they implied not only a lack of independence, in which they took great pride, but specifically dependence on their traditional rivals across the Pan-American Highway. Thus, ambitious Guanansi leaders, led by the energetic thirty-five-year-old Ricardo, developed a plan; they would build a community center that would aid in state-of-the-art production (approaching a factory setting) and, at the same time, provide a location to receive foreign tourists and wholesalers.

In the early 1990s, a Peace Corps worker was instrumental in helping the community gain funding to build such a community center. By 1993, most of the two-story structure had been completed. Plans for the community house are as ambitious as any in Peguche: as the community leader looked down from his unfinished office on the second floor, which has a spectacular view of the valley and Mount Cotacachi, he was proud to point out where the electric weaving machines would be located. The bottom floor was used as a traditional meeting place, while the top floor was being transformed into a small factory, including a collection of wooden looms, electric sewing machines, and a fax machine—though neither electricity nor telephone lines had arrived yet to the village, community leaders were ready to hit the ground running when they did arrive. Of special pride to my host were two boxlike concrete structures adjacent to the small dirt parking lot (though none of the villagers owns a vehicle; he explained that foreigners require flush toilets, not cornfields. Ricardo asked me to find out, on my next trip back to Quito, how he could get a grant from a development foundation for start-up capital for the community house project, especially a cultural display room and library for visitors.

Because the community house is associated with the agricultural cooperative, several households not belonging to the cooperative are also excluded from the planned commercial handicraft venture. Hence, while Ricardo, the leader of the cooperative, has traveled abroad and has plans to do so in the future, thus far most migrants leaving Guanansi have been precisely those excluded from the cooperative. Most of these Guanansi migrants, however, travel back and forth across the Colombian border on small selling trips. Three have traveled to Europe.

The contact and ease of interaction with outsiders on the part of some of the young leaders, leading to important extralocal social networks such as those with Peace Corps volunteers, has been possible because of formal schooling and the political mobilizations of several years earlier—not just the human capital of learning to read and write Spanish but also the social networks made available by such education. The leader of the community house and cooperative, Ricardo, was also one of the principal organizers of the uprising and expropriation of hacienda lands, bringing him into contact with a range of indigenous, mestizo, and foreign sympathizers and activists. Not surprisingly, Ricardo was the first from Guanansi to travel beyond Colombia. He traveled to Germany in 1991 to demonstrate weaving and Andean music at the invitation of a German handicraft association. He could be called the Rosa Lema of Guanansi, though pioneering a somewhat more cooperative path of export-led development rather than the household competition found among the merchant class in Peguche.

Yet, while Rosa Lema was empowered by her "noble" background within Peguche, Ricardo was empowered by a sort of symbolic capital based not on nobility but rather on cultural authenticity. Ricardo had also formed a musical group of mostly family members. After returning to the United States, I received a letter from Ricardo's group, complete with customized letterhead, seeking my help in obtaining a U.S. cultural visa. The letter "reminded" me that they "are the true representatives of Otavalan culture." In a region selling cultural commodities, moral claims to "authenticity" become a comparative economic advantage. Community members, who are primarily full-time farmers, derive much of their moral authority in issues of authenticity from their continuing connection to the land; land is at the center of the Otavalan sociocultural universe, a fact that even the most successful middlemen merchants in Peguche would readily admit. Thus, would-be merchant-weavers from Guanansi have found an opening into the ethnic economy.

The emerging entrepreneurial activities of Guanansi are also aided by the cultural capital of wider group membership. With the exception of foreign wholesalers, whether a sweater is made in Guanansi or Peguche is of little concern to outsiders, only that it is "Otavalan," or, more specifically, "handmade by Indians." The significance of this sort of coethnic public good for Guanansi is best underscored by examining a neighboring, though non-Otavalan, indigenous group living just on the other side of San Pablo Lake. They, too, were peasants working on hacienda lands with a nearly identical lifestyle and standard of living as that found in Guanansi. However, the only development projects introduced in the region are in the areas of public health and infrastructure (latrines), not the marketing of handicrafts and music in European plazas. The principal difference between Guanansi and the neighboring community of Angla is the cultural capital of group identity and membership in a "miracle" indigenous group.

A Household Perspective on Transnational Merchant Migration

Examining the results of the household survey, we lose some of the narrative richness but are compensated with a more generalizable and comparable analysis of transnational migration from Peguche and Guanansi. Regarding the spatial patterning of the onset of transnational migration in the two Otavalan research sites, with the Peguche data we are able to analyze the percentage of adult migration within each of the seven neighborhoods; all seven barrios have similar levels of transnational migration, ranging from 20 percent in two of the barrios to 34 percent in another. Thus, although we are not able to map household clusters of transnational migration as we did with Azuayan villages, we can conclude that none of the Peguche barrios is "shut out" from transnational migration.

Similar overall levels of transnational migration, however, by barrio do not reveal the composition of transnational migration regarding economic activities abroad (i.e., selling artesanía or making music). Music making has been seen as a temporary strategy to make enough capital to enter the more lucrative handicraft trade. A cross-tabulation of the type of activity abroad by barrio reveals that some barrios send more musicians per migrant household than others. It is noteworthy that the newest barrio, Provivienda, is sending the most *musicians* abroad, while the more established barrios in the center of the community are sending comparatively fewer.

Music making is also useful for opening new markets less amenable to selling items on the street, especially in North America and Europe, where street peddling is not always condoned and is sometimes done at considerable risk. The commercial nature of musicians playing exotic instruments is more ambiguous and somewhat less offensive to state authorities, though Otavalan musicians have been deported home for it, as in the case of Pedro. Music making, whether by itself or supplemented with handicraft sales, is a prominent activity among those going to North America and, especially, Europe. In this respect, the strategy of music making exploits the lucrative markets of the

First World, not just for compelling economic reasons but also because it is there that their cultural exoticism can be commodified. As Bobby, the Canadian "Otalavan," explained, "We don't mind overcharging people when they hire us for special occasions because they view us as cute little brown people." In Guanansi, similar to Azuay, there is a spatial clustering of households sending migrants abroad, mostly to Colombia. This corroborates the qualitative data, which found a village divided by cooperative membership and, therefore, by households and families, not by individuals. With the exception of Ricardo, most of the migrant households do not belong to the cooperative. Few households have sent migrants to Europe, and none has sent members to North America. Although the type of migration to Colombia and Europe is different from the labor migration found in Azuay, we find a similar nonrandom, social patterning of transnational migration, pointing to its underlying social process.

As in Azuay, an important aspect of the social process of transnational migration is how it is financed. In the case of Otavalo, however, the legality of the trip itself presents little need for the elaborate system of migration merchants in Azuay. Transnational migration from Peguche is largely financed by personal savings and the travel agency from which the airline ticket is purchased. It is also significant that some migrants are able to obtain bank loans, a fact indicating both their business reputation and the linkage between the informal and formal economies in Otavalo. Another interesting feature is that travel agency financing seems to be increasing with more household transnational migration. This makes sense given the ability of a son to obtain credit based on his father's (or family's) reputation and collateral. In Guanansi, most migrants use personal savings, since crossing the Colombian border by bus is relatively inexpensive. Given Guanansi's historical remoteness from urban life, it is significant that migrants traveling to Europe were still able to obtain formal financing through a bank and travel agency.

In describing the development of household transnational social structures from Peguche, the household survey data is somewhat limited in capturing its totality, since some Peguche households have now moved permanently to Otavalo or Quito. Yet, there is no indication that many families have completely abandoned their Peguche homes altogether; rather, most families seem to maintain a sort of dual residence, with some family members, such as grown children, living in Otavalo and others remaining in Peguche. Nonetheless, we must recognize that our survey may be missing this segment of the population. On the other hand, I have purposively excluded the mestizo families from the following analyses; we should note, however, that the

**Table 6.1. Presence of Cottage Industry in Migrant Households,
by Village, 1993 (percentage)**

Number of Migrants in Household	Households with No Cottage Industry	Households with Cottage Industry, with No Employees	Households with Cottage Industry, with Employees
Peguche[a]			
n	72	179	99
0	66.7	61.4	37.4
1	19.4	22.9	31.1
2	9.7	11.7	19.2
3+	4.2	3.9	12.1
Guanansi			
n	20	22	7
0	80.0	77.3	57.1
1+	20.0	22.7	42.8

Source: Adult study data, 1993.
[a] For columns 2 and 3, Cramer $V = .192$**.

household survey reveals that none of the mestizos living in Peguche has ever traveled abroad nor is engaged in cottage craft industry.

Of prime interest is the nature of the relationship of household transnational migration to commercial handicraft production and, in the case of Guanansi, commercial agriculture. Greater household migration levels are strongly associated with handicraft production using cottage industry, as we see in table 6.1. Furthermore, higher levels of household migration are also associated with an emerging bourgeoisie as evidenced by their greater use of wage laborers and increased numbers of employees. In Guanansi, we find that migrant households are overwhelmingly engaged primarily in cottage industry, with a few even using wage laborers.

Building on our previous findings, we find that migrant households are more likely to be engaged not only in the production of handicrafts but also in their direct marketing as middlemen. The problem with examining the middleman status, loom ownership, and use of employees is that our cross-sectional data do not allow for causal analyses, since we do not know the causal direction, if any. Yet, having a selling stall in Otavalo is a different matter, in that most of them have been retained by the original families to which they were granted in 1973. Indeed, maintaining a stall in Otavalo is associated with greater household transnational migration in both communities.

In Guanansi the agricultural cooperative has socially and economically divided the community. Most transnational travel from Guanansi to Colombia is largely composed of those who were excluded from the cooperative. From both the quantitative and qualitative data presented so far, we can see that there are essentially two groups with two economic strategies in Guanansi. The first group, composed of cooperative members, dedicate nearly all of their time to agricultural production and domestic chores. The charismatic leaders of this group, however, are attempting to use this base of resources to enter into the handicraft trade at its most industrialized and developed phase (i.e., the factory-style "community house"). The second group, excluded or unwilling to join the cooperative, have turned to handicraft production and marketing as best they can, using older technologies and the tried-and-true markets of Otavalo and nearby Colombia. Some simply buy their sweaters in Otavalo (having already passed through one intermediary) and sell them in Colombia, where they "are treated better than in Ecuador." As one can imagine in such a small community, the acrimony from such a community division is palpable; one family from the second group told me of their intention to completely move to Colombia because they could more efficiently weave and sell in the same place and because they could not withstand village life anymore.

In either Peguche or Guanansi, the desire for more land was nearly uniform among migrant and nonmigrant households in the survey. What is noteworthy is the difference in the desire for more land between the two villages. Although it is not a surprising finding, Peguche villagers are clearly desperate for more land, as they have been for decades. My six research assistants from Peguche were unanimous in their lack of faith that they would one day own their own plot of land in Peguche. Although Guanansi has sufficient land for now as a community, it is land that has become politicized and lacks the stability of household ownership and the ability to be handed down to the next generation. Thus, a substantial percentage from Guanansi, though lower than that from Peguche, would still like more land.

Transnational migration from these Otavalan communities does not entail the complete abandonment of farming their small plots but rather the use of paid laborers (*jornaleros*) to work their lands when necessary. The maintenance of the growing cycle is as much symbolic as economic in Peguche households, especially the growing of corn. A household must have corn and animals for both everyday reciprocal exchanges and, above all, for special celebrations. Thus, corn is still a sort of currency in Peguche, though wallets may not only contain Ecuadorian sucres but also German marks, Italian lira, and U.S. dollars. Viewed from a different angle, the transnational social structures are able to evolve as long as traditional activities can be commodified in a politically stable manner.

Turning to the material conditions of the emerging transnational social structures, we see a pattern similar to that of Azuay: migrant households are more likely to own more household consumer goods, a car, and a multistory house. In other words, migrants are considerably more wealthy than their nonmigrant counterparts. In some ways, this is not as obvious a finding as one would think, for two reasons: first, wealth is not generally flaunted in the construction of extravagant and exotic-looking houses as in Azuay; second, Peguche, unlike Azuayan communities, is literally buzzing with industry. That is, while one sees cars and other consumer items in Peguche homes, there is not an obvious relationship between their ownership and migration per se, as in the case of Azuay. Nonetheless, the data clearly show that transnational migration and the direct marketing it entails is quite profitable.

Transnational Social Structures and Social Change

Just as in Azuay, one of the new social formations arising from ever greater levels of transnational migration is what I have called the "transnational social structures," as opposed to the more diffuse, nation-based concept of a "transnational community." A feature of Azuayan transnational migration and the formation of transnational social structures is that even though households join the transnational social structures at different times and in somewhat different ways, there is a more or less common experience of adaptation to New York City, or a handful of other locations, reinforced by the advantages of mutual aid abroad from fellow villagers, or *paisanos.*

The entrepreneurial transnational migration of the Otavalan ethnic economy has engendered transnational social structures that differ from Azuayan transnational social structures in two ways. First, households and kinship groups in the same home community develop fairly distinct transnational social structures; neighboring households in Peguche or Guanansi may be in constant contact with family members not only in different countries but in different continents. Second, Otavalan transnational social structures are more fluid constructions that may change from year to year yet are firmly anchored in the "home base" of the sending household. To be sure, colonies of Otavalans have formed in Bogotá, Madrid, and New York City. However, long-term stays in one location by the same individual seem to be uncommon. A more common strategy for providing a stable base of operations is to rent a house or apartment abroad and have it manned by various family members and associates as they cycle back and forth. Appropriate to this strategy, many young sellers and musicians simply buy a van in which they can both travel and live, punctuated by hotel stays or the hospitality of sympathetic admirers (such as women with romantic interests).

Although we have seen few parallels between the social construction of transnational migration in Azuay and that of Otavalo given their different strategies, both have developed transnational social structures deeply embedded in, and facilitated by, gender stratification. While Parsons implies that Otavalan women are never bossed around by their husbands (1945, 10), it is also clear from her ethnography that women are beholden to their husbands and have a multitude of household chores to complete. The preexisting gender stratification in Otavalo, as in Azuay, has allowed the development of transnational social structures in which the men do most of the "adventuring." Once again, the women are expected and required to maintain the home as the economic and cultural foundation of the household. Aside from their material contribution to household production, which is great, two examples of the rôle of women in the emerging transnational social structures are also evident: first, the expectation that they will maintain the cultural anchor of the group's identity, and, second, the expectation that they will accept the "adventures" of their boyfriends and husbands as they establish romantic liaisons with gringas, both in Otavalo and while abroad.

With the exception of their long hair, middle-aged and young men have increasingly stopped wearing full traditional garb (*traje*); women have largely continued to wear the complete costume. Even the long hair worn by men takes on a new meaning in the transnational context, denoting both "primitive" and "hip." According to survey data, migration abroad clearly diminishes the daily use of the full traje in both men and women, but especially men. Are women naturally more "traditional" than men? In Otavalo, where cultural identity is of economic importance, there is an especially strong pressure for the women not to adopt Western dress. As one informant put it, "If the women didn't wear the traditional costume, we would be just like mestizos." To be sure, some younger women have taken to modifying their dress in subtle ways, such as wearing different hairstyles. A more obvious change has been the use of designer jackets instead of the *fachalinas,* or shawls, worn over the rest of the traditional dress. However, even at large parties of young adults in Peguche, which can look and sound like a scene from an MTV dance party, it is striking to seeing the fashionable and affluent young men dancing with women in full traditional regalia. Of course, the same phenomenon can be observed among other indigenous groups, where the men are typically the first to use more Western dress styles, such as the Cuna of Panama.

Similarly, to understand the frequent sexual encounters and longer relationships developed between young Otavalan men and foreign women, known as gringas, one must focus on gender stratification in Otavalan households. As Lynn Meisch observes (1995), and my fieldwork corroborates, these are not simply romantic adventures for the Otavalans, especially musicians; it is an economic opportunity. While the foreign women may see in the face of the "Indian" the noblesse of innocence past, some Otavalans see not only the ultimate transnational "prize" but also literally a free lunch and, possibly, a place to stay while abroad. Otavalans are so successful at "winning" gringas that there is now the prospect of a sort of cultural free-riding by local mestizos posing as Otavalans. If this description sounds harsh, it is only because we are unaccustomed to seeing indigenous people as anything but victims of First World exploitation and destruction (ibid.). This is clearly not the case with the Otavalans, who will sometimes lie about their marital status back home. Stories abound in Otavalo of gringas who have lost not only their hearts but also their pocketbooks to a young Otavaleño. One young German women, whom I met at a Peguche wedding party of a wealthy family, explained how she had been duped into providing room and board at home for an Otavalan who had lied about his marital status, a revelation precipitated after she had bought airline tickets for both to go to Ecuador. She decided to go ahead and use the ticket to Ecuador anyway so she could see "where he came from." "Besides, this is my only luxury [to travel], he has better clothes than I do and even a car which I don't own—I would warn them (looking at the five or six gringas dancing with Otavalans) never trust an Otavalan." If the German woman was feeling heartbroken and conned, his Otavalan wife must endure the pain of encountering adventurous gringas, in her own community—a sort of side effect of the wider transnational social field. Rosa Lema, in her day, did not have to put up with gringas.

In sum, the "subsidization" of the household economy and facilitation of foreign travel by wooing and "scamming" foreign women would probably not be tolerated under conditions of greater gender equality within Otavalan households. As more and more young women are also traveling to sell or to attend universities, it is difficult to predict whether the evolving political economy of transnational households will ultimately alter gender relations toward greater equality or greater conflict. Meanwhile, the gendered division of economic and cultural labor on which the transnational social structures is built shows no signs of weakening: when I met several young Otavalan women at the Indian Cultural Center in Manhattan, where they were preparing to celebrate the Incan "Inti-Raymi" that evening, they emphasized that selling artesanía was secondary to their mission as cultural representatives.

There is much confusion over the nature of cultural change among Otavalans as they become more integrated economically and socially with urban society. Specifically, I want to reexamine the oft-repeated truism that Otavalans have retained "their culture" in the face of modernization and industrialization. Touristic, and even some scholarly, publications have long implied that Otavalans have managed to change their economic and political statuses with little or no cultural assimilation. Not only are they admired because of this fact, it has been viewed as the social foundation of their economic independence and overall cultural tenacity. However, one question arises that is generally not asked in this regard: which Otavalans are we referring to, those historically tied to the haciendas or those tied to the looms and, thus, external markets? As late as the mid-1980s, professional observers could always point to the Otavalans' nearly uniform traditional dress, which made them look like "penguins," in the words of an American hotel owner in Otavalo. Furthermore, there were no (obvious) signs that the use of Quichua was diminishing even in the face of education and jet travel; in fact, there had been a self-conscious cultural renaissance among the educated economic elite of Peguche and Otavalo (Korovkin 1998).

Whatever the level and nature of cultural change in the past, today there are obvious, though ambiguous, signs of acculturation, especially among the younger generation. In fact, if postmodern culture has arrived anywhere it has arrived in Otavalo, with its mix of indígenas aping foreigners and foreigners aping indígenas, all coming together at the local Hard Rock Café, which fronts the Poncho Plaza (the café is reportedly no longer there). Alongside an elderly woman wearing a traditional costume that has changed little in centuries stands her grandson dressed in the latest European or North American fashions, including earrings and designer tennis shoes. The reason these outward cultural changes are somewhat ambiguous in their indication of cultural change is that many of the young men sporting a "hip" look bought their clothing on trips in which they were either selling "native handicrafts" or making "Andean music." In addition, they are adamant that they would never cut their hair, a traditional social marker of indígena status within the local and national contexts.

Peguche households, whether engaged in migration or not, are far from being closed social groups. Most of those surveyed would not object to a son or daughter marrying a foreigner; in fact, a few young men in the village have done precisely that, marrying Dutch, Spanish, American, and Japanese women, also attesting to the fact that not all Otavalan men treat foreign women as disposable. Nonetheless, it has been the foreign women who have conformed to Otavalan life, some even adopting the traditional female costume of the Otavaleña. The principal point here is that there is no great sanction against those who want to adopt nontraditional lifestyles as long as they maintain respect for some of the core values and mores. I suspect that this does not represent a significant change for Peguche and is indicative of its historical pragmatism.

In contrast, the nature of socialization in Peguche for the current generation now coming of age has been profoundly altered by several factors, including temporary migration of one or both parents, the reorganization of household production to include wage laborers, and greater levels of formal education. It was, in fact, the parents of the current generation of young adults who first began to make small changes in clothing styles, to travel widely to Europe and North America, and to have some formal schooling. As one of the young musicians explained: "It's our parents fault—they didn't teach us all of the traditions." As part of this study, I convened a group of ten migrants to discuss their experiences abroad and community life back home. It was clear that there was a generation gap between the middle-aged and younger teenage migrants; the older migrants could not understand how the younger ones could "lose their culture" and not wear the traditional hat or sandals; for their part, the younger migrants blamed their older brothers and fathers for not teaching them, or for not being around to teach them, and for increasing "greed." Nearly all at the table agreed that the popularity of such musical groups as Charijayak, with their Western style and economic success, has generated a lot of envy and, thus, desire to mimic them. Common replies to the open-ended household survey question regarding their view of return migrants were that they were "changed," "proud of themselves," and "egotistical."

Of course, part of the change in the socialization process toward greater individualism, probably unnoticeable at first, was the greater emphasis and dependence on urban life. Since land has been the traditional centerpiece of community membership, it is one's relation and proximity to the rural community and agriculture that forms the primary yardstick for cultural "authenticity," no matter what style of dress is used. For Guanansi migrants, Peguche's success in commerce and industry and failure to retain traditional rituals and clothing is a sign of cultural denial; among Peguche migrants, those who have moved to Otavalo or Quito are referred to as "indios plásticos" or "indios 2000." A Peguche community member wrote the following scathing critique, entitled "Los Indios Plásticos":

> It is no longer admirable to see a group of young indígenas wearing Nike's, blue jeans, Walkmen in their ears, and a empty "Canguro" bag covering the front part of their belt, asking about places to dance "rap music," plus using hippie words, agreeing with "Okay"! These young people want to eat, more and more, hamburgers and hot dogs with French fries and Coca-Cola instead of the traditional lunch. They do not appreciate our own music and only want to play it when they drink in groups, not for its value, and even less for its message, but because they want to be the "hermosas" [beautiful people] of the "Kjarkas" [popular Andean musical group]. (Terán 1991, 20; translation is mine)

These urban styles and behaviors are viewed with ambiguity even by those engaging in them. Many feel like something is being lost, but at the same time, no young man is willing to be the only one wearing the full traditional garb, what may be considered, in another cultural context, as being "square." In sum, unlike previous periods in Otavalan history, the rise of transnational social structures in the current period, as Otavalans shuttle back and forth across time zones, has brought about increasing individualism and a debate within Peguche regarding the value of recent cultural changes.

Some of the superficial cultural changes, however, are more instrumental and calculated than simply a "bright lights" phenomenon. That is, they facilitate the economic activities in the region and abroad. For example, it is simply not practical to sell on European streets in November wearing straw sandals and knee-length cotton pants. Similarly, on some North American or European streets, sellers and musicians must be ready to close up shop (e.g., into a duffel bag) and meld into the crowd when police approach, something better accomplished wearing tennis shoes and a baseball cap.

The above provide examples of outward sociocultural changes more in line with the preexisting ideology of the merchant-weavers and the exigencies of operating industrial looms and selling or playing music on northern streets. Other cultural changes are occurring, however, that may ultimately affect the ethnic economy, especially Quichua usage. Without land and without the traditional dress, Quichua represents an important bastion of group identity and a common culture, and, therefore, a social resource. While anecdotal information from Peguche indicates that many have now begun to give their children Quichua names, a practice previously forbidden by the Catholic Church, the household survey data reveals that the level of household

Table 6.2. Language Spoken in Peguche Migrant Households, 1993 (percentage)

Number of Migrants in Household	n	Quichua	Quichua/Spanish	Spanish	Other
0	182	77.4	18.5	3.8	0.0
1	82	69.5	21.9	8.5	0.0
2	44	55.6	31.1	9.1	2.3
3+	21	42.7	38.1	19.0	0.0

Source: Household study data, 1993.

Note: Cramer $V = .157$**.

transnational migration has a clear impact on the level of everyday Quichua usage among household members (see table 6.2). Even among those households without migrants, nearly one-fourth speak Spanish part or all of the time. In addition, many young people speak Quichua with Spanish and foreign words mixed in. Unlike its influence on clothing styles, the impact of transnational migration on Quichua usage is an especially important change, which can go unnoticed by outsiders, who normally communicate in Spanish or a foreign language when conversing with Otavalans.

Instead of viewing these cultural changes as examples of the loss of native culture, I would argue that the strength of the independent weaving communities, such as Peguche, has always been their ability to adapt economically, politically, and culturally to their social environment when the need arises. Those Otavalans who have been most engaged in market activities are essentially pragmatists, the sine qua non of all entrepreneurs; they are now adapting to the reality of global marketing and the development of transnational social structures. Nonetheless, the recent economic strategy of music making abroad by young men does entail a subtle decoupling from household production and, with it, greater individualism and alienation, not unlike the labor migration of young men from the Azuayan communities. Concerning the classic sociological marker of individualism and alienation, a significant turning point for Peguche occurred in early 1993, when a young adult male hung himself after a fight with his father. It is precisely these sorts of sociocultural changes that members of the cooperative and community house in Guanansi hope to avoid as it enters into the booming ethnic economy.

Even within the Otavalan region, the development of transnational merchant migration is embedded in preexisting social structures, especially at the community level. Where Azuayan communities are culturally diverse and economically similar in their insertion into regional institutions and transnational social structures, the opposite is true of Otavalo. The socioeconomic and ideological differences between Guanansi and Peguche are nearly as great as those between Peguche and Tomebamba. These preexisting social structures have produced a more self-selective migration process than the Azuayan case, whereby there has been a fifty-year lag in the initiation of transnational migration between some neighboring villages. Nevertheless, communities such as Guanansi, until now largely left out of the ethnic economy, are attempting the same strategy that has produced an indigenous economic "miracle" in other communities.

Second, though the strategy for capital accumulation is different from that of a labor migration, merchant migration is also embedded within the historical ethnic economy. Far from being atomized actors, Otavalan weavers, merchants, and musicians depend very much on what other Otavalans have done before them and are currently doing. Group membership carries with it the possibility for social capital as a public good (Coleman 1990), though not necessarily in the form of direct aid, and also sets parameters on what is acceptable and what is not. For some fully engaged in transnational processes of capital accumulation, allowing members to remain a part of that community while changing the way they are structurally embedded in that community (e.g., by religious conversion, by moving to city) renders some group sanctions impotent.

Finally, commercial transnational migration from Otavalo has also led to the formation of transnational social structures as many aspects of its society have been transnationalized. Although they are more anchored in the home region than the transnational social structures of Azuay, we can see similar features, including economic and sociocultural adaptations to a personal world of people and foreign places. Ironically, while the attempts of Azuayan migrants to live in two places at the same time produce outwardly tragic consequences for predominantly young families, Otavalan migrants, who would never confuse Amsterdam with home, are more at risk for anomie and individualism as each must find his own street corner (and girlfriend) abroad.

The latest phase of the development of the Otavalan economy has been one of significant widening of household craft production and marketing and regional integration, both vertically within the region and horizontally around the globe. It has been a process closely tied to the intersection of class, ethnicity, and gender. Lynn Walter's analysis of Otavalan society in the 1970s clearly demonstrates the characteristics of an emerging ethnic economy. She summarizes her findings thus:

> The specific form of Otavaleño economic development: (1) Is weakening the boundaries of the closed corporate community. (2) Is heightening identification with the ethnic group. (3) Is creating class differences within the ethnic group. (4) Is challenging the non-Indian attitude that "Indian" means "lowest class." (5) Involves the Otavaleño in increased participation in the national economy and, to a lesser degree, in the dominant society. (6) Leads some Otavaleño to adopt elements of the dominant culture without "becoming white." (1981, 326–27)

The ethnic economy has matured in the past twenty years, expanding into wider areas of cultural commodification such as music making. Yet, the deepening of internal class relations and the development of far-reaching, diverse transnational social structures carry new risks for the cultural foundations and political stability of the group, and, therefore, for the foundation of the ethnic economy itself.

CHAPTER SEVEN

Conclusion: Of Migration Merchants and Merchant Migrants

Soy Cholo Boy, y me voy a viajar! La próxima vez a Florida me iré donde el cuye grandote anima Disney World y Mundial de soquer, yo will go. Yea, that's right, next time, voy de tourist! Me fui a la YANY, me fui a trabajar, no importa en que, pero pude triunfar. Los dólares vienen, los dólares van, con todo ese money, llegué a comprar: ropita, casita, y el Trooper manejar. Soy Cholo Boy y me voy a disfrutar. You know, man. . . . chulla life!

[I am a Cholo Boy, and I'm going to travel! The next time I'll go to Florida where that giant guinea pig enlivens Disney World and to the World Cup, I will go. Yea, that's right, next time, I'll go as a tourist! I've been to la YANY, I went to work, it didn't matter in what, but I was able to triumph. The dollars come, and the dollars go, and with all that money, I was able to buy clothes, a little house, and a Trooper to drive. I am a Cholo Boy and I'm going to have fun. You know, man . . . only one life to live!]

New immigrant groups may share certain features with other immigrants, past and present, but their story must be told anew, explained from the ground up. Apart from establishing the existence and contours of transnational migration from rural Andean communities in Ecuador, I have attempted to understand why and how two groups pursue divergent transnational strategies to overcome barriers to social mobility based on class, ethnicity, and gender. Unlike many other cases of international immigration, nearly all of the transnational migrants of this study who leave their regions do so despite—and even because of—the fundamental physical and social attractiveness of their home communities: they leave because they feel blocked by others in their attempts to secure economic mobility at home (see Carpio 1992, 23, for a similar conclusion regarding migration from Azuay). Of course, for the communities of this study this is not the end of a story but only the beginning. During the past six years since I concluded research in Ecuador, several things have happened at the community and national levels in Ecuador that are worth reporting because they bear on study findings; they also underscore a need for caution as we rush to construct new narratives of transnational mobility, the primary theme of this chapter.

In contrast to the academically descriptive subtitle of this book, the title "transnational peasants" is meant to communicate a reality beyond our normal language rather than a precise label describing a new social type. Though the "transnational" part is accurate in conveying an important feature of migrations from these communities, the historically resonant "peasant" is a problematic concept applied to the Andean region (Orlove 1977) and, especially, within a context of transnational social relations (Kearney 1996); even in its everyday usage by many in Ecuador, not all of the subjects of my study would have identified themselves as campesinos, precisely because they were now shuttling between their smallholdings planted with corn and Manhattan or Amsterdam. However, the group in my study who most typified the label "peasant" was the indigenous group in the community of Quipal known as "los naturales" (probably descendants of the Cañari) whose dependent relations with locals fit the following sociological description of peasant relationships to outsiders within Ecuador: "Peasant links to city, region, and nation were mediated through powerful outsiders, such as foreman, landowners, merchants, priests, or law enforcement officials" (Kluck 1991, 73). Though no one from this ethnie had sent a migrant abroad at the time of my survey of Quipal in 1993, since the first one left in 1994 more and more have migrated every year to work in the United States. Just as the other two ethnic groups of the community had forged semi-independent networks of migration to different destinations in the northeastern United States, this third group now has several members working in lumber operations in rural Pennsylvania, a continuation of one of their primary activities in Azuay. Once again, we find that a group has turned to transnational migration as a route to social mobility, though, in this case, they had to forge their own transnational networks, since it was other co-villagers who had been, in part, the powerful intermediaries.

Given that this entire study was premised on different kinds of transnational migration strategies from Azuay and Otavalo, a surprising develop-ment in Otavalo has occurred. Lynn Meisch reports that several young Otavalan men are taking seasonal wage labor jobs during the harvest season in Europe (personal communication, February 10, 2000). They have com-plained about the saturation of overseas markets by their coethnics; in the re-cent "running of the bulls" festival in Pamplona there were no fewer than forty stalls of Otavalan merchants offering similar merchandise. It seems that for the merchant migrants of Otavalo, the term *global markets* is misleading; there are only so many urban settings in the world amenable to their brand of cultural commodity. More important, given the Western European ro-manticization of indigenous peoples of the Americas as a comparative advantage for this ethnie (which seemingly embodies some of the most stereotypical portrayals of primitive nobility), the ubiquity of Otavalans throughout European and North American urban centers produces the per-ception that perhaps they are not that different from the local souvenir shops. In fact, on recent trips I have found Otavalans in Florence, Italy, selling not only folkloric handicrafts but key-chain souvenirs of the famous Duomo cathedral, and in Chicago one Otavalan sold exclusively contemporary silver jewelry, which he buys in Tasco, Mexico. With increasing competition from more and more Otavalan communities joining the transnationalized ethnic economy—communities, such as Guanansi, that traditionally had not been part of the "awakening"—it is not surprising that some are turning either to wage labor abroad or to an expansion of wares into nonethnic merchandise. Both present a qualitative shift in the logic and structure of the ethnic enclave in Ecuador in that transnational migration until now has been viewed as both an economic and a cultural mission to the world of wealthy nations.

Though not in danger of full convergence anytime soon, this nascent de-terioration of the sharp socioeconomic distinctions between Azuayan and Otavalan migrants will probably be intensified by recent national trends and events. Throughout the 1990s, the economy of Ecuador weakened, reaching the dubious distinction by 1999 of having the highest inflation rate (60 per-cent) in Latin America. Throughout 1999, several economic measures urged by the International Monetary Fund provoked political unrest and social chaos, especially the freezing of dollar bank accounts. In January 2000, Ecuador undertook one of the most dramatic economic measures a state can take: President Jamil Mahuad made the U.S. dollar the official currency of the country, with a final exchange rate of twenty-five thousand sucres to the dol-lar. Indigenous peoples from around Ecuador shut down major roads and marched to Quito in protest, calling for Mahaud's resignation. Financial markets within Ecuador responded immediately by dropping interest rates from 200 to 20 percent. Others responded very differently; following a massive march to Quito by indigenous campesinos, a short-lived military coup, which also included an indigenous leader, succeeded in removing Mahuad from office. However, military generals, facing complete isolation from other countries and from the International Monetary Fund, quickly returned the government to Mahuad's vice president, Gustavo Naboa, on January 23. President Naboa declared that he would continue most of the economic policies of his predecessor, including the dollarization of the economy. There is a widespread belief among Ecuadorians that this measure will benefit only wealthy elites, the international bankers, and corrupt politicians; political conflict over the social, political, and economic future of the country will surely continue.

Over the past few years, I have received information from a research assistant in Quipal via e-mail who logs on to a high school computer in Cuenca (though it was extremely difficult for her to get access, given the long lines of people wanting to use it). Migrants working abroad and remitting dollars took special note of recent political and economic upheavals back home. There are now several websites designed to keep migrants abroad informed of the very latest events in Azuay and Ecuador. My assistant explained that migrants from her village living in New York City were worried that replacing the sucre with the dollar would reduce their spending power and economic security back in Ecuador. Thus, they are reevaluating the sacrifice of a transnational life and its economic benefits; the result might be not a return to Ecuador but consideration of more permanent residence in the United States. She also noted that many more now want to leave Quipal.

Surely the even closer intermingling of Ecuadorian and American societies (and, by extension, other NAFTA [North American Free Trade Agreement] countries) through a common currency will have long-term implications for transnational migration from Ecuador to the United States. Such a link provides both a cultural bridge and an ability for Ecuadorian workers to make comparisons between their incomes and those of American citizens more easily, while the cost of living in Ecuador is regressing toward the U.S. mean. Though such invidious comparisons are not sufficient to initiate mass migration from a region, it is likely that local and foreign migration merchants, building on existing transnational social networks, will attempt to meet the greater demand for migration from Ecuador stemming from economic chaos and political unrest.

Hence, with these recent developments two facts are salient: an increasing transnationalization of Ecuadorian society through both migration abroad and state policies and the possibility that continuing social upheaval will alter the local, regional, and hemispheric contexts in ways that make it difficult to predict even the short-term outcome for the four communities of my study. Not unlike most areas of social life in the world today, this dynamic complexity of interpenetrating sociocultural milieus and ideologies is precisely why static theories can be both useful guides and intellectual enclosures allowing only a limited range of questions with which to query social settings and imagine differently abstract macrosocial and political relationships.

Regardless of how states construct migration and immigrants, this social complexity that international migration engenders has provided one of the most energetic and lasting debates in the social sciences. From its inception, the scientific study of international migration in the age of strong nation-states has been a struggle between abstract theory building, on the one hand, and ad hoc accounts based on a seemingly unique combination of migration characteristics at the local level. E. G. Ravenstein's (1885, 1889) initial attempts in the 1880s to discover "laws of migration," using national and international census data, present the principal theoretical challenges that have endured until today. His presentations before the Royal Statistical Society in London, and subsequent commentary by its members, marked one the first systematic analyses of the available data using prevailing theory—today characterized as "push-pull": there are incentives for leaving and disincentives for staying, which, in turn, affect subsequent levels of "dispersion" away from the sending region and "absorption" within the receiving region.

Given the reduction by subsequent migration scholars of Ravenstein's research into a largely discredited push-pull camp, it is surprising to find that his analyses are not that alien to contemporary approaches to transnational migration. Although he spoke heuristically of "laws of migration"—using the language of his day—he also spoke of the "migration process" and of "currents of migration," pointing to a phenomenon much richer than individuals' making abstract calculations and acting mechanically to bring a social system to equilibrium (1885). There may be push and pull factors, but there are also a variety of economic, social, demographic, and geographic contingencies affecting the mobility levels and destinations of specific segments of the population: rural to urban migration can be characterized as "multiple displacements" occurring through a series of short-distance stages or steps; females are more migratory than males, though they typically travel shorter distances in search of wage work; every migration gives rise to a socially heterogeneous counterflow in the opposite direction.

Ravenstein did such a good job of uncovering the variety of migration patterns that others at his lectures wondered if general "laws of migration" were even possible. For example, Dr. Longstaff asked why Irish immigrants, who "in Ireland talked about nothing but the land . . . [their] idea of bliss," would concentrate so intensely in urban areas of the United States, unlike the Germans, who were settling in the Midwest. Other members scoffed at the appropriateness of comparing mobility patterns of the United States, a nation of immigrants and untapped territory, with those of the European continent, where all of the hinterlands were already populated and were being put to productive use. Thus, Ravenstein's systematic examination of migration had left in the minds of many a question that has never been fully resolved, regarding the different assumptions and methods of disciplinary approaches to the study of migration: How can we—or should we—develop universal theories regarding human mobility with so many different national contexts composed of myriad social groupings by class, ethnicity, trade, gender, geography, culture, and citizenship? Considering what Stephen Castles and Mark Miller (1998, 8–9), refer to as the "globalization, acceleration, and differentiation" of contemporary international migrations from a wide variety of sending regions to a growing set of receiving countries during the current post–Cold War period, this question is especially appropriate today. The new transnational migrations of Azuay and Otavalo typify these global trends in migration and provide an opportunity to measure how far we have come and how far we need to go in understanding current mobility patterns by those seeking wages and profit well beyond their home communities.

Old Theories, New Migrations

A central question from labor market theory concerns the role that individual-level attributes play in determining who goes or stays; this is why I surveyed four villages. Although transnational migration patterns differ between the Azuayan and Otavalan regions, the demographic and socioeconomic profiles of migrants are remarkably similar across communities: most migrants are male and, in comparison with nonmigrants, relatively young and educated. Migrants also tend to be either single or recently married, indicating that most are at the early stages of independent household formation. Thus, there is support in the Ecuadorian case for the basic insights of the equilibrium perspective that is prevalent in the economic literature. In the first instance, people are motivated by potential rewards unevenly distributed across the population according to individual skills and resources. The group of individual-level attributes categorized as human capital can be viewed as one of the most significant proximate determinants of transnational migration in all four villages. However, in this case it is the success of the conventional labor market approach at the individual level that also reveals the limits of using human capital to predict migration. Most important, differentials in human capital cannot explain the different patterns and strategies and forms of transnational migration in the two regions studied.

In contrast with the atomistic approach to migration by labor market theories, the history of Ecuador's national and regional development, especially its historical insertion into the global system of capital accumulation dominated by core countries, forms the backdrop for understanding common social processes affecting diverse villages. However, it is subnational regions (or labor markets), rather than nations, that are integrated into the world economy in a variegated fashion. The early Republic of Ecuador was marked by considerable heterogeneity in the economic mix of distinct regions and their connections to foreign markets. Of course, these differences were shaped by even older variations in their sociodemographic makeup and elite strategies for the accumulation of wealth and power during the colonial period. Interestingly, the rural indigenous and mestizo populations of both Azuay and Otavalo were distinctive among other neighboring regions of Ecuador in their ability to retain a level of independence from the complete dominance of the agricultural encomienda and hacienda institutions. In addition, a striking feature of both Azuay and Otavalo is the early and nearly complete integration of their handicraft economies into global markets, mediated by usurious middlemen.

Yet, the two regions diverged precisely in regard to the role and economic power of handicraft middlemen and other (white) regional elites. In Azuay, transnational migrant communities seek to avoid the old middleman structure of the Panama hat trade and other patronal relationships only to develop yet another pyramidal structure of migration merchants in which local financial institutions, owned and managed by white elites, continue to reap the most benefits. Thus, the notion of a periphery-centered dynamic in Azuay and Otavalo recognizes important politicoeconomic linkages with core states and, therefore, is not the same as a one-sided "push factor," though it does draw more attention to the development decisions made by a range of regional and national actors and institutions over time. As Ronald Skeldon (1997) points out, migration and regional development are locked in an embrace such that we cannot understand one without the other; in a more connected but decentralized world economy, the variety of local development patterns implies much more variegated migration systems.

It is the general logic of the preexisting transnationalized ethnic economies that has shaped the emerging patterns of transnational migration, though once migration begins it continues to transform the local economy. Following long-standing patterns of "trails" in and out of the regions of study, Otavalan sellers fan out in centrifugal fashion across the globe in search for buyers of indigenous handicrafts, whereas among Azuayans the selling of one's labor abroad is centripetal, mostly concentrating in several urban neighborhoods in New York and New Jersey. There are two additional dimensions of Otavalan transnational migration that are different from that of Azuay: first, transnational migration does not represent a "new" strategy for capital accumulation, and thus a break with the past, but rather is part of an economic repertoire that reaches back to the pre-Incan period; second, whereas Azuayan communities are culturally diverse and economically similar in their insertion into regional institutions and social structures, the opposite is true of Otavalo. Indeed, the Otavalan ethnie is surprisingly diverse in the socioeconomic makeup of the many communities that identify with it; and it would not be incorrect to posit a well-defined class structure around ownership of industrial looms. In this regard, some of the specific economic, social, and cultural strategies we find in Otavalo, such as the sharp increase in transnational migration to play music, are the result of class formations stemming from the dynamic growth of capitalist modes of production and commodified social relations in that region.

Another striking difference between the two artisanal regions is that whereas Otavalans sell handicrafts made in Panama as their own (e.g., molas made by the Cuna), the Azuayans have long produced a hat called the "Panama." In other words, there is a fundamental cultural alienation from handicraft work in Azuay, which is, nonetheless, one of the Centers of Artesanía for Latin America designated by the Organization of American States. In the 1980s, the government of Ecuador placed a phrase at the bottom of its official letterhead in an attempt to right the injustice of this famous but mislabeled export: "Panama Hats Are Made in Ecuador." It was removed when officials realized that foreigners interpreted it as, "Oh, Ecuador now makes straw hats," and were not changing their perception that the real Panama hat must come from Panama. In Otavalo, the reverse is true: seemingly, nearly anything they sell is considered by foreigners as socially noble and culturally "authentic," even when much of their inventory is made by other Latin American groups, including the wives of transnational migrants from Azuay.

However, this attention to the ideological and cultural dimensions of migration patterns takes us afield from the core assumptions of the historical-structural approach. New approaches to economic sociology are more attuned to the interplay among cultural narratives, social structures, and human agency (see chapter 4). These approaches draw, in part, on the well-developed notion of the social construction of reality. With transnational migration, cultural and social structures change in ways that affect each another: For example, cultural change can often lead, whether through diffusion, borrowing, or intentional engineering by both elites and others, to changes in the social structures of the group, including the splintering of the group into new subgroups (see Hall and Neitz 1993). With global communications and transportation, built on the foundation of stored media (print, photos, film, video, magnetic tape, etc.), the tacit assumption of a uniformity of cultural flows within a group has become untenable, especially when it is the transnational flow of culture itself that is an important explanatory dimension. As Ulf Hannerz (1992) notes, "cultural complexity" (or a lack of in-group cultural uniformity) has come to characterize many postindustrial and industrializing societies around the world and is directly related to increasing social complexity, though without a fixed direction of causality.

This distinction between social structure and culture, however, also stands apart from the related concept of ethnic identities, which are often based as much on stereotypical portrayals from the "outside" as from actual group beliefs and norms. Hence, the everyday culture of a group, region, or state, can be distinguished from the loosely related concept of ethnic identity as a self-conscious culture. Ethnic identities imply a stable and recognizable relationship between social structure and culture because they are politically motivated social constructions, typically the result of political and military coercion based on the strategic economic and symbolic value of the ethnic group to internal and external elites. Even group membership itself (regardless of everyday culture) is often decided by powerful group members.

Thus, an assumption of the social constructivist perspective is that social structures cannot be separated from processes of ideological domination and cultural interpretation. Stated differently, ethnic identity and group membership can be conceptualized as forms of social structure affecting not only everyday cultural practices but also the social status and economic opportunities of individuals. It is through everyday politics, executed in a web of social networks, that cultural production is wedded to economic production. In this sense, culture is not a static set of ideas or practices but rather what David Sabean has defined as a series of arguments among people about the common things of their everyday lives. . . . If we consider culture as the "medium," as it were, in which conflicts are worked out, faulty and partial visions are adjusted, domination is attempted, and resistances set into play, then we can use the concept as an instrument for investigating the dynamics of power, the distribution of resources, and the nature of hierarchy. . . . It is precisely because it is an argument, or a set of exchanges, or an attempt to wield or resist power, that we learn more about it by starting with the relations of the people who share a culture than we do by assuming that culture is about a set of tools or ideas, a unified set of notions which a people share. (Sabean 1984, 95)

Although the Andean region has been the arena for dramatic conquests, violent uprisings, and national revolutions, often along ethnic divides, much of the political conflict continues to be played out symbolically over the on-going creation of ethnic identities. Within this milieu, community and group leaders emerge, often with a keen perception of the resources available to them by virtue of their multiple statuses in a variety of social settings. There is no natural reason that peasants, or what Michael Kearney calls "peasant-types" (1996), wanting to retain a household mode of production in their communities, would not actively seek out every social, cultural, and techno-logical resource available to them, including using their stereotypical ethnic identity in an instrumental manner. It is in this context that we are to under-stand the leadership and pioneering efforts of actual people—Rosa Lema of Peguche and Jesus of Tomebamba—as they react to, and anticipate, eco-nomic, political, and social change in their home communities and in the bar-rios of New York City or Amsterdam.

In addition, the social construction of the Otavalan ethnic economy, as it moved toward more touristic items in the 1950s, can only be understood within the broader context of how dimensions of our own (Western) identi-ties have required them to do so. In Otavalo, tourists with the time and money to travel to a foreign country hope to disguise their First World status through the low-brow earthiness of purchasing items from primitive natives. As Mary Crabb observes, the typical tourist to Otavalo is an adventurous "antitourist" not wanting to be identified as the "package-tour" type (1993, 80), an adjec-tive that certainly could not be applied to the American and European women looking for romance with an Otavalan. For some tourists, both the seller and the merchandise have to be "authentic"; to the enormous dismay of Otavalan merchants, tourists (or antitourists) in the 1990s began searching out the more "authentic" animal market, just outside of town, where Otavalan agriculturists trade and sell livestock. In sum, our own social construction of reality in the core (the First World) has shaped differently the transnational opportunities of Azuayans and Otavalans.

To the extent that transnational migration is not driven entirely by the discrete calculations of atomized individuals but rather is made up of migrants whose decision and ability to migrate was affected by the previous migration of others and by the preexisting social structures within their community, we can recognize that transnational migration is a thoroughly social activity tending toward the formation of new social structures. Recent migration research and theorizing emphasizing the role of social networks have gone far in bringing back a more close-range analysis of transnational migration that focuses on individual and household decision making without relying on individual attributes (coded as variables) to do all of the heavy lifting analytically. For example, I have used the heuristic devise of two separate "migration moments" to conceptualize the difference between the pioneering efforts of migrants and the actual onset of mass migration within their communities and social networks. As this study confirms once again, the reasons for outmigration after the second migration moment are more diverse than those of the original pioneers and include the desire for members to know both sides of the transnationalized household and community and to spend time with a distant parent or sibling. As migrants return, build modern houses, and emphasize their foreign adventures, social networks provide not only a social resource for leaving but also the main reference point for young adults who increasingly perceive the reality of relative deprivation between migrants and nonmigrants (Massey et al. 1998, 26). Social networks communicate powerful economic and social information about opportunities spread unevenly around the world in ways that make staying home seem more like a morally imbued act of cowardice than a rational economic decision on the part of an individual actor.

However, social network theories come close to "oversocializing" migrants in their treatment of migration network building as a process with a high degree of internal momentum: once a migration flow begins, the "internal logic" of network building acts as a sort of macrostructural force to migration. Recognizing that transnational migration is a social activity, grounded in social networks, does not provide an explanation of a specific outflow but rather provides us with a starting point for analysis, much like recognizing the law of gravity without specifying its effects on a given configuration of object size, weight, and form or the object's relation to other environmental conditions. This is one of the central observations of the economic sociology approach: individuals and social units are always embedded in larger social structures, but the actual "effect" of these social structures must be examined inductively as a set of socially constructed (historical) relations in dynamic interchange with individual agents.

As a metaphor for social resources available to specific kinds of social relations—and the price of those resources—social capital is a useful concept for understanding those intermediate-level social processes and structures (associated with transnational migration), which builds on the simple recognition that networks matter. Pierre Bourdieu (1986) conceptualized "cultural capital" and "social capital" as metaphors for understanding how the accumulation of social history affects individuals differently and how they can then be converted into financial capital. For example, in Azuay, to understand the operation of the informal money-lending network we must examine the level of social closure along kinship and community lines that allows for high levels of trust, a primary conceptual component of social capital by some formulations of the concept (Coleman 1990; Portes and Sensenbrenner 1993). A certain level of reasonable trust built on community ties is necessary before a migration merchant will offer a loan. An even higher level of confidence is necessary among the lenders so that issues of security and price-fixing can be overcome. This high level of confidence is achieved through close ties of kinship—even separate, large-scale lending groups are interrelated by marriage in some Azuayan towns.

Yet, the comparative analysis between and within the regions of Azuay and Otavalo also demonstrate the limits of the "social capital" metaphor. Otavalans instrumentally use their centuries-old positive identity to help gain resources from a wide variety of external people and agencies, including travel agencies, banks, foreign governments, and wholesalers, to name a few. If we are to use the capital metaphor at all, it is the more exclusive cultural capital (Bourdieu 1986, 243) that best accounts for the divergent transnational strategies of these regions, though it is typically applied to those who have, for example, elite educations (Kyle 1999). Both social and cultural capitals, however, must themselves be explained historically and are not simply placeholders for such an analysis.

It is the multiple conjunctural configuration of such things as historical resources, socially constructed identities, ethnic repertoires, and individual human capital (not an exhaustive list), rather than the additive independent effects of each, that best explains the different transnational migration patterns found in Azuay and Otavalo. For example, the sixth-grade educational level of the Azuayan migrant washing dishes in a Manhattan restaurant can be used to "explain" his position as an undocumented immigrant compelled to take a menial labor job; in contrast, a young Otavalan's same level of education will not be used to explain his activities in the same way but will instead be used as counterpoint to a morality story in which even "common Indians" can become jet-setters. To understand why this is so requires a much deeper historical and sociological understanding of their sending communities and our own societies than is typically available within a strictly "independent variables" approach to social analysis.

In sum, the basic inductive findings of this study guided by existing theories of international migration, are the following:

- Transnational migration has become a significant economic strategy in all of the highland villages forming the research sites, yet characteristics of the historical development of mobility and economic activity have varied across the four communities (wage labor abroad facilitated by migration merchants versus merchant migration based on the commodification and global marketing of their own and others' indigenous culture).
- The concept of human capital is useful for understanding the set of primary proximate determinants for individual migration; migrants across all four research sites tend to be men who are younger, more educated, and more skilled than their nonmigrant counterparts.
- The "decision" to migrate, however, is best characterized not as a discrete decision by an individual but rather as a social process deeply wedded to the premigratory processes of dynamic social change at the household, village, and regional levels. Although they pursue different transnational strategies, Azuayan and Otavalan migrants leave their home communities not to escape their regions but to better position themselves structurally in a well-articulated, migrant export economy.
- Rather than stemming from a "core-centered" dynamic, whereby rural semiproletarianized peasants are directly recruited or otherwise disrupted by destination countries, transnational migration from Ecuador is based on a "periphery-centered" dynamic, whereby strategies of capital accumulation in the sending regions produce both the compelling conditions for transnational mobility and the specific nature of the local economy.
- Though specific patterns of migration (destination, activity abroad, duration, etc.) may vary from region to region—or even from village to

village—the organization of the migration process through social networks (based on kinship and friendship) and market relations (both formal and informal) is similar in function but not in form across the two groups. A common feature, in this regard, is the increasing commodification of the migration process itself within either the informal economy (human smugglers) or the formal economy (travel agencies) by what I have labeled "migration merchants."

– The concept of social capital (or capitals) is helpful to the extent that it sensitizes us to resources available only to those identified with a particular community or ethnic group; hence, it describes a distinctly sociological aspect of transnational migration. However, it is external social capital beyond one's immediate social network, not just internal social capital, that provides opportunities for transnational economic activities in both regions. The extent and type of external social capital is closely related to a group's cultural capital, a historical political resource less affected by individual or group agency.

– Transnational migration may be fundamentally rooted in economic processes of capital accumulation (class) but is often impossible to disentangle from other important areas such as ethnic and gender discrimination (caste) and historical social norms and ideologies of the migrating group (culture) because all three have a synergistic or multiple conjunctural effect. Thus, similar economic and technological contexts can still lead to different development paths because of the sociocultural embeddedness of the group.

Echoing a recent evaluation of theories and evidence concerning international migration to North America, which found support in the research literature for all of the major approaches (Massey et al. 1998, 106), this study also lends additional support to all of the theories that helped guide my research design and analysis. Yet, I also designed the study to push these theories to their limits in that I did not limit my field of study to strictly international labor migration within the same ethnic group but also included entrepreneurial migrations and a complex array of ethnic and class identities; I did, however, control for rural origins and nationality to allow a basis for comparison. I conclude from the experience of this novel approach that though existing theories do relatively well at answering the questions they ask, they limit our ability to imagine other social realities and ask questions other than the demographic ones of central interest to states: who, and how many, are crossing our borders? Past theories of international migration are still powerful tools, but they are reaching their conceptual limits within a highly dynamic global political economy and an equally dynamic array of transnational actions by corporate and noncorporate actors for economic gain and sociopolitical maneuvering. A new set of essays and research under the rubric of "transnationalism" seeks to better understand the complexity of contemporary transnational migration beyond its sociodemographic dimension.

A Transnational Research Agenda: Migration Merchants and Merchant Migrants

Recently increasing attention has been paid to distinctly transnational migrations, with some viewing it as a qualitative shift in migration patterns requiring new concepts and methodologies (Basch, Schiller, and Blanc 1994; Kearney 1996). Proponents of transnationalism argue for a dialectical approach that integrates the economic, political, and cultural dimensions of processes not easily captured by the implicit discreteness of such labels as "international immigration." It is a conscious effort to redirect what its proponents view as "bounded" and "dichotomous" analyses concerning contemporary migration flows back and forth across national borders, with particular attention to its subjects of analysis—"transmigrants" (Basch, Schiller, and Blanc 1994). Thus far, the contribution of those examining transnationalism lies in ambitiously presenting a multistranded vision better suited to contemporary migrant groups within "transnational social fields" rather than a set of well-defined concepts and theoretical propositions. Though it is promoted as a novel approach, many of its insights and methods are not that different from some of the strides in international migration research in the 1970s and 1980s, such as the desirability of studying multiple migration poles at multiple levels of aggregation with multiple methods. In addition to this study of Azuay and Otavalo, a growing set of compelling empirical cases do suggest that some contemporary migrations from a range of sending countries to the traditional receiving countries of North America and Europe may be considered transnational to the extent that they do not reside in a single locale nor do they have unitary political identities (Sutton 1987; Georges 1990; Goldring 1992; Rouse 1992; Guarnizo 1994; Smith 1994; Mahler 1995).

As more social scientists conduct research on myriad transnational social processes and settings, two trends in research approaches are clear: first, a move to limit the conceptual reach of transnationalism through more refined definitions and typologies (Portes, Guarnizo, and Landholt 1999) and, relatedly, the call for more attention to the social and political variegations of transnationalized social groups (Smith and Guarnizo 1998; Mahler 1998; Goldring 1998; Morawska forthcoming); and second, a broadening empirically of the range of social phenomenon to be considered under the transnationalism rubric (Vertovec 1999), often by reaching back to historical "migrant flows" to parse out what is truly novel about current migration patterns, considering that many of the things we are witnessing today were also experienced by immigrant groups during the last great waves of immigration (Foner 1997; Smith 2000). For example, many European immigrants a century ago returned home frequently, including a sizable portion who returned home permanently after building their "American houses" (for a photographic example, see Wyman 1993, 128), similar to migrant houses in Azuay; William Thomas and Florian Znanieki (1927, 1575) have documented the intense nationalism of Polish peasant immigrants at the beginning of this century and even their attempts to build "super-territorial" institutions. This has led nearly all scholars working in this area to emphasize the speed, scale, and scope of contemporary transnational migration and related activities as the novel dimensions; today, a campesino from Tomebamba can be in Manhattan by tomorrow, give his wife authorization to buy a cow by fax, and send her videotape of his weekend activities in Flushing Meadow Park.

Attempts at a reconceptualization of the analytic problems posed by the fact of transnational migration, multiple ethnic identities, dual nationality, and distinctly transnational development patterns in the origin communities are now in full swing, and it would be premature to predict the directions this emerging perspective will take. One of the most exciting trends in this regard is that it has attracted a much more diverse range of scholars than those who have traditionally identified themselves as international migration specialists. For this reason I want to examine this present study through a somewhat different lens by considering what we would not have learned had I omitted a particular community from my study. The significance of this methodological exercise of imagination is that differing perceptions and definitions of what constitute a more disciplined approach to transnationalism might have eliminated either Azuayan migrants (since they are possibly a first-generation immigrant phenomenon) or Otavalan migrants (since they do not form a counterhegemonic resistance force to global capitalism, a leitmotif of many essays concerning "grassroots transnationalism"). Likewise, some researchers may want to avoid, for political reasons, studies that would bring attention to transnational activities linking migrants to crime and the appearance of coethnic exploitation, whether in the sending or receiving country. As a legitimate concern, given the importance of the ways in which groups and activities are socially constructed by states for domestic and foreign policy purposes, it makes it that much more important to evaluate what we learn by taking a more inclusive approach to transnational brokering of all sorts.

If I had limited my study to Otavalo, which has received by far the most attention from Ecuadorian and foreign researchers of any region in Ecuador, we would not have understood how Azuayans have forged their own transnational development project based on an articulated regional economy structured to export people along with its hats. We would be more likely to impute special qualities to an essentialized Otavalan ethnie, since the lack of another region would not impel us to explore the historical social construction of the Otavalan identity. Variations on the theme of "the awakening valley" could have been constructed unhindered by a reminder of the consequences for other mestizo and indigenous campesinos not considered special by urban elites and foreigners.

In contrast, without the inclusion of the Otavalo canton and its prominent indigenous ethnie, we could not have understood the full range of transnational opportunities available to some rural smallholders of Ecuador in the 1990s; it is in that region that we take notice of the cross-cultural brokering at the heart of its sociological foundations, removing our gaze from the fetishism of transnational flows as the sine qua non of transnationalism. It forces us, ironically, to take more notice of the cross-cultural brokers of Azuay who participate in the business of migration. An exclusive focus on the mass transnational migration from Azuayan villages would have better supported, though not completely, dominant sociological theories of migration and development that assume that rural folk would leave their beloved land only as a last resort for survival, and when they do leave, the experience is generally negative and exploitative; Otavalo clearly does not fit that model. We certainly found exploitation and hardship among the women of Tomebamba who began to migrate using human smugglers against the wishes of their husbands in Queens and at great financial and personal risk, including—as they were well aware—the possibility of rape by those who prey on clandestine migrants along the journey through Central America and Mexico.

In fact, within Azuay, without the inclusion of Tomebamba, we would not have seen the full extent to which a community can sustain, though tenuously, transnational households divided by gender, such that they are referred to as "villages of women" within the region; nor would we understand why some ethnic minority communities find it difficult to resolve the social tension between living in one distant locale that offers work and another that offers social status based on conspicuous consumption. It would have also been difficult, without Tomebamba, to see the subtle connection between the buyers and exporters of Panama hats and the local migration merchants. Without the inclusion of Quipal, which is not a traditional hat-weaving community, we would not have understood how a small rural community can be completely divided by ethnicity yet still manage to send migrants abroad through separate networks resulting in parallel transnational social structures. With Tomebamba alone in the study, we might have been tempted to overgeneralize about the ambiguous role of women in emergent transnational social structures; Quipal demonstrated that in some Azuayan communities women are leaving to work alongside their brothers, fathers, and husbands, though still not in equal numbers.

Without the Otavalan village of Peguche we would not know one of the most amazing findings of this study: in one rural community merchant migrants were traveling to at least twenty-three different countries and generally returning in the same year. In observing a village with only one telephone—but with a centuries-old history of transnational, cross-cultural relations—we need to reevaluate our globalization narratives that emphasize contemporary communication and transportation technologies as the driving force to increased transnational flows of all sorts, including people. Without Guanansi, we could not appreciate the fact that not all Otavalan communities have participated in the transnational economic miracle, though these communities are trying to catch up as rapidly as possible, even when lacking electricity and telephones. Guanansi teaches us to continue to pay close attention to historical social stratifications even when the uniform dress and ideology of an ethnie disguises this social reality.

==

A search for what accounts for the differences in transnational migration strategies between two regions and among four communities in the same country has led me to consider its mirror image, which remains fuzzy and distorted by our ideologies of global networks and mercurial flows as the guts of both globalization from above and transnationalism from below: how can we conceptualize and understand the *similarities* between the transnationalized social settings of the four communities of this study, given the differences of sociocultural and economic histories, including distinctive migration patterns? This has led me to consider a different kind of transnational metaphor from the "flows of migrants" generally said to be at the heart of "transnationalism from below," which is the primary focus of this book. The imagery of conical funnels—with many people left behind but still transformed by transnational activities and ideologies—may be a useful companion image to flows across territorial borders, which primarily reflects the state-centered fetish of enumerating and describing those who cross its borders. The image of the funnel can be used to remind us that flows come from somewhere and include heterogeneous groups of people with social histories. I can only wonder what I would have found in another corner of Ecuador and what lessons it would teach us about the possibilities for historically embedded transnational projects funneling flows of migrants in different directions, speeds, and shapes. Until we collect more descriptions and comparisons of these different transnationalized social settings around the world at multiple levels of analysis, ambitious typologies and theory construction are premature, and we will probably continue to use old theories to find "new" things rather than more inductive approaches to find older but recurrent social processes manifested in contemporary forms.

Although Azuayan and Otavalan migrations represent different transnational strategies for short-term capital accumulation, a surprising commonality is their development of truly transnational social, economic, and cultural spaces, as both groups shuttle back and forth. It is accurate to say that few of the migrant members of the four rural communities on which the present study is based feel any great allegiance to Ecuador, or any other nation-state, as ill-fated state census takers have found out. From their perspective, states ask of them much more than they receive. Nonetheless, transnational migrants from Ecuador have attempted to mold the nation-centered basis of citizenship to their own transnational reality by lobbying for dual citizenship and by successfully winning a national (Ecuadorian) day in their honor, El Día de los Ausentes.

The two regions do share a common feature: The long-standing middleman social and financial institutions arising from cottage industry have been modified, but not discarded, as mass migration in both regions has developed. In Azuay, both community- and kinship-based networks and the informal economy of migration now play the crucial recruitment role once played by the actual employers or their go-betweens during periods of absolute labor shortage in the North America or Europe. A range of migration merchants profit by facilitating some aspect of the migration process, such as money-lending, activities available to nearly all return migrants. This brokering has reproduced the pyramidal structure of the straw hat export economy, although this structure is more open to entrepreneurial migrants who are not part of the local financial elite. While the image of the coyote helping a Mexican immigrant cross the Rio Grande has been common since World War II, the global business of migration is a qualitatively different and historically novel development—one that does not swim upstream with global capitalism. Connecting labor with capital is now a multibillion-dollar industry worldwide. Similarly, some Otavalans have retained positions as middlemen locally by abandoning it altogether in search of new markets and commodities. Because of the way those merchant migrants have exploited their group's ethnic identity in pursuit of expanding global opportunities, other nonmerchants have been able to use their common cultural capital to overcome a lack of financial capital needed to enter the local cottage industry. Both are fragile projects still susceptible to national economic and, especially, political crises. The growing politicization of international migration in receiving societies, especially focused on migrants working illegally, could also jeopardize both region's migration-led regional development projects by creating physical and legal barriers. However, migration merchants will surely attempt to meet the need for more professional migration services to overcome such barriers to entry.

In both regions of this study, the export of either commodified alien workers or cultural commodities is vertically integrated into a local economy in which those who broker the commodities, over great physical and cultural distances, profit most. Merchants from a community or ethnie pursuing long-distance, cross-cultural trade, such as some Otavalans and Azuayans, are rare precisely because they represent a sort of Jurassic Park of transnational enterprises. They are involved in the type of trade networks Philip Curtin labels "cross-cultural trade diasporas," which he found to be "one of the most widespread of all human institutions over a very long period of history, yet limited to the long period of human history that began with the invention of agriculture and ended with the coming of the industrial age" (1984, 3). Though such cross-cultural trade diasporas came in many different organizational forms—some lasting only a few years, others a few centuries—Curtin has found that they nearly all became anachronistic with advanced Western colonization facilitated by industrial military power and its global infrastructure of steamships and postal services.

> One could pursue the theme of Western technological superiority and its impact on the world of commerce into the field of banking, insurance, international monetary exchange, and much else. But, for trade diasporas, the conclusion is obvious. They could survive for a time in some places beyond the fringes of the international economy, but they had long since served their purpose in uniting an extremely diverse world. . . . Where the West dominates world commerce, and in circumstances where the competitive success or failure depends on using appropriate technology, the sweep of industrial technology is undeniable, and it has ended the era of the trade diaspora in cross-cultural trade. (Ibid., 253)

Thus, the historical force of Westernization, a large part of the contemporary "globalization project" (McMichael 1996), implies a world in which more and more countries must adopt U.S. and European business practices and standards in order to compete with Western firms and sell to Western consumers; we also now have multilateral organizations, such as the International Monetary Fund, that attempt to impose Western business norms in the form of anticorruption programs touting "transparency," with the goal of harmonizing global business practices and the limiting of political interference in markets. Of course, these extramarket activities by powerful states and transnational organizations simply underscore, ironically, the continual need for state and other institutional actions in supporting global markets (Block 1994). It is, in fact, the twin forces of more ecumenical transnational trade organized by monopolistic firms and state policies promoting a borderless world of capital and commodities—but not of its citizenry—that led to a relative lull in cross-cultural brokering during most of the twentieth-century, a century characterized, nonetheless, by enormous strides in the development of transportation and communication technologies.

Globalization notwithstanding, the forces that led to the demise of cross-cultural trade diasporas are still in effect, but there is an exception, or window of opportunity, that exists in a world in which production and distribution are organized globally by transnational corporations: commodities traded transnationally that either are off-limits to legal firms or obtain their value by remaining foreign at the point of sale are open to this older form of cross-cultural trade since they still require a specifically cross-cultural, transnational broker. This can even be a matter of degree: the same handicrafts sold by an Otavalan family in native dress in a street fair in San Francisco are more valuable and attract more attention than when they are sold in an ethnic novelty shop in the same neighborhood and are worth less still when sold by a large transnational firm such as Pier One Imports. As in the past, the cross-cultural broker of today continues to be viewed as a strange anomaly operating in the liminal spaces of more legitimate mainstream economic activities and is just as likely to attract the ire of state enforcement agencies as admiration for entrepreneurial prowess. Arguing against this view, Robin Cohen asserts that "trade diasporas can be seen as an enduring and perhaps innovatory model of social organization that may be advantageous to the diaspora itself, its homeland, and its place of settlement" (1997, 104). This book has explored, in part, the ambiguous but very real benefits of transnational brokering and mobility for four communities in Ecuador. People at their places of destination also benefit from their transnational projects; to the extent that we in the wealthiest countries seek illegal alien labor to build our houses and create exotic, but authentic, handicrafts with which to decorate them, cross-cultural traders will make it convenient for us to find them within our own homeland.

That is not to say that Otavalan merchant migrants and Azuayan migration merchants are functional equivalents or mirror images of each other; there are some fundamental social, legal, and moral differences between exporting legal goods and exporting people clandestinely. More important, if globalization means anything it is greater instability and unpredictability for those operating at the grass roots as laborers or traders. Zygmunt Bauman has pointed out that "what appears as globalization for some means localization for others; signalling a new freedom for some, upon others it descends as an uninvited and cruel fate. Mobility climbs to the rank of the uppermost among the coveted values—and the freedom to move, perpetually a scarce and unequally distributed commodity, fast becomes the main stratifying factor of our late-modern or post-modern times" (1998, 2).

It is noteworthy that the Otavalan transnational project is much more exposed to negative events and trends within Ecuador and to states' actions in general than is the Azuayan transnational project. National economic and political upheaval have immediate impacts on levels of tourism and on the economic activities of those using legal services to exit and enter the country, communicate with buyers and sellers, and produce and ship goods all over the world. Likewise, in a world already getting too small for Otavalan sellers and musicians, it must be remembered that many of their activities abroad are illicit since their visas generally do not allow for business activities and they are now regularly sent home after being caught with their duffel bags down in some urban plaza. Many Azuayans, both migrants and nonmigrant brokers, participate in a different sort of transnational project that funnels workers to distant labor markets in spite of concerted state opposition to stop the entry of "illegal aliens." This is a region in which they have struggled against the wrath of the gods of globalization for nearly two centuries rather than two decades and have forged their own paths through the back alleys of nation-states and global capitalism. One day, the merchant migrants of Otavalo may find themselves using the services of the migration merchants of Azuay. Ultimately, it remains to be seen whether the experiences of the "transnational peasants" of Azuay and Otavalo are part of an enduring trend around the world or temporary anomalies found within a transitional period toward an era of even greater state control over human mobility.

Study Design

The central feature of this study is its comparative design at the community and regional levels; the sociocultural and economic diversity of regions within Ecuador, even within the Andean highlands, provides a unique opportunity to reexamine theories of international migration that make predictions based on both individual and broader social characteristics. This study employs a triangular strategy of data collection combining household surveys, ethnographic data, and historical primary and secondary sources. Specifically, four types of data are used throughout the study: (1) household surveys of 723 households and their adult members ($n = 2{,}185$) conducted in four diverse Andean villages, including a panel study in the village of Quipal; (2) ethnographic research in the four Ecuadorian villages and New York City, using a range of migrant and nonmigrant informants in Ecuador; (3) secondary historical and demographic information concerning Ecuador, the regions under study, and their past mobility patterns; and (4) household maps of three of the four villages, used to show the dynamic spatial patterning of the onset of migration.

Past research on transnational migration have utilized probability sampling methods, which estimate attributes of the general population of a region. A complete census of the universe of households, instead of a probability sample, was used in the present study for two reasons: because the villages were small enough to warrant it, and to capture rare but important occurrences, such as the existence of migrant households or the diversity of their destinations. Sampling is especially appropriate when general characteristics of the population, or even aspects of it under study, are already known and can be compared with the sampled population. In this case, only anecdotal information for most of these villages was available before the surveys were carried out. If, as in the case of Guanansi, only a few had migrated abroad at the time of the survey, a sample would risk failing to include them at all. Most statistical analyses are based on the assumption of a probability sample rather than a census; however, the extremely high levels of cooperation in all four communities warrant its use.

A drawback to the design of this present study is that most of the survey data were collected at a single point in time. Given the limitations of time and funding for this study, the possibility of a full-blown longitudinal study in all villages was precluded. Nevertheless, the limitations of cross-sectional data were mitigated in four ways:

1. Since the original household survey in the spring of 1993, further data concerning who has left the village of Quipal was collected by a research assistant, allowing for a one-year panel design in that community.

2. The initiation of mass transnational migration flows is so recent in the four villages that many of the pioneers or their families are included in the survey and in the in-depth case studies.

3. Information collected on inactive and active migrants is retrospective; that is, the survey covers not only their current status but also characteristics of their first and subsequent trips abroad.

4. Primary and secondary historical data collected in the home villages, including localized studies of transnational migration, provides a dynamic context in which the more static survey data can be viewed.

The research design used in this study is also not well suited for estimating the general magnitude of transnational migration from Ecuador, or even from the Andean regions in which the villages are located—though it does point to a significant phenomenon. This study is, however, well suited to examining theories that hypothesize the centrality of a particular constellation of economic and social factors in initiating and sustaining transnational migration, ranging from personal attributes to the social structure and cultural norms of the village to recruitment by employers.

Data Collection

My research on this topic began with two exploratory five-month trips to Ecuador in September 1990 and October 1991. Most of my research for this book was carried out during a year of fieldwork from August 1992 to July 1993, with the exception of the longitudinal data collected in Quipal since this period. In between the three research trips to Ecuador, I made four trips to New York City that ranged from five days to one month. Three aspects of this final phase of data collection will be presented more closely: site selection, questionnaire design and survey application, and the interviews and ethnographic research.

Research Sites

Similar to past studies, the original plan of this study was to select one urban and one rural community in each of the northern and southern regions of Ecuador. It became obvious, however, that comparisons based on the two major dimensions of community size and ethnicity would be confusing and indeterminate. Furthermore, there is a problem in this case that would confound any attempt to study ethnicity across urban and rural areas and then relate it to transnational migration: in Ecuador, indigenous persons living in the city, wearing Western dress and hairstyles, are no longer considered Indian: they are now considered cholo, or mestizo. Throughout the Andean cultural region, race and ethnicity are very fluid social constructions, based largely on lifestyle and dress rather than phenotype or place of birth. The innovative element of this study design is that it seeks to minimize the effects of demographic size (rural versus urban) among sending communities, a common comparison in migration research, so that sociocultural factors and their relation to the structure of the migration process can be brought to the foreground. Thus, the four rural villages that form the primary research sites of this study are comparable in size (100–350 households), and all rely on some combination of agriculture, cottage industry, and wage work. However, all of the villages vary in their degree of assimilation to the dominant national culture, ranging from acculturated blanco-mestizos to Quichua speakers who are actively attempting to maintain their indigenous culture.

The Household Survey

Although a census does not use a probability sampling technique, similar preparations and controls are needed to determine the universe and carry out the survey. In Guanansi, Quipal, and Tomebamba, geographic maps were drawn indicating every dwelling and the principal roads and footpaths. Next, each dwelling on the map was assigned a number that would be recorded on the survey. Owing to the much larger size of Peguche and time constraints on the survey team, a different method was devised that would ensure that every household was surveyed: fluorescent stickers were placed on the front door after completion of the survey. Instead of recording the household identification numbers, the neighborhood (or barrio) was recorded in Peguche. Thus, although the geographic mapping of key variables is precluded in Peguche, we can, nonetheless, show their spatial relationships using seven barrio divisions.

Survey data were gathered in all four villages from March through June of 1993. The questionnaires were filled out by the interviewers after the questions were asked verbally. The survey team for Guanansi and Peguche consisted of six native-born interviewers associated with the Incapirca Community House in Peguche. Although the survey instrument was written in Spanish, the Otavalan survey team asked the questions in Quichua (the local term for *Quechua,* which is the language spoken in the southern Andes) and Spanish. Conceptual equivalence between the Spanish and Quichua versions was attained by several hours of discussion among the research team members and Incapirca staff, who are fluent in both languages. Out of these discussions a common translation was agreed upon and used by all of the interviewers.*

The surveys in Quipal and Tomebamba were administered by two separate survey teams; in Quipal the team included a high school teacher native to the village; in Tomebamba the team included the local school teacher, who had worked in the village for several years, and an Ecuadorian anthropologist already known to the villagers. Research assistants were careful to note any inconsistencies between the response and their preexisting knowledge of the family and would ask for clarification when such inconsistencies occurred. Table A.1 presents details of survey data collection by village. The very low refusal rate across the four villages (.02%) indicates the familiarity and trust that interviewers enjoyed by virtue of their membership and common ethnic identity in the communities surveyed.

The number of vacant dwellings is significantly higher in Tomebamba and Quipal than in the Otavalan villages. This is a function, in part, of the type of migration in each region but also of the rapid cultural transformation occurring in Azuay, where more traditional houses built of adobe and straw are being abandoned in favor of cement cinder-block construction by migrants.

---

* The Quichua spoken in the Otavalo region has incorporated many Spanish words or derivatives. Hence, the distinction between a purely Spanish and Quichua version of the survey instrument is less clear-cut in this regard.

Table A.1. Household Survey, 1993

Village	Number of Dwellings on Frame	Vacant Dwellings	Refusals	Other Problems[a]	Number of Households Surveyed	Number of Adults in Survey
n	897	113	14	57	723	2,185
Quipal	213	29	1	21	162	511
Tomebamba	222	65	2	5	150	404
Guanansi	68	8	1	10	49	112
Peguche	394	11	10	21	362	1,158

Source: Study data, 1993.

[a] This category includes dwellings that were not inhabited but were still used for other purposes; households in which an adult member was never located after repeated attempts; and interrupted, incomplete, or incorrectly administered surveys.

Often the older structures are not torn down but are converted into storage houses. In some cases the family of a current migrant continues to live in the older house, though the new one is complete. In Quipal, a research assistant native to the community, and part of the original research team, recorded all return migration and new emigration from the village up to August 1994. As we expected, transnational migration was poised to take off in Quipal; fully thirty new migrants left during the fourteen-month period after July 1993.

The design of the questionnaire reflects a balance between the need to collect a range of information and the limitations posed by respondents with little time or education. Since in-depth case studies were being compiled in each village, the principal goals of the survey were validity, reliability, and a high response rate, attained by not overtaxing respondents with a lengthy and complex questionnaire. Thus, the survey interviews were generally less than one hour in duration.

The questionnaire is divided into nine sections. The first two sections record control information concerning the identification of the households surveyed. Sections 3 through 5 ask questions regarding household-level characteristics: language spoken, demographic data, type and condition of dwelling, and information on the household economy, including size of landholdings, use of modern agricultural inputs (e.g., fertilizers), and the other nonagricultural economic activity (cottage industry). This last section also asks how many modern consumer items the household has, such as televisions, VCRs, gas stoves, and electric looms.

The following section of the survey obtains general socioeconomic data on every adult member of the household between the ages of sixteen and sixty. Adult members who had migrated, but formed part of the household at the time of migration, were also included in the survey. Section 7 asks questions regarding the characteristics of the migration, including years abroad, whether they crossed with or without legal documents, their destination, and how the trip was financed. Since questions regarding migrant household members were answered by nonmigrant members, few questions regarding immigrant adaptation abroad were included in the household survey, since their validity would be extremely suspect.

Section 8 attempts to find out the degree of social closure and level of intervillage contact by asking whether the marriage of a daughter or son to a foreigner would be acceptable to the family. Other questions ask who the godparents were for family births and marriages in terms of kinship, community membership, and ethnicity: the response could range from a close relative of the same village to a foreign visitor. It was important to capture the institution of *compadrazgo* (fictive kinship), since it provides a way of examining the extent of social networks carrying important mutual obligations.

The last section asks questions regarding possible future migration, including why it was or was not being contemplated, and the duration and destination of the proposed trip. Finally, the respondent was asked an open-ended question concerning any changes he or she saw in the return migrants. In Guanansi and Peguche, the survey instrument asked a few additional questions concerning economic activities and specific sociocultural changes that had been noted in these villages through ethnographic research. For example, in Peguche, religious membership was of interest, since there were reports that many had converted to Protestantism, whereas Guanansi was thought to be homogeneously Catholic, often running off any Protestant missionaries unlucky enough to enter the village.

For each village, survey data were coded and then entered into two separate household and individual databases; individual data were then matched with household data to form a combined database for that village. An even larger database was formed by combining the merged village data, containing more than four hundred thousand data points.

Ethnographic Data

The more qualitative ethnographic research can be divided into two categories: case studies and participant observation. The case studies, which range from five to twenty for each village, were gathered by the author, who mostly interviewed male informants, and three female research assistants, who interviewed women in the Azuayan villages. The research team included a village member and two Ecuadorian social scientists, one of whom had conducted research on women in Tomebamba the previous year and was able to offer a number of insights into changes that had occurred in that village. The case studies were strategically chosen (using a purposive sample) to reflect the diversity of situations found by men and women in a particular village, ranging from a spouse left behind while the husband is abroad to young males who have not migrated.

During the initial trips to New York City, my primary research goal was to learn about aspects of the migrants' lives as individuals and as participants in a larger network or diaspora of Ecuadorians. Community civic and business leaders were asked to share their observations regarding the Ecuadorian exodus and their adaptation to the New York metro area. However, the last two trips, which were made after extensive fieldwork in Ecuador, were focused on contacting specific village members from Quipal and Tomebamba. Given the homogenous nature of migration from the latter village, I was much more successful in contacting its migrant members, virtually all of whom were living in the same Queens neighborhood. Migration from Quipal reflects its preexisting social and ethnic divisions, whereby trust must be gained within each subvillage network. Thus, given time and resource constraints, and the desire to attain a variety of migration paths, I focused on the "whites" from Quipal who were living in the Boston area. Although I never visited them in Boston, I talked to one of the pioneers in Quipal, who had returned for a visit and was about to take several friends and relatives back across the Mexican border with him. I then talked with him several times by telephone after his successful border crossing. Once again, the trust gained by meeting active migrants in their home villages, where a more natural rapport can be developed, was crucial for enabling me to contact them in the much more threatening environment of New York City and Boston, since most were undocumented or falsely documented.

In addition to the interviews, participant observation also provided a different type of "qualitative" data gained through a more unstructured role that plays down the researcher's status as researcher. In Azuay, I participated in a folkloric musical group from August to December 1993 (described in chapter 4). In Peguche, participant observation took the form of fictive kinship with a local indigenous family (described in chapter 6).

Statistical Overview of Migration

Using original household survey data, the following sections present a statistical overview of the prevalence of migration among individuals and households and their demographic and socioeconomic backgrounds, which are then compared with those of nonmigrants. These survey data provide a snapshot of transnational migration in each of the four villages from the time of its inception to the time of the survey in 1993, providing a basic set of information comparable across villages and with other cases of transnational migration.

Migration Prevalence in Four Rural Villages

As can be seen from table B.1, transnational migration is, indeed, a common strategy in the four research sites in Azuay and Otavalo, the rates of migration ranging from 9 percent of all adults (ages 16–60) in Quipal to 28.1 percent in Tomebamba. Apart from the overall high levels of migration, the table also indicates that the variation of sending levels within regions (Quipal versus Tomebamba) is as great as the variation between regions (Azuay versus Otavalo). "Active migrants" are those who were out of the country at the time of the survey, while "return migrants" are those migrants who were in their home village at the time of the survey. However, these categories do not imply that return migrants have returned permanently and will remain inactive. The data on the levels of return migrants reveal an important difference between regions: unlike the Azuayans to the south, the Otavalans were nearly all back in their home village during the April 1993 household survey.

The percentage of migrating adults is only one measure of the extent of

Table B.1. Migrant Status, by Village, Age Sixteen to Sixty, 1993 (percentage)

Migrant Status	Quipal	Tomebamba	Guanansi	Peguche
n	513	402	110	1,132
Active Migrant	8.4	26.4	1.8	3.5
Return Migrant	0.6	1.7	12.7	20.0
Never Migrated	91.0	71.9	85.5	76.5

Source: Study data, 1993.

migration; another method is to examine the levels of migration of adult members per household. In some villages most of the migration is highly concentrated in a few households; in others, the migrants may be dispersed over several households, resulting in a higher ratio. Otavalan villages exhibit somewhat higher levels of concentration of migrants by households, reflected in the ratio of migrant adults to migrant households, whereby a ratio of one indicates an equal proportion of migrants and migrant households in a village. The proportion of migrant households in Guanansi and Peguche is equivalent to or slightly less than the proportion of the adult migrant population in these villages. In contrast, the proportion of migrant households in the Azuayan villages is nearly twice the proportion of the migrant adult population, indicating a more dispersed distribution pattern. Yet, given the high overall sending levels of Tomebamba, that village has the highest average number of migrating members per household (0.7), with more than 14 percent of the households containing two or more migrant members.

A major dimension to the development of migration is the year of its onset and the rapidity of its development. Figures B.1 through B.4 show the number of first-time male and female migrants by year for each of the four villages. The y-axis is the raw number of migrants leaving for the first time that year, not a percentage of the village population. In general, there is a direct relationship between the current extent of migration in a village and the year of its onset; that is, the earlier the year of onset, the greater the proportion of migrants. However, the Azuayan villages, though later in their initial onset of migration abroad, exhibit a more rapid increase in transnational migration than in the Otavalan villages. Similarly, although Quipal and Tomebamba both sent migrants for the first time in nearly the same year, the development of transnational migration in Tomebamba has been much more rapid.

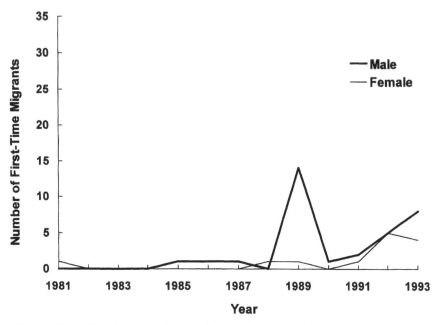

Figure B.1. Migration from Quipal, by Year of Onset and Sex
Source: Study data, 1993.

Figure B.1 shows that migration in Quipal, the village with the lowest level of migration in 1993, has developed fairly recently. The first village resident to migrate abroad was a young women who married a Peace Corps volunteer in 1981 and moved to the United States with her new husband. While the early years of migration abroad involved mostly men, in recent years women have migrated in nearly equal numbers. Another distinctive feature of the development of transnational migration in Quipal is the sudden rise in new, mostly male, migrants in 1989, reflecting a group migration whereby several friends and relatives cross the border en masse. This migration "spike" is common to all of the villages in varying degrees and typically occurs immediately after the first migrant pioneers have shown initial signs of success back home, such as constructing the first concrete house or buying the first new car or truck with foreign currency. In addition, the pioneers now attempt to help their immediate family members and friends to join them abroad. In this sense, the migration spike phenomenon is the first quantitative indication of the social origins of transnational migration in these villages.

In Tomebamba, the year of onset is only one year earlier than that in Quipal; yet, by 1988, nearly all of the males who were able to had already migrated abroad (figure B.2). Only in more recent years do we see that more

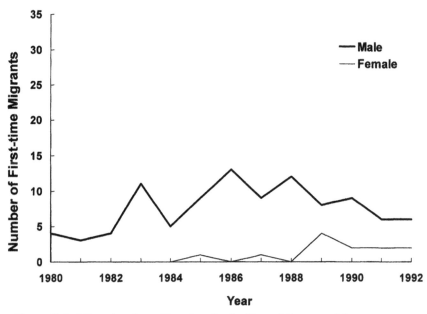

Figure B.2. Migration from Tomebamba, by Year of Onset and Sex
Source: Study data, 1993.

women have begun to migrate. Once again, there is a clear migration spike in 1983, when more than twice the number of villagers than the previous year migrated.

In contrast to Azuayan villages, the unfolding of transnational migration in Otavalan villages follows a distinctive pattern related to their entrepreneurial migration strategies. For example, while the first migrant abroad from Guanansi left in 1978, there was a lapse of nearly ten years before the next international migrant departed in 1987, from which time migration has steadily increased (figure B.3). However, all of the border crossings until 1991 were to Colombia, two hours to the north, or to Venezuela. In 1991, the first Guanansi residents headed for Germany and Holland. By the time of the survey in 1993, a "fever" to migrate to Europe and to the United States was beginning to be widespread in Guanansi—the year of the migration spike for that village, suggestive of a sociological process underlying migration similar to that of Azuayan sending communities.

The onset of migration abroad from Peguche began as early as 1949, when Rosa Lema, the subject of a well-known ethnography by Elsie Clews Parsons (1945), was invited by the president of Ecuador to accompany him on a tour

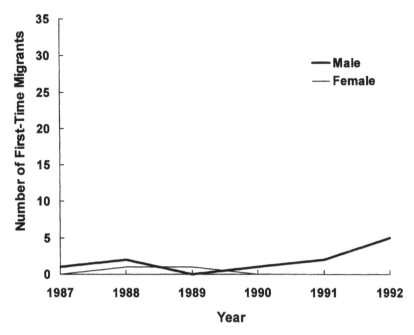

Figure B.3. Migration from Guanansi, by Year of Onset and Sex
Source: Study data, 1993.

of the United States.* Although her trip was diplomatic in nature, it never-theless dramatically revealed to Otavaleños the surprising interest by for-eigners, especially postwar Americans, in their native culture. While most of the transnational migrations from Peguche, through the early 1980s, were to other South American countries, especially to Colombia, the first regular transnational migrations to Europe began as early as 1970 (see figure B.4). During the late 1980s, migration abroad from Peguche rose sharply as more and more young men set off for Europe and North America, primarily to make music. The development of out-migration to South America first, and then the more recent development of migration to Europe and the United States, has also affected the sex ratio of migrants in both Otavalan villages: the more recent migrations to developed countries has been accompanied by a greater proportion of males. This is the opposite of the sex ratio trends found

* While 1949 is an appropriate year for dating the onset of contemporary transnational migration from the Otavalo region, not only from Peguche, it was not the first time that Otavalans traveled abroad.

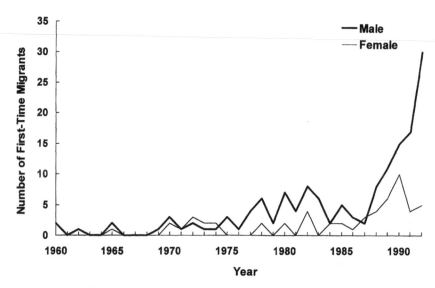

Figure B.4. Migration from Peguche, by Year of Onset and Sex
Source: Study data, 1993.

Table B.2. Migrant Status, by Sex and Village, 1993 (Percentage)

Village and Sex	Migrant	Nonmigrant
Quipal[a] ($n = 511$)		
Male	71.7	47.5
Female	28.3	52.5
Tomebamba[b] ($n = 404$)		
Male	87.7	30.0
Female	12.3	70.0
Guanansi[c] ($n = 112$)		
Male	81.5	43.6
Female	18.7	56.4
Peguche[d] ($n = 1,158$)		
Male	70.8	41.7
Female	29.2	58.3

Source: Study data, 1993.
[a] $\pi^2 = 9.811, p < .002.$
[b] $\pi^2 = 109.654, p < .000.$
[c] $\pi^2 = 7.748, p < .005.$
[d] $\pi^2 = 69.613, p < .000.$

in the Azuayan villages, where migration began as a predominantly male activity and then increasingly feminized.

The gender makeup of the migration flows from each village are overwhelmingly male (see table B.2). For example, in Tomebamba, nearly two-thirds of its inhabitants at any given time are women. This gender gap has begun to affect the social and cultural reproduction of the community. It should be noted, however, that the resulting gender imbalance of the nonmigrant population needs to be interpreted differently between the Azuayan and Otavalan villages: in Azuay, it represents real differences in the gender composition of communities over time owing to the longer stays of labor migrants, whereas in Otavalo the gender imbalance owing to migration is temporary. The survey in Otavalo was conducted in April and May, a peak period of migration for that region.

In sum, transnational migration from all four of the villages has become an important economic strategy for an increasing proportion of their inhabitants, with intriguing similarities in the development of migration in all four villages. Are the backgrounds of the migrants in these four villages similar or dissimilar? How do they differ from nonmigrants in their same village?

Individual Attributes of Migrants and Nonmigrants

A fundamental demographic characteristic of transnational migration is the sex distribution of the migrant flows, which was partly examined in figures B.1–B.4, when we looked at the development of transnational migration in each of the four villages. While all four villages exhibit a strong tendency for males to migrate, there are significant differences within regions regarding the sex distribution of migration. We saw in figure B.1 that Quipal's first emigrant was female and that female migration was significant in 1992. Indeed, to date, 28.3 percent of Quipal's international migrants have been women. Although the prevalence of transnational migration has been much higher in Tomebamba than in Quipal, women have only recently begun to migrate and still make up only 12.4 percent of Tomebamba's migrants.

In the Otavalo region, as we saw in figures B.3 and B.4, with the onset of greater transnational migration to the more developed countries, the proportion of women in the migrant flow has decreased somewhat. Traditionally, folkloric musical groups from the Andes are almost always exclusively male, hence the reduction in the proportion of females in more recent outflows. The making of music in the streets of foreign cities is a fairly recent addition to the commercial arsenal of Otavalans. In Guanansi, where transnational migration has developed under the more recent fashion of both selling crafts and music making, women constitute just 18.7 percent of the migrants. In Peguche, where a woman was the first international migrant, the overall proportion of women is the highest of the four villages, with 29.2 percent of migrant adults being female, reflecting the earlier period of somewhat more egalitarian migrations.

The age composition of transnational migration flows can tell us much about the possible purpose of out-migrations and, in more mature migration flows, the effects of migration on the age composition of those remaining behind. The migrant population of Quipal is extremely youthful, with the majority of migrants under the age of thirty. However, the relatively low levels of migration have not been enough to cause a noticeable impact thus far on the age composition of the nonmigrant population, which still takes a classic pyramid shape (in this case, one-half of a pyramid) of a so-called developing country. In contrast, while young adults predominate in Tomebamba's migration composition, the village also sees significant numbers of migrants throughout the working years. In addition, the high prevalence of out-migration has affected the pyramid structure of the age composition of the nonmigrant population, with a conspicuous drain on the population between the ages of twenty-one and thirty-five.

Similar to Quipal, Guanansi's age composition of migrants is very young, but its migrant population has not yet made a dent in the population pyramid to any significant degree. Peguche's more mature migration development is reflected in an age composition that is similar to that of Tomebamba; while generally youthful, significant numbers of migrants can be found at all age levels, which does seem to have flattened out the population pyramid somewhat.

Another demographic dimension related to the age composition is the marital status of international migrants. Marital status together with the age composition of migrants can indicate whether migration is a strategy for household formation. In all four villages, a majority of the migrants are married. However, in all of the villages except Guanansi, single migrants are overrepresented compared with the nonmigrant population. Approximately 40 percent of migrants are single in both Tomebamba and Peguche, communities similarly transformed by migration despite their different sociocultural contexts. However, the chi-square was not significant for Quipal nor Guanansi, indicating that these proportions could be attributed to chance.

Similarly, more than half the migrants in Quipal and 45 percent of the migrants in Tomebamba are the adult children of heads of households, representing the largest migrant categories for those villages. The Otavalan migrants, by contrast, tend to be household heads, though adult children of migrants do form fully one-third of the migrating group. Although the findings for Guanansi could be attributed to chance, in all of the villages the proportion of adult children migrating was greater than the proportion of adult children found among the nonmigrant population.

In the Azuayan villages of Quipal and Tomebamba, we also find two interesting anomalies in the data on household position and migrant status. In Quipal, the "other" category within a household accounts for 26 percent of migrant members, a greater percentage than those migrants described as household heads. A common strategy for newlyweds in Quipal who decide to migrate is for part of the family to move in with a parent while the husband, and sometimes the wife, work abroad. Young migrating couples, with or without children, are nominally part of an extended family in Ecuador, even though they are now living in New York or Boston.

In Tomebamba, the "spouse" category represents 38 percent of the predominantly male migrant population. Gender stratification is a common feature of Ecuadorian life, crosscutting all other forms of social stratification based on social class or caste. Under normal conditions, neither women nor men would recognize the wife as a household head, which would thereby make the husband a cohead or spouse. However, the long periods of absence by husbands that result from transnational migration has begun to alter women's self-identity, giving them a bittersweet feeling of independence, including the realization that they are, de facto, the household head. Thus, in migrant households 95 percent of "spouses" are male, while in nonmigrant households it is the exact opposite, with 95 percent of spouses being female.

In sum, given the nearly opposite migration strategies employed by the Azuayans and Otavalans, the demographic characteristics of migrants from both regions are similar: migrants from all four communities are mostly young males who have not yet, or have just recently, formed independent households. This suggests that transnational migration, whether to work or to sell, presents itself as an opportunity for young adult men to gain enough start-up capital to ensure an economic venture back home, a house and car, the ability to attract a desirable spouse, and a higher social status among the migrant's main reference group of community members.

Socioeconomic Background

The socioeconomic background of migrants and immigrants is of great interest to social scientists and the general public alike. As people traveling great physical and cultural distances in search of work, migrants are, not surprisingly, generally of lower socioeconomic status than the general population found at the destination. However, this observation tells us little about the relative socioeconomic position of migrants within their own regional and national societies. It has become a common finding of social researchers studying migration that nonrefugee migrants are generally positively self-selected and are often not the poorest of the poor of either their community or society. This finding seems to be upheld in our four research sites.

Before turning to the description of the occupational distribution of migrants, it should be noted that the sex distribution of migration has a direct impact on the occupational structure because of the sex-typing of some occupations. Furthermore, gender stratification develops within the parameters of the principal economic activities found within a particular cultural group.

In Quipal, a heterogeneous village near Cuenca that is now sending nearly as many women as men abroad, the occupational distribution of the migrant population is comparable to the nonmigrant population's distribution. However, migrants from Quipal do tend to have been trained in a modern skill—in this case, the use of sewing machines by both men and women—and are less likely to be farmers. In contrast to Quipal, the occupational distribution of migrants in Tomebamba is not at all comparable to that of the nonmigrant group, which is to be expected, given the disproportionate numbers of men who are migrating. Straw Panama hats, which in their heyday were woven by everyone, are now woven solely by women. Thus, the predominantly male migrant population comes largely from the ranks of those who held service jobs in nearby towns in Ecuador (72.4%), whereas the mostly female nonmigrant group are primarily engaged in the skilled traditional activities of hat weaving (62.7%) and subsistence agriculture (12.2%).

Similarly, the migrants, most of whom are male, from the agricultural community of Guanansi are less likely to be engaged in housework as their primary activity. Migrants from this village are more dedicated to traditional skills, such as weaving and acting as intermediaries for crafts made by others, than their nonmigrant counterparts. A similar, though more pronounced, occupational distribution can be found in Peguche between the migrant and nonmigrant groups. Nearly twice the proportion of migrants are engaged in traditional crafts than the nonmigrant population. It is also noteworthy that Peguche has now begun to export professionals, though they continue to retain households in the village.

Unlike the divergent patterns of occupational distribution found among the migrants of the four highland villages, educational attainment among those leaving their communities is consistently higher than among those who do not migrate. In Quipal, all of the migrants are literate, with at least four years of schooling. This is in contrast to the 20 percent of the nonmigrant population with less than four years of education. Migrants from Quipal are also more likely to have a high school diploma (28.3%) than nonmigrants (6%). However, both migrant and nonmigrant groups have nearly equal levels of postsecondary education (around 7%).

While the migrants in Tomebamba have considerably less education than those of Quipal, they are, nonetheless, better educated than their nonmigrant co-villagers. Unlike Quipal, there is no secondary school beyond the primary level in Tomebamba. While 8 percent of migrants in Tomebamba have no schooling, nearly 20 percent of nonmigrants in our study were illiterate. Similarly, more than half of the migrants had completed their primary training, though only 24 percent of nonmigrants had done so.

In Guanansi, which also has only a rudimentary primary school, the educational attainment pattern of migrants and nonmigrants is remarkably similar to that of Tomebamba. Although more than half of the nonmigrant population of Guanansi are illiterate, without any schooling (53.8%), only 12.5 percent of migrants had not attended school. Also, 37.5 percent of migrants had completed their primary education, while only 13 percent of the nonmigrant group had their primary diplomas.

While educational attainment patterns in Peguche are similar to those of the other three villages, differences between the migrant and nonmigrant groups are less divergent. For example, nonmigrants are three times more likely to be illiterate (30%) than migrants (8.6%), but the two groups have roughly equivalent levels of education until the secondary diploma, which more than one-fifth of the migrant group has attained compared with 7 percent of the nonmigrant group. A striking feature of both groups is the range of schooling levels: more than one-third of the village is illiterate, yet fully 10 percent have had some college, including several villagers with graduate degrees. This outcome is in keeping with the previous finding showing professional Otavalans working abroad.

By examining these two important measures of socioeconomic status among the four research sites—occupation and education—we have seen that while the occupational structure is highly sensitive to village-specific economic histories, educational attainment patterns for migrant and nonmigrant groups are strikingly similar across villages. The Azuayan villages demonstrate that even migrants from the same region can have a different mix of occupational backgrounds. With a much greater continuity between local economic activity and transnational migration patterns, both of the

Table B.3. Logistic Regressions of Selected Variables on Migration Status

Variable	Mean	Standard Deviation	Model 1 Parameter Estimate	Model 1 Log-Odds Ratio	Model 2 Parameter Estimate	Model 2 Log-Odds Ratio
n			1,820		1,820	
Age	35.336	15.695	−.029***	.971	−.027***	.974
Sex (0 = male, 1 = female)	0.516	0.500	−1.413***	.243	−1.467***	.231
Years of education	5.015	4.073	.058***	1.059	.105***	1.111
Marital status (0 = unmarried, 1 = married)	0.629	0.516	.434**	1.543	.554***	1.740
Village (dummy coded)						
Village 1					.304	1.355
Village 2					−1.193***	.303
Village 3					.897*	2.451
Degrees of freedom			4		7	
McFadden's r^2			.110		.169	

Source: Study data, 1993.
Note: *p < .05; **p < .01; ***p < .001. Cases with missing data have been deleted.

Otavalan communities draw most migrants from the ranks of those engaged in the production and merchandising of native crafts. Unlike these divergent patterns of occupational distribution, educational attainment patterns are virtually identical across villages, though the overall levels vary; migrants are decidedly better educated than their co-villagers.

Using a combined data set, table B.3 presents the results of two logistic regressions predicting migration abroad; the first includes some of the principal demographic and socioeconomic variables we have considered in this appendix; the second model adds village membership as a dummy-coded variable. Occupation was not included in the models, since it is highly correlated with village. The findings of the first model are consistent with previous descriptive observations; being young, male, educated, and married are all predictors of migration, with education and marital status especially strong, as shown in their log-odds ratio. Yet, with the addition of "village" in model

2, the log-odds ratio of one of its dummy codes is fully 2.451 and improves on the overall fit of the model as indicated by McFadden's rho-squared, which is similar to R-squared (though its size is expected to be somewhat smaller). While the variables remaining in the second model are little affected by the addition of "village," the fact that two of the dummy-coded variables are significant does indicate that migration from these communities is more complex than what can be captured in a model using only individual traits.

Spanish Terms Used in Text

agricultor-artesano	farmer-artisan
artesanía	artisanal products
artesano-agricultor	artisan-farmer
asiento	seat; Spanish settlement
ayllu	a communal kinship group under Incan rule
blanco	white
blanco-mestizo	preferred Ecuadorian term for *mestizo*
campesino	peasant; smallholding farmer
cargo	the responsibility of sponsoring a community feast
cascarilla	bark from which quinine is made
charango	stringed instrument made from the shell of an armadillo
chicha	a mild, fermented corn liquor
cholo	mestizo; can be pejorative or term of endearment, depending on context
cholo-Cuencanos	a distinctive class of peasants from the area surrounding Cuenca
chulquero	usurious moneylender; loan shark
comerciante	merchant; trader
comisionista	commission merchant
compadrazgo	fictive kinship
compadre	godfather
compañero	companion; comrade in arms
concertado	peon
concertaje	peonage system
corregimiento	a basic colonial administrative unit
coyote	a guide for illegal crossing of national borders
curaca	local indigenous leader; chief

efectos de Castilla	dry goods
encomendero	owner of the *encomienda*
encomienda	a labor system under which large estates were given to white elites along with the right to extract labor from the local Indian population
fachalina	traditional woven shawl
feria	local market
foresteros	internal refugees who sought to escape to more inaccessible highland areas or those communities perceived to be less egregious in their treatment of Indians
hacendado	hacienda owner
hacienda	large farm or ranch
huasipungero	an agricultural worker under the *huasipungo* system
huasipungo	a colonial labor system requiring laborers to "exchange" four days of work a week for the usufruct rights to a small plot, or *minifundio*
indígenas	indigenous people
indio	Indian; native
indio libre	free Indian
indio propio	owned Indian; agricultural peon
indio suelto	free Indian
jorga	group of friends
latifundia	large estate
la YANY	the Spanish translation of "I ♥ NY" ("Yo Amo New York"), the slogan of a bumper sticker popular in New York
mestizaje	miscegenation
mestizo	person of mixed European and Indian parentage; also, an Indian who adopts an urban lifestyle
mindalá	pre-Incan merchant class of traders
minifundio	small family farm
mita	an institution requiring that all adult males donate a year of labor for some public or private Spanish project once every five years.
mitayo	a worker under the *mita* system
mitimae; mitmakuna	an Incan institution of forced resettlement within the empire
naturale	indigenous person
obraje	textile sweatshop or primitive factory
paja toquilla	special type of straw used in hat weaving
parcialidad	small community
perro	a hat exporter's representative who travels to rural communities

pollera	traditional skirt worn by some cholas or campesinas
pucará	ritualized fighting during the San Juan festival
pueblo	commoner
quinta	small to medium hacienda
reducciónes	"reduced" settlements, created by the Spanish colonial policy of attempting to concentrate dispersed indigenous peasants into "feudalistic" corporate communities for greater political and religious control and for easier access to their labor
serrano	a person from the Sierra, or mountains
tramitador	a "facilitator" who provides the range of legal and illegal services needed to make a clandestine trip to the United States
vecino	neighbor; used to designate the founding families of Cuenca
yanapa	system of reciprocal obligations between peasants and hacendado
yanapero	an agricultural worker under the *yanapa* system

REFERENCES

Alexander, Jeffrey C. 1980–83. *Theoretical Logic in Sociology.* 4 vols. Berkeley: University of California Press.

Amin, Samir. 1974. "Modern Migrations in Western Africa." In *Modern Migrations in Western Africa,* edited by S. Amin. London: Oxford University Press.

Anderson, Patricia. 1988. "Manpower Losses and Employment Adequacy among Skilled Workers in Jamaica, 1976–1985." In *When Borders Don't Divide: Labor Migration and Refugee Movements in the Americas,* ed. Patricia Pessar. New York: Center for Migration Studies.

Astudillo, Jaime, and Claudio Cordero. 1990. *Huayrapamushcas en U.S.A.: Flujos migratorios de la región centro-sur del Ecuador.* Quito: Editorial el Conejo.

Basch, Linda, N. G. Schiller, and C. S. Blanc. 1994. *Nations Unbound: Transnational Projects, Postcolonial Predicaments, and Deterritorialized Nation-States.* Langhorne, Pa.: Gordon and Breach.

Bauman, Zygmunt. 1998. *Globalization: The Human Consequences.* New York: Columbia University Press.

Becker, G. S. 1975. *Human Capital.* New York: Columbia University Press.

Berger, Peter, and Thomas Luckmann. 1966. *The Social Construction of Reality.* New York: Doubleday.

Block, Fred. 1994. "The Roles of the State in the Economy." In *The Handbook of Economic Sociology,* ed. Neil J. Smelser and Richard Swedberg. Princeton: Princeton University Press.

Borjas, G. J. 1990. *Friends or Strangers: The Impact of Immigrants on the U.S. Economy.* New York: Basic Books.

Bourdieu, Pierre. 1986. "The Forms of Capital." In *Handbook of Theory and Research for the Sociology of Education,* ed. John G. Richardson. New York: Greenwood Press.

Buitrón, Anibel. 1947. "Situacion economica y social del indio otavaleno." *America Indígena* 7(1):45–67.

————. n.d. *Taita Imbabura: Vida indígena en los Andes*. Quito: Mision Andina.

Carpio, Patricio. 1992. *Entre pueblos y metropolis: La migración internacional en communidades austroandinas en el Ecuador*. Quito: Ediciones Abya-Yala.

Carrasco, Adrián. 1985. "La industrialización en el Azuay." *Azuay: Realidad de un Pueblo* 14 (June): 99–127.

Castles, Stephen, and Mark J. Miller. 1998. *The Age of Migration: International Population Movements in the Modern World*. 2d ed. New York: Guilford Press.

Chacón, Gerardo, and Sergio Chacón. 1991. *Mito y sobrevivencia en una comunidad mestiza*. Quito: Centro Ecuatoriano para Desarrollo de la Comunidad.

Chávez, Leo R. 1985. "'To Get Ahead': The Entrepreneurial Ethic and Political Behavior among Commercial Weavers in Otavalo." In *Political Anthropology in Ecuador: Perspectives from Indigenous Cultures*, ed. Jeffrey Ehrenreich. Albany, N.Y.: Society for Latin American Anthropology.

City of New York. 1992. *The Newest New Yorkers: An Analysis of Immigration into New York City during the 1980s*. New York: Department of City Planning.

Cohen, Robin. 1997. *Global Diasporas: An Introduction*. Seattle: University of Washington Press.

Coleman, James S. 1990. *Foundations of Social Theory*. Cambridge: Harvard University Press.

Collier, John, and Anibel Buitrón. 1949. *The Awakening Valley*. Chicago: University of Chicago Press.

Confederación de Nacionalidades de Indígenas del Ecuador (CONAIE). 1987. *Las Nacionalidades Indígenas en el Ecuador*. Quito: Ediciones Abya-Yala.

Consejo Nacional de Desarrollo (CONADE). 1989. *Poblacion y cambios sociales: Diagnostico sociodemografico del Ecuador, 1950–1982*. Quito: Corporacion Editora Nacional.

Crabb, Mary. 1993. "Otavalo: A Case Study of 'Successful' Ethnic Tourism." Master's thesis, Emory University.

Crain, Mary. 1991. "The Social Construction of National Identity in Highland Ecuador." *Anthropological Quarterly* 63 (1):43–59.

Curtin, Philip D. 1984. *Cross-Cultural Trade in World History*. Cambridge: Cambridge University Press.

D'Amico, Linda. 1993. "Expressivity and Ethnicity in Otavalo." Ph.D. diss., Indiana University.

de Janvry, Alain. 1982. *The Agrarian Question and Reformism in Latin America*. Baltimore: Johns Hopkins University Press.

Domínguez, Miguel E. 1991. *El sombrero de paja toquilla: Historia y economia*. Cuenca, Ecuador: Banco Central del Ecuador.

Dubly, Alain. 1990. *Los poblados del Ecuador*. Quito: Corporacion Editora Nacional.

Espinoza, Leonardo. 1979. "Politica fiscal de la Provincia de Cuenca: Resena historico pre supuestaria, 1779–1861." *Revista del Instituto de Investigaciones Sociales*, no. 6: 129–98.

Espinoza, Leonardo, and Lucas Achig. 1981. *Processo de desarrollo de las provincias de Azuay, Cañar, and Morona Santiago*. Cuenca, Ecuador: Center for Economic Reconversion of Azuay, Cañar, and Morona Santiago.

———. 1989. "De la sociedad comunitaria a la sociedad de clases." In *La sociedad azuayo-cañari: Pasado y presente,* ed. Leonardo Espinoza. Quito: El Conejo.

Espinoza Soriano, Waldemar. 1988a. *Etnohistoria Ecuatoriana: Estudios y documentos.* Quito: Ediciones Abya-Yala.

———. 1988b. *Los cayambes y carangues : siglos XV–XVI: El testimonio de la etnohistoria.* Otavalo, Ecuador: Instituto Otavaleño de Antropología.

Estudios Sociales. 1990. *Estudios sociales, segundo curso.* Cuenca, Ecuador: Edibosco.

Feld, S. L. 1981. "The Focused Organization of Social Ties." *American Journal of Sociology* 86(5): 1015–35.

Flores, Edmundo, and Tim Merrill. 1991. "The Economy." In *Ecuador: A Country Study,* ed. Dennis M. Hanratty. Washington, D.C.: Library of Congress, Federal Research Division.

Foner, Nancy. 1987. *New Immigrants in New York.* New York: Columbia University Press.

———. 1997. "What's New about Transnationalism? New York Immigrants Today and at the Turn of the Century." *Diaspora* 6(3): 355–75.

Frank, André Gunder. 1970. "The Development of Underdevelopment." In *Latin America: Underdevelopment of Revolution.* New York: Monthly Review Press.

Georges, Eugenia. 1990. *The Making of a Transnational Community: Migration, Development, and Cultural Change in the Dominican Republic.* New York: Columbia University Press.

Goldring, Luin. 1992. "La migración Mexico-EUA y la transnacionalización del espacio politíco y social: Perspectivas desde el Mexico rural." *Estudios Sociologicos,* no. 10: 315–40.

———. 1998. "The Power of Status in Transnational Social Fields." In "Transnationalism from Below," ed. Michael Peter Smith and Luis Guarnizo. *Comparative Urban and Community Research* (6):165–95.

Granovetter, Mark. 1974. *Getting a Job: A Study of Contacts and Careers.* Cambridge: Harvard University Press.

———. 1985. "Economic Action and Social Structure: The Problem of Embeddedness." *American Journal of Socioloy* 91(3): 481–510.

———. 1990. "The Old and the New Economic Sociology: A History and an Agenda." In *Beyond the Marketplace,* ed. Roger Friedland and A. F. Robertson. New York: Aldine de Gruyter.

Grasmuck, Sherri, and Patricia R. Pessar. 1991. *Between Two Islands: Dominican International Migration.* Berkeley: University of California Press.

Guarnizo, Luis-E. 1994. "Los Dominicanyorks: The Making of a Binational Society." *Annals of the American Academy of Political and Social Science* 533 (May): 70–86.

Guerrero, Andrés. 1991. *De la economia a las Mentalidades.* Quito: Editorial el Conejo.

Gurak, Douglas T., and Fe Caces. 1992. "Migration Networks and the Shaping of Migration Systems." In *International Migration Systems: A Global Approach,* ed. Mary Kritz, Lin Lim, and Hania Zlotnick. Oxford: Oxford University Press.

Hall, John R., and Mary Jo Neitz. 1993. *Culture: Sociological Perspectives.* Englewood Cliffs, N.J.: Prentice Hall.

Handlin, Oscar. 1951. *The Uprooted: The Epic Story of the Great Migrations That Made the American People.* Boston: Little, Brown.

Hannerz, Ulf. 1992. *Cultural Complexity: Studies in the Social Organization of Meaning.* New York: Columbia University Press.

Harvey, David. 1989. *The Condition of Postmodernity: An Enquiry into the Origins of Cultural Change.* Oxford: Basil Blackwell.

Hassaurek, Friedrich. 1967. *Four Years among the Ecuadorians.* 1867. Carbondale: Southern Illinois Press.

Hirschkind, Lynn. 1980. "On Conforming in Cuenca." Ph.D. diss., University of Wisconsin.

Hugo, G. J. 1981. "Village-Community Ties, Village Norms, and Ethnic and Social Ties: A Review of Evidence from the Third World." In *Migration Decision Making,* ed. Gordon F. DeJong and Robert W. Gardner. New York: Pergamon Press.

Hurtado, Osvaldo. 1980. *Political Power in Ecuador.* Translated by Nick D. Mills, Jr. 1977. Albuquerque: University of New Mexico Press.

Inkeles, Alex, and David H. Smith. 1974. *Becoming Modern: Individual Change in Six Developing Countries.* Cambridge: Harvard University Press.

Instituto de Investigaciones Sociales (IDIS). 1990. "Propuesta para la investigación de migración al exterior." Unpublished manuscript, Universidad de Cuenca, Ecuador.

Instituto Nacional de Estadistica y Censos (INEC). 1991. *Anuario de estadisticas de migracion internacional.* Quito: Republica del Ecuador.

Jaramillo Alvarado, Pio. 1954. *El indio Ecuatoriano.* Quito: Corporacion Editora Nacional.

Jaramillo Cisneros, Hernán. 1987. "Apuntes sobre la artesanía textil de Otavalo." *Sarance* (Instituto Otavaleno de Antropología) 11 (August): 11–20.

Kalberg, Stephen. 1994. *Max Weber's Comparative Historical Sociology.* Chicago: Chicago University Press.

Kearney, Michael. 1996. *Reconceptualizing the Peasantry: Anthropology in Global Perspective.* Boulder: Westview Press.

Kluck, Patricia. 1991. "The Society and Its Environment." In *Ecuador: A Country Study,* ed. Dennis M. Hanratty. Washington, D.C.: Library of Congress, Federal Research Division.

Korovkin, Tanya. 1998. "Commodity Production and Ethnic Culture: Otavalo, Northern Ecuador." *Economic Development and Cultural Change* 47(1):125–54.

Kritz, Mary, Lin Lim, and Hania Zlotnick, eds. 1992. *International Migration Systems: A Global Approach.* Oxford: Oxford University Press.

Kyle, David. 1996. "The Transnational Peasant: The Social Construction of International Economic Migration from the Ecuadoran Andes." Ph.D. diss., Johns Hopkins University.

———. 1999. "The Otavalo Trade Diaspora: Social Capital and Transnational Entrepreneurship." *Ethnic and Racial Studies* 22(2):422–46.

Lerner, Daniel. 1965. *The Passing of Traditional Society: Modernizing the Middle East.* New York: Free Press.

Lomnitz, Larissa. 1977. *Networks and Marginality: Life in a Mexican Shantytown.* New York: Academic Press.

Lucas, Robert E. B. 1992. "International Migration: Economic Causes, Consequences, and Evaluations." In *Global Trends in Migration,* ed. Mary Kritz, Lin Lim, and Hania Zlotnick. New York: Center for Migration Studies.

Mabogunje, A. L. 1970. "Systems Approach to a Theory of Rural-Urban Migration," *Geographical Analysis,* 2(1): 1–18.

Mahler, Sarah. 1995. *American Dreaming: Immigrant Life on the Margins.* Princeton: Princeton University Press.

———. 1998. "Theoretical and Empirircal Contributions toward a Research Agenda for Transnationalism." In "Transnationalism from Below," ed. Michael Peter Smith and Luis Guarnizo. *Comparative Urban and Community Research* (6):64–102.

Marshall, Adriana. 1987. "New Immigrants in New York's Economy." In *New Immigrants in New York,* ed. Nancy Foner. New York: Columbia University Press.

Massey, Douglas, Rafael Alarcon, Jorge Durand, and Humberto Gonzalez. 1987. *Return to Aztlan: The Social Process of International Migration from Western Mexico.* Berkeley: University of California Press.

Massey, Douglas S., Joaquín Arango, Graeme Hugo, Ali Kouaouci, Adela Pellegrino, and J. Edward Taylor. 1998. *Worlds in Motion: Understanding International Migration at the End of the Millennium.* Oxford: Clarendon Press.

McClelland, David G. 1967. *The Achieving Society.* New York: Free Press.

McMichael, Philip. 1996. *Development and Social Change: A Global Perspective.* Thousand Oaks, Calif.: Pine Forge Press.

Meier, Peter. 1981. "Peasants' Crafts in Otavalo: A Study of Economic Development and Social Change in Rural Ecuador." Ph.D. diss., University of Toronto.

Meisch, Lynn. 1987. *Otavalo: Weaving, Costume, and the Market.* Quito: Ediciones Libri Mundi.

———. 1995. "Gringas and Otavaleños: Changing Tourist Relations." *Annals of Tourism Research* 22(2): 441–62.

———. 1997. *Transnational Communities, Transnational Lives: Coping with Globalization in Otavalo.* Ph.D. diss., Stanford University.

Miller, Tom. 1986. *The Panama Hat Trail.* New York: Vintage Books.

Monge Zari, Sergio I. 1992. "El impacto de la migración campesina a Estados Unidos de Norte América sobre la estratificación social." B.A. thesis, University of Cuenca, Ecuador.

Morawska, Eva. Forthcoming. "The New-Old Transmigrants, Their Transnational Lives, and Ethnicization: A Comparison of Nineteenth-, Twentieth-, and Twenty-first-Century Situations." In *Immigrants, Civic Culture, and Modes of Political Incorporation,* ed. Gary Gertle and John Mollenkopf. New York: Social Science Research Council.

Muratorio, Blanca. 1993. "Nationalism and Ethnicity: Images of Ecuadorian Indians and the Imagemakers at the Turn of the Century." In *Ethnicity and the State,* ed. Judith D. Toland. New Brunswick, N.J.: Transaction Books.

Myrdal, Gunnar. 1957. *Rich Lands and Poor*. New York: Harper and Row.

Oberem, Udo. 1981. "Los caranquis de la sierra norte del Ecuador y su incorporación al Tahuantinsuyo." In *Contribución a la etnohistoria Ecuatoriana*, ed. Segundo Moreno and Udo Oberem. Otavalo, Ecuador: Instituto Otavaleño de Antropología.

Orlove, Benjamin. 1977. "Against a Definition of Peasantries: Agrarian Production in Andean Peru." In *Peasant Livelihood: Studies in Economic Anthropology and Cultural Ecology*, ed. Rhoda Halperin and James Dow. New York: St. Martin's Press.

Palomeque, Silvia. 1990. *Cuenca en el siglo XIX: La articulacion de una region*. Quito: Ediciones Abya-Yala.

Papademetriou, Demetrios G. 1986. *New Immigrants to Brooklyn and Queens: Policy Implications, Especially with Regard to Housing*. Staten Island, N.Y.: Center for Migration Studies of New York.

Parsons, Elsie Clews. 1945. *Peguche: A Study of Andean Indians*. Chicago: University of Chicago Press.

Pearse, Andrew. 1975. *The Latin American Peasant*. London: Frank Cass.

Petersen, William. 1958. "A General Typology of Migration." *American Sociological Review* 23(3): 256–66.

Phelan, John Leddy. 1967. *The Kingdom of Quito in the Seventeenth Century: Bureaucratic Politics in the Spanish Empire*. Madison: University of Wisconsin Press.

Piore, M. J. 1979. *Birds of Passage: Migrant Labor and Industrial Societies*. New York: Cambridge University Press.

Polanyi, Karl. 1957. *The Great Transformation: The Political and Economic Origins of Our Time*. Boston: Beacon Press.

Portais, Michel. 1989. "Los intercambios internacionales del Ecuador: Su significacion geopolitica." In *Flujos geograficos en el Ecuador*, ed. Juan Moya. Quito: Corporacion Editora Nacional.

Portes, Alejandro. 1995. "Economic Sociology and the Sociology of Immigration: A Conceptual Overview." In *The Economic Sociology of Immigration: Essays on Networks, Ethnicity, and Entrepreneurship*, ed. Alejandro Portes. New York: Russell Sage Foundation.

Portes, Alejandro, and R. L. Bach. 1985. *Latin Journey: Cuban and Mexican Immigrants in the United States*. Berkeley: University of California Press.

Portes, Alejandro, Luis Guarnizo, and Patricia Landolt. 1999. "Introduction: Pitfalls and Promise of an Emergent Research Field." *Ethnic and Racial Studies* 22(2):217–37.

Portes, Alejandro, and Rubén G. Rumbaut. 1996. *Immigrant America: A Portrait*. 2d ed. Berkeley: University of California Press.

Portes, Alejandro, and Julia Sensenbrenner. 1993. "Embeddedness and Immigration: Notes on the Social Determinants of Economic Action." Paper presented at a meeting of the American Sociological Association, Cincinnati, Ohio, August 27.

Portes, Alejandro, and John Walton. 1981. *Labor, Class, and the International System*. New York: Academic Press.

Powers, Karen. 1995. *Andean Journeys: Migration, Ethnogenesis, and the State in Colonial Quito*. Albuquerque: University of New Mexico Press.

Ragin, Charles C. 1987. *The Comparative Method: Moving beyond Qualitative Strategies*. Berkeley: University of California Press.

Ravenstein, E. G. 1885. "The Laws of Migration." *Journal of the Statistical Society* 48(2): 167–235.

———. 1889. "The Laws of Migration." *Journal of the Statistical Society* 52 (2): 241–305.

Reichert, Joshua. 1981. "The Migrant Syndrome: Seasonal U.S. Wage Labor and Rural Development in Central Mexico." *Human Organization* 40(1): 56–66.

Ritchey, P. Neal. 1976. "Explanations of Migration." In *Annual Review of Sociology* 2:363–404.

Roberts, Bryan. 1978. *Cities of Peasants: The Political Economy of Urbanization in the Third World*. Beverly Hills, Calif.: Sage Publications.

Rouse, Roger. 1992. "Making Sense of Settlement: Class Transformation, Cultural Struggle, and Transnationalism among Mexican Migrants in the United States." In *Towards a Transnational Perspective on Migration: Race, Class, Ethnicity, and Nationalism Reconsidered*, ed. Nina Glick Schiller, Linda Basch, and Cristina Szanton Blanc. New York: New York Academy of Sciences.

Rowe, John Howland. 1963. "Inca Culture at the Time of the Spanish Conquest." In *Handbook of South American Indians*, vol. 2, *The Andean Civilizations*, ed. Julian Steward. New York: Cooper Square Publishers.

Rudolph, James D. 1991. "Historical Setting." In *Ecuador: A Country Study*, ed. Dennis M. Hanratty. Washington, D.C.: Library of Congress, Federal Research Division.

Sabean, David Warren. 1984. *Power in the Blood: Popular Culture and Village Discourse in Early Modern Germany*. New York: Cambridge University Press.

Salamea Cordero, Mario. 1979. "La emigracion international en Azuay entre los anos 1970–1976." B.A. thesis, University of Cuenca, Ecuador.

Salomon, Frank. 1981. "Weavers of Otavalo." In *Cultural Transformations and Ethnicity in Modern Ecuador*, ed. Norman Whitten. Urbana: University of Illinois Press.

———. 1986. *Native Lords of Quito in the Age of the Incas: The Political Economy of North Andean Chiefdoms*. Cambridge: Cambridge University Press.

Sassen-Koob, Saskia. 1978. "The International Circulation of Resources and Development: The Case of Migrant Labor." *Development and Change* 9(4): 509–45.

———. 1981. *Exporting Capital and Importing Labor: The Role of Caribbean Migration to New York City*. Occasional Paper 28. Center for Latin American and Caribbean Studies, New York University.

Sawyer, Suzana. 1997. *Marching to Nation across Ethnic Terrain: The Politics of Identity, Territory, and Resource Use in the Ecuadorian Amazon*. Ph.D. diss., Stanford University.

Schodt, David W. 1987. *Ecuador: An Andean Enigma*. Boulder: Westview Press.

Serrano, Alejandro. 1992. "El poder municipal: Situacion actual y tendencias." In *Cuenca y su futuro*. Quito: CORDES.

Siracusa, Christina. 1996. *Transnational Dimensions of Ethnic Politics: A Comparative Study of the Shuar and Huaorani of the Ecuadoran Amazon*. Ph.D. diss., Johns Hopkins University.

Skeldon, Ronald. 1997. *Migration and Development: A Global Perspective*. Edinburgh Gate, Harlow, Essex : Longman, Longman Press.

Smith, Michael Peter, and Luis Guarnizo. 1998. "The Locations of Transnationalism." In "Transnationalism from Below," ed. Michael Peter Smith and Luis Guarnizo. *Comparative Urban and Community Research* (6):3–34.

Smith, Robert. C. 1994. "Los ausentes siempre presentes: The Imagining, Making, and Politics of a Transnational Community between Ticuani, Puebla, Mexico, and New York City." Ph.D. diss., Columbia University.

———. 2000. "Comparing Local-Level Swedish and Mexican Transnational Life: An Essay in Historical Retrieval." Unpublished manuscript.

Soysal, Y. N. 1994. *Limits of Citizenship: Migrants and Postnational Membership in Europe*. Chicago: University of Chicago Press.

Stark, Louisa R. 1985. "The Role of Women in Peasant Uprisings in the Ecuadorian Highlands." In *Political Anthropology in Ecuador: Perspectives from Indigenous Cultures*, ed. Jeffrey Ehrenreich. Albany, New York: Society for Latin American Anthropology.

Sutton, C. R. 1987. "The Caribbeanization of New York City and the Emergence of a Transnational Socio-cultural System." In *Caribbean Life in New York City: Socio-cultural Dimensions*, ed. Constance R. Sutton and Elsa Chaney. Staten Island, N.Y.: Center for Migration Studies of New York.

Tartter, Jean R. 1991. "National Security." In *Ecuador: A Country Study*, ed. Dennis M. Hanratty. Washington, D.C.: Library of Congress, Federal Research Division.

Terán, Benjamín. 1991. "Los indios plásticos." *Shimishitachi: Información y Reflexión sobre Temas Indígenas* 9 (Dec.): 20–22.

Thomas, Brinley. 1973. *Migration and Economic Growth: A Study of Great Britain and the Atlantic Economy*. London: Cambridge University Press.

Thomas, William I., and Florian Znanieki. 1927. *The Polish Peasant in Europe and America*. Vol. 2. New York: Alfred A. Knopf.

Tilly, Charles. 1990. "Transplanted Networks." In *Immigration Reconsidered*, ed. Virginia Yans- McLaughlin. New York: Oxford University Press.

Tilly, Charles, and C. H. Brown. 1967. "On Uprooting, Kinship, and the Auspices of Migration." *Journal of Comparative Sociology* 8(2): 141–64.

Turner, Jonathan H. 1985. *The Structure of Sociological Theory*. Homewood, Ill.: Dorsey Press.

U.S. Bureau of the Census. 1993. *Statistical Abstract of the United States*. Washinton D.C.: U.S. Government Printing Office.

U.S. Immigration and Naturalization Service (INS). 1988. *Annual Report*. Washington D.C.: U.S. Government Printing Office.

Vertovec, Steven. 1999. "Conceiving and Researching Transnationalism." *Ethnic and Racial Studies* 22(2): 447–62.

Wachtel, Nathan. 1977. *The Vision of the Vanquished: The Spanish Conquest of Peru through Indian Eyes, 1530–1570*. New York: Harper and Row.

Wallerstein, Immanuel. 1974. *The Modern World-System*. New York: Academic Press.

Walter, Lynn. 1981. "Otavaleño Development, Ethnicity, and National Integration." *América Indígena* 41(2): 319–37.

Walton, John. 1983. "Marx for the Late Twentieth Century: Transnational Capital and Disenfranchised Labor." *Social Science Quarterly,* 64(4): 786–809.

Warren, Robert R. 1995. "Estimates of the Undocumented Immigrant Population Residing in the United States, by Country of Origin and State of Residence." Paper presented to the Population Association of America, April, San Francisco.

Wellman, Barry. 1979. "The Community Question: The Intimate Networks of East Yorkers." *American Journal of Sociology* 84(5): 1201–31.

Wrong, Dennis. 1961. "The Oversocialized Conception of Man in Modern Sociology." *American Sociological Review* 26(2): 183–93.

Wyman, Mark. 1993. *Round-Trip to America: The Immigrants Return to Europe, 1880–1930.* Ithaca: Cornell University Press.

Zlotnik, Hania. 1992. "The Identification of Migration Systems." In *International Migration Systems: A Global Approach,* ed. Mary Kritz, Lin Lim, and Hania Zlotnick. Oxford: Oxford University Press.

INDEX

Page numbers in *italics* indicate maps and tables.

"active migrants," 215

Agato, 138

agriculture: agrarian reforms and, 61, 62, 133–34, 135; altitude and, 115; in Azuay, 49; cultural "authenticity" and, 180; in Guanansi, 154–56, 170–71, 175; hacienda system, 128; migration and, 175; minifundio system, 21, 54, 55, 115; in Otavalo, 133; in Peguche, 175; in Quipal, 77–78, 103–4; in Tomebamba, 74, 103–4; women and, 103–4, 108–9; yanapa-hacienda relationship, 136–37, 154–55

Amazon, colonization of, 19, 25–26, 116

Andean tweed, 125–31

Angla, 171–72

asientos, 22

Atahualpa, 50, 117

Audencia of Quito, 53, 119, 120, 156

authority structure in Otavalo, 123–25

Awakening Valley, The (Collier and Buitrón), 114, 131

ayllu, 19–20

Aztra sugar plantation, 62

Azuay (province): agriculture in, 49; church hierarchy in, 51, 71–72; colonial period in, 50–55, 191; cultural alienation in, 192; economy of, 53–54, 55, 56, 57–61, 224; education in, 63, 225; gender in, 221; global market and, 10; hacienda system in, 52, 55, 61, 73; indigenous population in, 52–53, 110–11; land tenure in, 53, 102, 103–4; location of homes in, 97, *97, 98,* 98–99; mestizos in, 52; migration from, ix, 25, 29, 59–60, 64–65; migration merchants and, 66–71; modernization in, 61–64; "nobility" in, 51, 55, 59, 63; onset and development of migration in, 216; Otavalo compared to, 156–57, 182–83, 192, 203; pattern of migration from, 3–5, 192, 196–97; pre-Colombian period in, 48–50; Republican period in, 55–58; results from study of, 201–2; undocumented migration from, 33. *See also* Cuenca; labor migration; Quipal; Tomebamba

Bach, R. L., 10, 83

banana exports, 23, 25, 31

Baños, 76

Bauman, Zygmunt, 206

Benalcazar, Sebastian, 50

243

border, crossing without authorization, ix, 34–35, 70

Borja, Rodrigo, 27–28

Boston, migrants in, 95, 213

Bourdieu, Pierre, 196

Buitrón, Anibel: *The Awakening Valley*, 114, 127, 131; on education, 132; on Indians and authority, 164; on Otavalan communities, 167; on Saturday market, 128–29; on Señor Uribe, 125–26

cacao, 23, 25, 124

Caces, Fe, 84, 85

Cajas, José, 125–26, 133

campesino, 6–7n., 186

Cañari, 49–50

Cañar (province): coastal migration from, 25, 26, 70–71; hat weaving and, 57, 59, 61; history of, 48; migration from, 29, 33

capitalism, 46, 71, 152, 169, 192

Cara, 115, 116, 117

Caranqui, 115, 116, 117

cargo, 136, 153

Carpenter, Lawrence, 134

cascarilla exports, 58

caste in Andean region, 7, 28, 54, 123

Castles, Stephen, 1, 2, 190

census, 160

Center for Economic Reconversion of Azuay, Cañar, and Morona Santiago (CREA), 61

Charijayak, 141–42, 180

Chávez, Leo, 150

Checa, 73, 74–75

Chimborazo (province), 25, 26

cholo, 60, 90, 209

chulla vida, 90

chulquero, 66, 67

church hierarchy: in Azuay, 51, 73–74; in Tomebamba, 73–74

cloth: sewing of, 78–79, 105–6, 111; spinning and weaving of, 54–55, 60. *See also* weaving in Otavalo

Cohen, Robin, 205

Collier, John: *The Awakening Valley*, 114, 127, 131; on education, 132; on Saturday market, 128–29; on Señor Uribe, 125–26

colonial period: in Azuay, 50–55, 191; Azuay compared to Otavalo, 156–57; in Ecuador, 20–22; in Otavalo, 118–21, 191

colonization of Amazon, 19, 25–26, 116

community: nonterritorial concept of, 84–85; in Otavalo, 135–36; ritual fighting among communities, 137; transnational type, 9, 81–82

compadrazgo, 164–65, 212

comparative study design, 6–8, 11–12, 15, 160, 207

consumerism, 28–29, 48, 97, 104, 176

Cordero, Febres, 27

core-centered dynamic, 84

core country, 3, 83

Costa region: description of, 18; migration to, 19, 23, 25, 58, 60, 74, 79; Sierra region and, 22; transnational migration and, 94, 111

Cotacachi, 121

coyote, 66–67, 69, 203

Crabb, Mary, 163, 194

cross-cultural trade diasporas, 204–6

Cuba, 89–90

Cuenca: description of, 2, 15; economy of, 53–54, 91; growth of, 26; hat weaving and, 56; history of, 19, 21, 48, 50; migration and, 33, 65, 87–92; New York City and, 64; oil boom and, 62; status consciousness in, 51; vecinos in, 51

cultural capital, 196

cultural commodity: "authenticity" and, 171, 180, 192; indigenous groups and, 143–45, 147; music and, 141–42, 147–48; Otavalans and, 5–6, 15, 131–35, 179–82; overview of, x. *See also* weaving in Otavalo

culture, description of, 193–94

Curtin, Philip, 204

D'Amico, Linda, 130, 134
debt peonage, 21, 27, 121
Déleg, 93, 94
de Morga, Antonio, 119–20
destination of migrants: Boston, 95, 213; New York state, 2; from Otavalo, 40, 162, 165–66, 172–73; from Quipal, *99*, 99–101. *See also* New York City
development and migration, 46–48
Día de los Ausentes, El, 203
Diceney Tours, 142
dollarization of economy, 102–3, 187–88
Domínguez, Miguel, 57
dual citizenship, 2, 203
Duran-Ballén, Sixto, 29

economic sociology, 85–87, 195–96
economy: of Azuay, 53–54, 55, 56, 57–58, 224; CREA, 61; of Cuenca, 53–54, 91; dollarization of, 102–3, 187–88; of Ecuador, 11, 23–25, 48, 63–64, 187–88; encomienda system, 21, 50, 118; of Guanansi, 167, 169–72, 224; International Monetary Fund and, 187, 205; of Otavalo, 121–23, 135–38, 194–95; of Peguche, 152, 167–69, 192, 224; of Quipal, 77–80, 102–4; remittances and, 64, 70–71, 102–3, 104, 108–9; of Tomebamba, 74–76, 102–4; transnational household and, 102–4; vertical integration of, 204. *See also* exports; hacienda system; merchant class in Otavalo; Panama hat trade; weaving in Otavalo
Ecuador: agrarian reforms in, 61, 62, 133–34, 135; cultural heritage in, 27; economy of, 11, 23–25, 48, 63–64, 187–88; fieldwork in, 208–9; International Monetary Fund and, 187, 205; literacy in, 17–18, 28; migration from, 3, 4–5, 9–10, 29–35, 35–36, 42; migration within, 18–22, 25–26, 60, 74, 79; regionalism of, 18, 22, 191; research sites in, *14*, 209; social change and

protest in, 26–29, 62; societal themes in, 17–18; Spanish rule in, 20–22, 50–55, 118–21; transnationalization of, 188–89. *See also* indigenous groups
Ecuadorian Organizing Committee, 124
Ecuador Travel, 33, *34*
education: in Azuay, 63, 225; in Cuenca, 91; in Ecuador, 17–18, 28; of migrants, 31, 38, 47, 224–25; in Otavalo, 126–27, 132, 143, 225; in Peguche, 152–53, 225
embeddedness, 86
encomienda system, 21, 50, 118
entrepreneurial transnational migration. *See* market migration
equilibrium concept, 37–38, 46–47, 190–91
Espinoza, Leonardo, 53–54
Espinoza Soriano, Waldemar, 115
ethnicity: in Andean region, 27, 77, 209; conflict and, 194; data on, 212–13; economic activity and, 7, 135–38; market migration and, 183; migration and, 6, 12, 85; in Otavalo, 123–25, 159; in Peguche, 151; in Quipal, 76, 77, 80; stratification by, 18, 79–80, 135–38, 148; in Tomebamba, 75–76. *See also* indigenous groups; mestizos
exports: bananas, 23, 25, 31; cacao, 23, 25, 124; cascarilla, 58; petroleum, 23–25, 62. *See also* Panama hat trade; weaving in Otavalo
external economic dependence, 23–25, 48, 63–64

Feld, S. L., 85
Fisch, Olga, 134

gender: migration and, 8, 34, 177–79, *220*, 221–22; music and, 221; stratification by, 76, 77, 79, 104–6, 223, 224; urbanization and, 139–41; weaving and, 60, 150. *See also* women
General Tire Company, 61, 79
Girón, 65

globalization: Azuay economy and, 57–58; common currency and, 188; migration and, ix, x, 3–4; predictions of, 46; regionalism and, 191

godparents, role of, 164–65, 212

Granovetter, Mark, 72, 84, 86–87

Grasmuck, Sherri, 11, 83

Gualaceo, 68–69

Guanansi: agriculture in, 154–56, 170–71, 175; Angla compared to, 171–72; community center of, 170; demographic characteristics of, 221–22, 223; description of, 6, 12–13, *13*, 15; destination of migrants from, 40; economy of, 167, 169–72, 224; financing of migration from, 173; hacienda system and, 136, 154–56; land and, 155, 175; before mass migration, 148–49, 153–56; migration from, *41, 42, 43*, 173; onset and development of migration in, 218, *219*; Peguche and, 169; results from study of, 202; socioeconomic background in, 224, 225

Guayaquil, 24, 25, 26, 30–31, 33

Guerrero, Andrés, 55, 136, 154, 155, 161

Guevara, Ché, 89

Gurak, Douglas, 84, 85

hacienda system: in Azuay, 52, 55, 61, 73; in Guanansi, 154–56; in Otavalo, 128, 136–37; in Sierra region, 23

handicrafts. *See* cloth; Panama hat trade; weaving in Otavalo

Hassaurek, Friedrich, 121–22, 123

Hirschkind, Lynn, 50–52, 53, 54, 61–62, 63

historical-structural perspective, 46–48, 83–84, 191–92

household: as economic unit, 102–4; survey of, 160, 207–8, 209–12, *211. See also* transnational household

Huáscar, 50

huasipungo: description of, 15, 21, 22, 121; end of, 27; "huasipungo times," 159; latifundia and, 120

human capital, x, 38, 191, 197

human smuggling, ix, 66–67, 69–71

Hurtado, Osvaldo, 27

Imbabura (province): migration from, 25, 26, 33–34. *See also* Otavalo (canton)

immigration, definition of, 30

Immigration and Naturalization Service (INS), 35

Incapirca Community House (Peguche), 210

Inca regime, 18–20, 49–50, 115

indigenous groups: authority and, 164; in Azuay, 52–53, 110–11; in cities, 209; culture of, 143–45, 147; exploitation of, 22, 26–27; indios libres or indios sueltos, 151, 168; "indios plásticos," 180–81; "los naturales," 186; in Quipal, 79, 99–100; uprising by, 28

international migration: macrosociological theories of, 45–46, 82–83; push and pull factors, 37–38, 189; theories, application and function of, xi, 10, 189, 190, 198–99. *See also* labor migration; mass migration; transnational migration

International Monetary Fund, 187, 205

jorga, 88

Juan Antonio de Ulloa, Jorge, 120–21

Kearney, Michael, 194

labor market theory, 42–44, 190–91

labor migration: beginnings of, 64–65; dimensions of, 91–92; dollarization of economy and, 188; as familial strategy, 64–65; financing of, *100*, 101; onset of, 96–99, *97, 98*; overview of, 3, 39–41, 47; past compared to current, 83–84; permanent compared to temporary, 110n., 188; pioneers of, 30–31, 65, 91, 92–93; wage differentials and, 3–4, 38, 42

La Mar, Mariscal José de, 54n.
land tenure: analyses of, 168; in Azuay, 53, 102, 103–4; in Guanansi, 155, 175; in Otavalo, 122–23, 171; in Peguche, 150–51, 175
latifundism, 120
"laws of migration" (Ravenstein), 189–90
Lema, Rosa: on land, 122; as merchant, 129–31, 151, 171; migration of, 218–19; as pioneer, 126, 194
liquor smuggling, 78–79
literacy in Ecuador, 17–18, 28
Lucas, Robert, 42–43

Mahuad, Jamil, 187–88
Manabí (province), 56
market migration: cultural change and, 179–82; current generation and, 180; ethnicity and, 183; financing of, 173; gender and, 177–79; godparents, role of in, 164–65; handicraft production and, 174, *174;* individualism and, 181, 182; information about, 162, 165–66; overview of, ix, 39–42, 160–63; pattern of, 172, 173; profits from, 176; saturation of market and, 187; socialization for, 163; social networks for, 163–64, 176–77
Marx, Karl, 46
massacre at Aztra sugar plantation, 62
Massey, Douglas, 10–11, 83
mass migration: from Azuay to New York City, 64–65, 72; definition of, 30; from Ecuador to U.S., 4–5, 30–31; migration fever and, 161
Meier, Peter, 136, 137, 146, 147
Meisch, Lynn: on clothing, 116, 135; on current migration patterns, 187, 188; on innovation in design, 134; on musicians, 178; on Plaza de Poncho, 144
merchant class in Otavalo, 129–31, 132–33, 140–41, 168–69, 192
merchant migration. *See* market migration
mestizaje, 124

mestizos: in Azuay, 52; in Cuenca, 91; in Ecuador, 209; in Otavalo, 122, 143, 146, 152, 173–74, 178; in Quipal, 94
methodology: analysis omitting each community, 200–202; case studies, 212–13; characteristics of research study, 11; comparative design, 6–8, 11–12, 15, 160, 207; data collection, xi, 12, 207–9; ethnographic data, 212–13; household survey, 160, 207–8, 209–12, *211;* logistic regressions, *226,* 226–27; participant observation, 88–91, 212, 213; qualitative part of study, 88; research sites, *14,* 209; research team, 160, 210
migration merchants: description of, 198; financing and, *100,* 101; human smuggling and, ix, 66–67, 69–71; as middlemen, 66–71; pioneer migrants as, 95, 96; role of, 203–4; structure of, 191; trust and, 196. *See also* travel agencies
migration spike phenomena, 217, 218
migration systems approach, 84–85
Miller, Mark, 1, 2, 190
minifundio system, 21, 54, 55, 115
mita, 21, 120
mitimae, 19, 20, 49, 116, 117
money lending, 67–69, 196
Monsalve Pozo, Luis, 57
Morono Santiago (province), 48, 61
Muratorio, Blanca, 123–24, 124–25
music as export: author and, 165; class relations and, 141–42; cultural change and, 182; deportation and, 167; destinations for, 165–66, 172–73; gender and, 221; group formation, 162; migration and, 161, 172; skills for, 147–48, 169

Naboa, Gustavo, 188
NAFTA (North American Free Trade Agreement), 188
naturalization, 35
networks. *See* social networks

New York City: fieldwork in, 213; labor migration to, 31, *32*, 64–65, 72; Otavalans in, 158–59; perception of life in, 29; undocumented immigrants in, 35–37, *36*, 45; women migrants to, 109

New York state, 2

"nobility" in Azuay, 51, 55, 59, 63

obrajes: colonial period and, 118, 119, 120; end of, 121; in Peguche, 120, 149, 154

Organization of Petroleum Exporting Countries (OPEC), 24

Oriente region, 18, 25–26

Ortman, John, 134

Otavalo (canton): agriculture in, 133; authority structure in, 123–25; Azuay compared to, 156–57, 182–83, 192, 203; colonial period in, 118–21, 191; crafts of, 137, *138;* culture of, 5–6, 15, 131–35, 179–82; description of, ix–x, 113–15; economy of, 121–23, 135–38, 194–95; education in, 126–27, 132, 143, 225; gender in, 221; global market and, 10; land tenure and, 122–23, 171; men of, 177, 179; migrants by household, 216; migration from, 5–6, 33–34, 160–63, 192, 196–97; onset and development of migration in, 216, 218; Pan-American Highway and, 139; pre-Colombian period in, 115–17; Republican period in, 121–25; results from study of, 201; social networks in, 130, 162, 163–64, 176–77, 184; socioeconomic history of, 121–23; stratification of, 135–38, 148; tourism in, 163, 194–95; traje in, 177–78, 179, 181; vulnerability of migration in, 206. *See also* Guanansi; market migration; music as export; Peguche; weaving in Otavalo

Otavalo (town): description of, 114–15; Plaza de Ponchos in, 141; recent developments in, 146–47; Saturday market in, 128–29, 139, 144, 163; urbanization of, 142–43

Paccha, 117

Palomeque, Silvia, 55, 58

Panama hat trade: in Azuay, 4, 7, 14, 25, 55–59; collapse of, 58–61; comeback of, 62; culture and, 192; in Tomebamba, 74, 93

Pan-American Highway, 139

parcialidades, 114

Parsons, Elsie Clews: on colonization, 116; on economic strategy, 125–26; on education, 126–27, 132; on hacienda system, 128; on land, 122; Lema and, 129, 130, 218; on Peguche, 150, 152; on women, 177

participant observation, 88–91, 212, 213

Peace Corps, 94, 134, 153, 170, 171

Pearse, Andrew, 132–33

peasant, description of, 6–7n., 186

Peguche: capitalism in, 152, 169, 192; corn in, 175; demographic characteristics of, 222; description of, 6, 12–13, *13,* 15; destination of migrants from, 40; economy of, 167–69, 224; education in, 152–53; financing of migration from, 173; foreigners in, 179–80; Guanansi and, 169; Incapirca Community House, 210; indios libres or indios sueltos in, 151, 168; land competition in, 150–51, 175; before mass migration, 148–53; migration from, *41, 42, 43,* 172; obraje at, 120, 149, 154; onset and development of migration in, 218–19, *220,* 221; results from study of, 202; socioeconomic background in, 224, 225; weaving in, 128, 133, 136, 150, 151

periphery-centered approach, 47–48, 83–84, 191–92, 197

Pessar, Patricia, 11, 83

petroleum exports, 23–25, 62

Phelan, John, 119, 120

Pichincha (province), 26

pioneer migrant, 92–93, 194

Pizarro, Francisco, 20

Polanyi, Karl, 86

Portes, Alejandro, 10, 83
pre-Colombian period: in Azuay, 48–50; in Ecuador, 19–20; in Otavalo, 115–17

Quichua language: household survey and, 210; Peguche and, 181–82; Tombebamba and, 7, 13, 73, 75
Quinchuquí, 133, 138, 140, 149, 154–56
Quipal: agriculture in, 77–78, 103–4; demographic characteristics of, 221, 222, 223; description of, 7, 12–13, *13*, 15; destination of migration from, *99,* 99–101; economy of, 77- 80, 102–4; financing of migration in, *100,* 101; gender and migration in, 105–6; household in, 102; indigenous population of, 110–11; before mass migration, 76–80, 82; migration from, 39, 40–41, *41, 42, 43,* 106–7; migration moments in, 93–95; "los naturales" in, 186; onset and development of migration in, 96–99, *98,* 186, 216–17, *217;* pioneer migrants from, 94, 95; results from study of, 202; socioeconomic background in, 224, 225; Tomebamba compared to, 110–11
Quito: Audencia of, 53, 119, 120, 156; history of, 19, 21, 24, 26, 50

Ravenstein, E. G., 82, 189–90
"Reconquest of Otavalo, The" (documentary), 143
reduccíones, 19, 21–22
remittances from migrants, 64, 70–71, 102–3, 104, 108–9
Republican period: in Azuay, 55–58; in Ecuador, 20–22; in Otavalo, 121–25
research agenda, 199–200
"return migrants," 215
Riobamba, 20, 21
road, homes of migrants as clustering along, 97, *97, 98,* 98–99
Rowe, J. H., 19
Rumiñuahi, 141

Sabean, David, 193–94
Salazar, Rodrigo, 118
Salomon, Frank: on Cara, 116–17; on economy of Otavalo, 122–23, 125; on latifundia, 120; on obrajes, 118; on Otavalan region, 138; on "points of stress," 145–46; on textile merchants, 135; on weaving, 125, 126
Sandoval, Diego, 50
San Juan, festival of, 137, 142
San Luis obraje, 120
seasonal migration pattern, 60, 74, 79
Sierra region: Costa region and, 22; description of, 18; migration from, 23, 33; urbanization of, 26. *See also* Azuay; Cañar
Skeldon, Ronald, 191
social capital, 5, 87, 196
social class: migration, 30–31, 59–60, 198; music and, 141–42. *See also* caste in Andean region; merchant class in Otavalo
social constructivist perspective, 193–95
social networks: analysis of, 84–85, 86; Azuay compared to Otavalo, 182–83; business of migration and, ix, 70; godparents, role of, 164–65; Guanansi and, 170, 171; macrosociological theory and, 82–83; migration moments and, 92–101, 195; Otavalo and, 130, 162, 163–64, 176–77, 184; research on, 46; role in migration, 2–3, 5, 112, 195–96, 197–98
Soviet Union, breakup of, 89
"Soy Cholo Boy" (Utopía): story of, 90–91; words to, 17, 45, 81, 113, 158, 185
Spain: Otavalans in, 164, 187; rule by, 20–22, 50–55, 118–21
straw hats. *See* Panama hat trade

target earners, 33, 34
Thomas, William, 200
"Tiempo de Mujeres" (documentary), 71
Tilly, Charles, 82, 83, 101

Tomebamba: agriculture in, 74, 103–4; church hierarchy in, 73–74; colonial period in, 50; demographic characteristics of, 221, 222, 223; description of, 1, 7, 12–14, *13;* economy of, 74–76, 102–4; financing of migration in, *100,* 101, 196; gender and migration in, 8, 105; household in, 102; indigenous population of, 110; before mass migration, 73–76, 82; migrants by household, 216; migration from, 39, 40–41, *41, 42, 43;* migration moments in, 93, 94, 95–96; onset and development of migration in, 96–98, *97,* 216, 217–18, *218;* overview of, 1; Quipal compared to, 110–11; results from study of, 201–2; socioeconomic background in, 224, 225; technology in, 4; vacant dwellings in, 210–11; as village of women, 107–10

tourism: migration and, 29–30; in Otavalo, 163, 194–95

tourist visa, 34–35, 70, 166, 167

traje, 177–78, 179, 181

tramitadores, 66–67, 69–71

transnational economic migration, 11

transnational household: in Azuay, 82; definition of, 102; economic change in, 102–4; gender roles in, 104–6

transnational investment and migration, 3, 83

transnationalism, 9, 199–200

transnational migration: characteristics of, 40–42, *41, 42, 43,* 197; class, caste, and culture in, 198; demographic and socioeconomic characteristics of, 38–39, 221–27; dimensions of, 91–92; gender and, 8, *220,* 221–22; multiple conjunctural causes of, 12; nonrefugee status and, 9–10, 224; onset and development of, 216–21, *217, 218, 219, 220;* past patterns in current, x–xi; politicization of, 204; rates of, 215, *216;* regional variations in, 4–5; social forces in, 2–3; types of, 11, 39–40. *See also* international migration; labor migration; market migration; mass migration

travel agencies: mail and, 33, *34;* as migration merchants, 66, 93; musicians and, 142, 147

tribute laws, 118–19

undocumented migration: overview of, 33–35, 35–37, 39, 66; thwarted legal migration and, 47

United States: Boston, 95, 213; mass migration to, 4–5, 30–31; New York state, 2; "third wave" of immigration to, 35. *See also* New York City

urbanization: Azuay and, 61–62; gender and, 139–41; Otavalo (town) and, 142–43, 146–47; overview of, 19; Peguche and, 173–74; Sierra region and, 26

Uribe, Señor, 125, 126

U.S. Peace Corps. *See* Peace Corps

Utopía, 17, 88–92

vecino, 51

villages of women, 4–5, 107–10, 201

Wachtel, Nathan, 20

wage differentials, 3–4, 38, 42

Walter, Lynn, 183–84

weaving in Otavalo: adaptation and, 182; Andean tweed, 125–31; Azuay compared to, 156; colonial period and, 118–21; commodification of, 143–45, 147; competition in, 140; foreign interest in, 134–35, 168; gender and, 150; innovations in, 132–33, 134–35; marketing of, 129, 133, 135, 174; merchant class and, 129–31, 132–33, 140–41, 168–69, 192; Peguche and, 136, 150, 151; Plaza de Ponchos and, 139, 141, 162, 174; profit from, 169–70; Republican period and, 121–23; Saturday market and, 128–29, 139, 144, 163; skills for, 169; specialization in, 127–28; transnational migration and, 160–

63; urbanization and, 139–41, 142–43, 146–47, 173–74

Weber, Max, 123

Wellman, Barry, 84

Westernization, historical force of, 205

women: combination households and, 104; dress of, 116; marriage to Peguche men, 179–80; migration of, 8, 101, 105–6, 107, 108, 109; "Tiempo de Mujeres" (documentary), 71; villages of, 4–5, 107–10, 201; weaving, handicrafts, and, 60. *See also* gender

world-system (capitalist), 46

Yamor, annual parade of, 141

yanapa-hacienda relationship, 136–37, 154–55

"YANY, la," 2

Znanieki, Florian, 200

Lightning Source UK Ltd.
Milton Keynes UK
UKHW041430021019
350868UK00001B/83/P